Inside Picture Books

Inside
Picture
Books

Ellen Handler Spitz

Yale Nota Bene

Yale University Press

New Haven & London

Published with assistance from the foundation established
in memory of Amasa Stone Mather of the Class of 1907, Yale College.

"In the Dark" by A. A. Milne, from *Now We Are Six* by A. A. Milne, illustrations
by E. H. Shepard, copyright 1927 by E. P. Dutton, renewed © 1998 by A. A. Milne.
Used by permission of Dutton Children's Books, a division of Penguin Putnam Inc.
(U.S. and Canada); also published and reprinted by permission of Methuen
Children's Books, a division of Egmont Children's Books Limited
(U.K. and Commonwealth excluding Canada).

First published as a Yale Nota Bene book in 2000.

For information about this and other
Yale University Press publications, please contact:
U.S. office   sales.press@yale.edu
Europe office   sales@yaleup.co.uk

Printed in the United States of America.

The Library of Congress has cataloged the hardcover edition as follows:

Spitz, Ellen Handler
Inside picture books / Ellen Handler Spitz.
p.   cm.
Includes bibliographical references and index.
ISBN 0-300-07602-9 (alk. paper)
1. Children—Books and reading—Psychological aspects.
2. Picture books for children—Psychological aspects.
3. Reading—Parent participation   I. Title.
BF456.R2S685   1999
028.5'01'9—dc21   98-26327

ISBN 0-300-08476-5 (pbk.)
A catalogue record for this book is available from the British Library.

10 9 8 7 6 5 4 3 2 1

for my sister,
Constance Ann

Contents

Foreword

Sometimes the most obvious and important aspects of our lives go unnoticed, unexamined by those of us whose business it is to understand the way children grow up, the way family life works. We who practice child psychiatry or psychoanalysis—not to mention those who observe and try to make sense of families as they vary across regions and nations, classes and races—have learned in this century to watch closely how children are fed, how they are taught to control their bodily functions, how they learn to get along with other children, what happens when they go to school and, of course, how they get along with their parents, their brothers and sisters, their relatives and friends. This is the complex psychological development of childhood and too, the "socialization" of youngsters, by which we mean their gradual introduction into a particular (economic, cultural) world. Yet, for all our evident interest in such matters during this fast-receding century, we have paid relatively little attention to what our sons and daughters read (or hear read), and to what moral and psychological consequence—a significant oversight now corrected by this knowing, wise book.

For many years Ellen Handler Spitz has worked in a field best described as applied psychoanalysis—she has been interested in, among other subjects, the imaginative life of children as it expresses itself in words and pictures and as it, in turn, gets shaped by the words and pictures of others, those who write and illustrate books. Her interest has been aesthetic, moral, and not least, psychological, and her interest has been strongly influenced by her long-standing and thorough knowledge of psychoanalytic work with the young. She understands the conflicts with which our young sons and daughters must contend as they become old enough to understand language, to read. She understands the strong desires that assert themselves in the young, the wishes and resentments and fears and worries and anxieties that they must struggle to keep under wraps as they make their accommodations to home life, and later, school life. She understands how the mind, in the course of that struggle, relies upon others to offer not only love but moral guidance—a sense of what matters and why, as well as a clear sense of what is desirable and what is not at all allowable. Finally, she understands that we who are parents or teachers or relatives, and so have the opportunity to spend a lot of time with children, are ourselves as needy, in our own way, of direction, of help in articulating the rights and wrongs of this world, the promises life offers and the dangers it presents, as our children are needy of that articulation and direction from us.

This book is, then, an effort on the part of a psychoanalytically informed educator to offer some considered thought to those of us who love reading, love reading to children, and want these children, down the line, to love reading too. In effect, we have in the pages ahead reflections on what a broad range of familiar picture books have to say—what their stories mean to the youngsters who first listen to them and then read them on their own. Further, this book is refreshingly free of a facile reductionism that, for awhile, tarnished a substantial body of psychoanalytic psychology—an interest in explaining the mind's life through constant resort to a kind of psychological archeology: *this* is due to or proves *that*. Rather, we are asked here to understand and appreciate the psychological complexity of stories, and the complexity, as well, of the reception they receive from young readers. Very important, also, is the author's emphasis on the aesthetics of "children's" literature. She refuses a single-minded emphasis on psychology or psychopathology; she wants us to realize that certain books have endured as hugely popular ones because they were written (and illustrated) by individuals of real literary and artistic capability and achievement. Under such circumstances, children (and those who read to them) are excited not only by a message, by its symbolic meaning, by themes in a book that connect with themes in lives, but also by a persuasive, compelling, or stirring manner of presentation.

What follows then, are the thoughtful and candid reflections of a serious-minded, psychologically knowing, and subtle reader who also has a sense of humor and recognizes that writers and artists work in exceedingly varied ways to engage with us, to win us over, to prompt us to sit at the edge of our chairs. We are given careful, sensitive descriptions of plots. We are given, for each book, a good deal of "character analysis"—a commentary on how so-and-so does such-and-such, as well as speculations on motives and reasons. We are given, graciously, not interpretations categorically handed down, but a more contemplative tone throughout: a particular essayist's take on certain books as she has thought hard about them for these many years.

There is in this book a larger message that comes to us both forthrightly and by implication. Ellen Handler Spitz obviously has fond and vivid memories of her own childhood experiences with the picture books she so much wants to celebrate, or figure out, or describe with reservations and concerns. But she is not only telling us how gratefully she recalls certain books, how affectionately she still regards them. She is also making plain her life-long delight with books—her belief that children today also ought be nurtured and excited just as she was, that the television set and the latest gadgets and gimmicks of our toy stores are not at all worthy substitutes or equivalents of the various picture books she attends and commends in the pages ahead. Indeed, in its sum, this book is not only a book about books, but a book that calls us to books, that reminds us of their singular aesthetic power, their moral energy, their ability to reach us mind, heart, soul, to tell us about the world, to help us figure it out, and very important, to affirm our humanity as the one creature who has been endowed with language, who uses words to try to fathom the nature of things. Picture books are "signs" that help us start thoughtfully on this life's journey.

Robert Coles, M.D.

A Greeting to My Reader

We never seem to forget our first books: the look, feel, and smell of pages daubed with color that pulled us in when we were small. Just a name—Madeline, Ferdinand, Corduroy, Babar, Max and his wild things, Peter Rabbit—brings a smile, a bright image, or the fragments of a story; the timbre of someone's reading voice; the faint odor of a pipe or a favorite cologne; the folds of a quilt; the sensation of being held. Best of all, perhaps, these books evoke the memory of having someone all to ourselves and sensing that we are, together with that someone, enveloped in fantasy.

This book is for mothers, fathers, grandparents, teachers, therapists, and scholars. Most of all, though indirectly, it is for children. It is they especially who I hope will benefit from its pages.

Reading aloud is an activity fraught with advantages—for grown-ups as well as for youthful listeners—and it is a quintessentially *relational* activity. My overarching purpose is to underscore this relational aspect and to point out just how, through the shared cultural experience of reading aloud and being read to, adults and young children—in moments of intensely pleasurable rapport—participate in the traditional task of passing on values from one generation to the next. Occasionally people argue about the extent to which children's tastes and preferences are formed by early reading, but rarely is effort spent trying to understand *how* this influence comes about, how psychic tasks are portrayed in picture books—for example, how moral lessons are conveyed, how prejudices are subtly implanted. These are questions I will take up.

And, in keeping with the relational focus, I want to stress the notion of "conversational reading," by which I mean the interactive participation of adults in children's cultural experience. This participation, by the way, does not end in the primary years. Long after they have learned the alphabet and acquired a substantial written vocabulary, children love to be read to. They ask us to read to them, and we do. Sitting close and sharing their books, we enter imaginary spaces with them. We communicate across the intervening years to transcend the routines of their daily lives and ours and render it—artfully—more real.

Parenting, never a simple task, seems especially complex in times like ours when widely accepted ideologies and hierarchies that have supported parental authority have been eroded and advocates of a multitude of competing priorities vie with one another in a progressively strident disharmony. In the midst of this fray, self-proclaimed proponents of "children's rights" speak out, but even these apparently well-meaning advocates propound agendas that, on careful examination, often prove naive or troubling. Conscientious parents trying to function in this scene may feel pulled apart—rather like those medieval images of poor St. Bartholomew on the verge of his martyrdom. Picture him splayed out in the center of a painted panel, with each limb tied to a colored horse about to be whipped off toward one of the four corners of the picture—north, south, east, and west. Not a comfortable position, to say the least.

As the end of the twentieth century approaches, families in the United States are becoming increasingly mobile and diverse. The paradigm myth of mother, father, and child living comfortably together in a stable dwelling place matches the reality of only a fraction of today's families. Important issues of race, gender, and class have complicated this simple image. I want to highlight this fact because many of the images and stories we will encounter in this book reflect a world at least superficially different from that which swirls around us today. Aided by the intuitive leaps children love to make, however, the picture books discussed in these pages speak messages of enduring value.

If anyone were to ask me what I consider to be the most important feature of parenting, I would say, without hesitation and without wishing to beg the question, simply, enjoyment—enjoy your children. Delight in them, rejoice with them, have good times together, treasure the days of your life that are spent in their company. Days that—although it may not seem so to harried and often worried young parents—are limited. A great deal follows from this simple thought.

Let me tell a story. During my high school years, I had a boyfriend whose family had emigrated to this country from Norway in the aftermath of World War II. With his beautiful, austere mother I had, at least from my viewpoint, a somewhat tense relationship. Her command of English was somewhat limited, and her interest in me even more so. Nevertheless, one day we had a serious conversation. She spoke words I never forgot, words that have followed me throughout my adult life and occasionally led me. What she said was this: "A mother's children are *lent* to her for a brief time. Children are not a permanent possession." I can still feel how that idea struck me at age sixteen. It was my first look across the massive divide between being a child and being a parent. In that conversation, Mrs. Annie Aagaard made me try to peer all the way from the land of Moab into the land of Gilead. What I saw seemed terrifying and absolutely unknown. As I have subsequently learned, parents *and* children are lent to one another. Time is of the essence. This wise, terse message echoes through the years. Its force impels me to write—not with a sense of frantic urgency, but with an awareness that the rabbinic saying also makes explicit: "The day is short; the task is great; the workers are sluggish; the wages are high; and the Master of the house is pressing" (Rabbi Tarfon, *Sayings of the Fathers*, quoted in *Gates of Prayer*, 1975).

Another story complements this one, and it involves my own search, several years later, for the perfect pediatrician for my firstborn child. Jennifer was a tiny infant, just over five-and-a-half pounds, and I was a young, somewhat physically frail mother with all the usual concerns about safety and health and questions about how to nurture this precious young creature who had become my primary responsibility. The first couple of doctors who saw her were highly recommended, but to me they seemed efficient, perfunctory, and routine. From my perspective, a miraculous event had occurred, and I sought a physician who could understand this. Not yet in despair of finding such a person but growing restive, I made an appointment with a pediatrician who had been recommended by one of my husband's university colleagues. The day came, and it was unforgettable. After a short period of pacing in the waiting room and filling out forms, I was admitted, baby in arms, into a consulting room. There, Dr. Leonard Bellin of Providence, Rhode Island, greeted me with a gentle smile, extended his hand for a shake, and then asked whether I would be comfortable placing tiny Jennifer on the examining table or would prefer to continue holding her in my arms. I gingerly put her down. Standing on the other side of the examining table from me, Dr. Bellin looked down at the wriggling human creature that lay before him and said: "Hello there, Jennifer! You are one beautiful little girl." I still do not understand fully why I reacted so strongly, but tears flooded my eyes and in that instant I knew that, for as long as I lived in that city, this man would be my daughter's pediatrician.

Why? Because here was a doctor who saw my child, barely four weeks old, as a fully formed, viable human being—a *person*—who could be addressed in language and treated as though she possessed an emergent subjectivity. He saw her as I did. He saw her as a living child, not merely a specimen. Beyond that, he understood the special value of the moment of a new beginning; it was, after all, an important beginning—for her, for me, and for himself; for all three of us.

With these two stories, my unknown reader, I begin my relationship with you. The stories are meant to convey my sense that the topic of this book, parenting through cultural experience, is one of immediate importance, that it has to do with individual books and individual children as well as with themes of overarching concern, and that it is a project best undertaken with pleasure, passion, and conviction. We care, and we take care, to know a great deal about what goes into our children's bodies; we need to be no less attentive to what goes into their minds.

When I was a little girl, there was an old book I especially treasured, a collection of illustrated stories called *Walt Disney's Surprise Package*. The cover was drawn to look like a birthday present wrapped in striped paper and tied with a pink bow that was being pulled apart in a tug of war by characters who appeared inside when the book was opened. One of the stories was an adaptation of Hans Christian Andersen's "Through the Picture Frame." In this tale, a little boy named Hialmar climbs magically inside an oil painting that has been hanging on his bedroom wall. The painting itself is a rather dark landscape, but once he is actually within it, Hialmar can smell springtime, hear birds singing in the trees, and perceive small animals such as frogs, moles, and groundhogs—even tiny ants and beetles that were invisible from outside the picture. The space inside the frame seems noisy and vibrant. As he walks farther in, he follows the twists and turns of a mysterious river and comes upon a red boat tied to a tree, its sails rigged. He climbs aboard, and his adventures continue. He rides a talking horse and rescues a little princess. At length, Hialmar finds himself sitting once more just inside the frame of the painting with his legs dangling out. The story ends when he jumps down and discovers that he is back again on the floor of his own bedroom.

This tale captures something about my own relation to visual art—something I have tried to convey in this book. It is a story that speaks to those magical acts of projection we perform with respect to works of art and literature—the way in which we put ourselves into these works and incorporate them into our lives. As children, we all performed such acts, and we continue to do so despite our adult sophistication—a sophistication, I might add, that the presence of young children can force us very quickly to abandon.

Charles Baudelaire, writing on the Exposition Universelle of 1855 in Paris, told a relevant story about Honoré de Balzac, the great French novelist, who one day found himself standing before a painting of a melancholy winter scene. Balzac gazed at the image of a small house from which a thin wisp of smoke was rising and exclaimed: "How beautiful it is! But what are they *doing* in that cottage? What are their thoughts? What are their sorrows? Has it been a good harvest? No doubt they have bills to pay?" Commenting on this response, Baudelaire wrote that Balzac's reaction to the painting contained an important lesson: namely, that art is "an evocation, a magical operation" (Baudelaire 1956, pp. 197–98). He added that it might not be a bad idea to consult the hearts of children on this matter. Taking his injunction seriously, I have, throughout the pages of this book, made sure to include the voices of children.

And so, as you settle down in a cozy spot to read a favorite picture book to a child you know, you yourself may find that you have been transported into the realm of the uncanny. Unexpected sensations may bubble up, words and images may combine to ignite memories, lines and colors may radiate and spin in your mind like spokes on a moving wheel, and associations may fly wildly like glints of light from a holiday sparkler.

Resting expectantly on their shelves, in copies that have faded under the gaze of generations and been made soft by the touch of eager hands, or in shiny new paperback versions with sharper edges and brightly colored surfaces, the picture books discussed in these pages are treasures that glow as soon as they are opened. If you snuggle up with them in the company of a young son or daughter, a grandchild or grandniece, a pupil or small neighbor, they will enchant you both. As you read and look, they will transport, amuse, console, inform, and inspire you. They may even untie you from the horses of St. Bartholomew and connect you with the empathy of Balzac or the daring of little Hialmar, who actually climbed right in.

As you read and reflect on the chapters that follow, I hope that you will feel linked through cultural experience, and with ever-increasing pleasure and understanding, to the children you love and to the shared worlds you and they bring to life as you turn pages together.

Acknowledgments

In this space, I wish to thank many people for their love, concern, and support. Their voices form the harmony that sustains the melodies of this book. No one but myself, however, should be held responsible for its dissonances.

As a resident fellow at The Bunting Institute of Radcliffe College, 1995–96, I was privileged to be part of a unique community of women writers, artists, scholars, and scientists, each of whom inspired me and taught me to see my own work and theirs in surprising and even now unforeseen ways. The following year, at the Center for Advanced Study in the Behavioral Sciences, Stanford University, with financial support from the Andrew W. Mellon Foundation, I was blessed with the intellectual companionship of a distinguished group of international scholars who refocused my perspective once again. I want to express my heartfelt thanks to the directors of those institutes, all of whom gave generously to me of their time and wisdom. Florence Ladd, Renny Harrigan, Neil Smelser, and Robert Scott. I would like to thank the staff members of these research centers: at the Bunting, in particular, Lyn O'Connor, Gretchen Elmendorf, Linda Roach, Reece Michaelson, and Marilyn Bibeau; at the Center, Felicia Whiteside, Christine Duignan, Julie Shumacher, Nancy Pinkerton, Jesse Lewis, Van Cook, and librarians Joy Scott and Jean Michel. No request was ever too much for these kind and dedicated individuals. When books or supplies were needed posthaste, they made them available; when someone's nose bumped into a glass door on the day of a big lecture, they were ready with ice; when a person's leg was mangled in a grating and she could barely walk, they sprang to her aid; when FedEx decided not to materialize on the day page proofs were due on another continent, they found a way. Above all, each one of them made me feel that the sort of work I am trying to do matters. At moments when that work itself is making faces at you, scowling back at you from the monitor screen, refusing to cooperate and behave itself, no gift seems more valuable. I am immensely grateful to all these "collaborators" at the Bunting and at the Center. Their contributions to these pages, tangible and intangible, are beyond measure.

During my year at the Bunting, two Harvard undergraduates, Talia Milgrom-Elcott and Sandra Youngmie Lee, worked closely with me as Radcliffe Research Partners. We read to young children together; they interviewed their peers on the subject of early reading, discussed their reactions to the material with me, and wrote up their findings. Throughout our months together, these gifted young women buoyed my spirits with their effervescence and enthusiasm. I miss them dearly, and I want them to know how grateful I am for their devotion to this project.

As a fellow at the Center, I also had two young "research assistants." These were four-year-olds—Alex Krosnick and Haley Wegner, daughters of other scholars in my year, Jon Krosnick and Dan Wegner. Alex and Haley came individually to my study on the hill, settled down amid my vast collection of picture books, old and new, and "read" with me. Only a fraction of what they taught me could be included here, but the pleasure their visits afforded will be evident. These delightful children gave me the opportunity to repeat my favorite parenting activity. Listen for their voices as you turn the pages of this book. I would like to express my thanks to them and to their parents.

Alex and Haley, however, are but two of the children whose words and thoughts and feelings appear here. I wish to acknowledge the Peabody Children's Center of Cambridge, Massachusetts, for granting me permission to come on a weekly basis and, with Talia and Sandra, read to their three- and four-year-olds. This book would have been less rich without the spoken and unspoken responses of all those wonderful children.

In addition, I would like to acknowledge a number of colleagues and friends whose help to me has ranged from the spiritual to the practical, including everything in between—from calling books and secondary materials to my attention to finding me a quiet, cozy space in which to work when there seemed to be no place to go. Everyone listed here, precious and dear to me in different ways, will know why he or she has been included. I beg forgiveness if, by accident, I have omitted anyone. I wish to thank Joanna and Peter Strauss, Gilles Fabre, Anne Griffin-Lefer and Jay Lefer, Knut Aagaard, John Toews, Peter Jelavich, Yael Feldman, Jane Celwyn, Sander Gilman, Suzaan Boettger, M. G. Lord, Martha Saxton, Elka Spoerri, Mieke Bal, Svetlana Boym, Ellen Harris, Judith Aissen, Dubravka Ugresic, Gillian Feeley-Harnik, Catherine Soussloff, Lucie White, Bonnie Kaufman, Susan Wolf, Hortense Spillers, Carol Shloss, Mary Steedly, Joss Marsh, Cay Craig, Eric Simonoff, Robert and Judith Wallerstein, Cynthia Rostankowski, Mimi Spengnether, Mina Friedkin, Katherine Dalsimer, Maria Tatar, Lisby Mayer, Nancy Chodorow, Wanda Corn, Anan Ameri, Lorraine O'Grady, Csaba Pleh, Judy DeLoach, Tom Weisner, Lois Weithorn, Sarah Burns, Alan Code, Martin Shulman, Joan Baudouine, Anita Silvers, Elliot Eisner, Hank Aaron, Carolyn Feigelson, Martin Gliserman, Louise Kaplan, Lucy Daniels Inman, Claire Kahane, Donald Kuspit, Patrick O'Brien, George Locker, Barbara Press, Philip Muskin, Michael Nassau, Elizabeth Leonard, Tara Fitzpatrick, Liz Martin, Larry Zacharias, Sonia Alexander, Alla Efimova, Barbara Gelpi, and Nicole Squires.

As for my family, my mother's picture books adorn my shelves; perhaps my very choice of subject matter is a way of keeping her alive. Each of my children, as well, Jenny and Paul, Nathaniel, and Rivi, has taught me valuable lessons concerning the subject of this book, as did my father, Leslie, my maternal aunt Sylvia, and my paternal aunt Ruth. Their love is written into these pages.

Finally, I wish to thank my editors at Yale University Press, Gladys Topkis, who has always maintained her faith in me and in my work; Julie Carlson, my outstanding manuscript editor; Margaret Otzel; I-Huei Go; my designer, Charles Ellertson; and my dust jacket designer, Rebecca Gibb.

Inside Picture Books

☞ Chapter 1 ☜

Pictures, Words, and Voices

If I close my eyes and concentrate, I can even now hear my mother's voice as she read to me each evening when I was a child—both picture books and poetry. I remember the cadences and inflections, the lilt and verve, of her special reading voice. Nuanced and expressive, it pronounced each word slowly and distinctly and lingered lovingly over syllables or phrases. Not at all like her normal "hurry-up" voice, this one had the capacity to transport me to faraway times and places, to send tremors through my spine, to conjure exotic pictures in my mind even as her fingers pointed to details of images on the pages of a book. Best of all, it embraced me with an auditory ambience of coziness and warmth. In those evening hours, we stretched and grew together. We could be anywhere, with anyone; it was anytime; I was sure I could do, or have, or feel anything; and then, when it was over and all the clouds of make-believe dissolved, the safety of her presence remained to hold me.

Unlike my mother, my father rarely read to me at bedtime; he would come in quietly, sit down beside me, and sing a lullaby. "Sweet and low, sweet and low, wind of the western sea. . . ." The quality of his voice seemed to match the words as I lay under the covers with eyes closed, imagining blue waves, smelling salt air, waiting for the special kiss I knew would come when the last notes faded.

In early childhood, the separations among different spheres of functioning are not yet firmly established, and young children come only gradually to distinguish clearly between dreams, fantasies, and waking states, between the self and others, between a picture and the thing pictured. Thus, the artifacts presented to them make a deep and lasting impression. Favorite songs and stories are repeated endlessly, and just as tastes are registered with high intensity, feelings too have a pungency, immediacy, and lability that may diminish in later years. In studying imagery in picture books, I have come to realize ever more poignantly the added power of the context of children's cultural lives — the crucial role of parents, teachers, other adults, and older siblings as mediators between them and the cultural objects they encounter.

Taking up themes important in children's lives as my organizational device, I shall explore ways in which these themes have been treated through the medium of picture books. At the same time, however, the books themselves, as works of art in their own right, can be seen as generating a multitude of questions. Because my effort is in no way meant to be comprehensive, my hope is that these pages will serve as a guide from which you can freely extrapolate to develop your own approaches not only to the books discussed here but also to other books and to works in other media. I have set down reflections that are meant to be helpful in choosing, introducing, rendering, and interpreting cultural objects for young children.

Picture books, unlike television and the other electronic media ubiquitously available today, require the participation of warm, breathing adult human partners who have available laps, keen eyes and ears, arms adept at holding while turning pages, and perhaps a flair for the dramatic. The political agenda of this book is thus to advocate for the practice of reading aloud to young children. Here are a few brief stories to support this project:

In Los Angeles a few years ago, after a talk I gave on picture books at the Getty Center for the History of Art and the Humanities, a graphic artist approached me. Brimming with reminiscences, she recalled her delight when, as a little girl, she would nestle up to someone big who would put his arm around her and read her a story. In this case, the someone was a beloved grandfather. To my astonishment, she reached into her bag on the spot and produced an old black-and-white photograph. There she was, not more than four or five years old, enraptured, her thumb in her mouth, her favorite doll, "Baby Snooks," cradled in her lap. She was listening intently as her grandfather read aloud. Contemplating that photograph in her presence, I became another witness to the scene, and as we gazed at the image together, the artist asked me to try and hear in my imagination the sonorous voice of this special granddad, who had been, she told me proudly, one of the last oldtime southern preachers. Visiting her family homestead in Georgia, she had spied a worn copy of the very children's book depicted in the photograph; opening it for the first time in thirty years, she realized with amazement that she could recall every scene: "As I turned each page, the images glowed in my memory."

Last spring, in the course of several interviews with Harvard undergraduates concerning their memories of being read to as children, one sophomore recalled an incident that occurred when she was about six years old. Her mother had come into her room to read the usual bedtime story. Climbing into bed and under the covers with her little daughter, as was her wont, she selected, on this particular night, *The Velveteen Rabbit* by Margery Williams, originally published in 1922. The little girl's fourteen-year-old brother happened to be passing by. Realizing that his mother was reading his own special favorite, he could not bear to walk away. Despite embarrassed feelings of being much too grown-up to stay, he lingered, trying to seem nonchalant and hoping no one would notice. Finally, unable to restrain himself any longer, he plunged headlong into his sister's room, climbed into her bed, and, settling himself under the covers, he continued to listen as their mother read the last pages of the story to them both. Teenage machismo proved no match for a spotted brown Rabbit with floppy ears, a Skin Horse, and the Boy who loved them.

Some months ago, over coffee in my favorite Cambridge cafe, a fellow devotee of children's literature was debating with me the ethical implications of Father Rabbit's "accident" in Mr. McGregor's garden. Father Rabbit was put in a pie, you may remember, by Mrs. McGregor. A palpable silence revealed that our somewhat unusual conversation was being monitored by an elderly couple seated nearby. At length, leaning toward us, one of them broke in. It was a gray-haired lady who politely confided that, although she was not normally in the habit of eavesdropping on other people's private conversations, she had not been able to resist once she recognized our topic because (believe it or not, as she put it) in all the years of her life she had strenuously avoided drinking chamomile tea. This, she explained, was due to the fact that she had always supposed that Mother Rabbit gave chamomile tea to Peter as a punishment for his disobedience in going into Mr. McGregor's garden. Unlike his better-behaved siblings, Flopsy, Mopsy, and Cotton-tail, Peter had not received any bread, milk, or blackberries. All he got was chamomile tea. If, her little girl-self had reasoned, chamomile tea was a punishment, it must be a disagreeable substance. Recently, however, she had been persuaded to take a sip and, to her surprise, found its taste both distinctive and delicious. This discovery had prompted her entry into our conversation. Listening to us, she reflected that the change in her perception of chamomile tea might require a radical change in her understanding of its import and of the character of Mother Rabbit. Was, she wondered aloud, the chamomile tea given to Peter by his mother *actually* a punishment (as she had presumed), or was it a soothing remedy administered to the shivering little bunny in order to calm him down and settle his stomach after he had been so frightened and had consumed so many lettuces, French beans, and radishes? Was Mother Rabbit's behavior disciplinary and depriving or kind and restorative? And how might the answers to these questions change the meaning of the story as a whole?

My companion and I were charmed with this interruption. We were struck by the fact that this elderly stranger had been so taken with a book encountered in her childhood that she had allowed an aspect of it to influence her lifelong culinary habits and keep her from even trying a certain beverage. Beyond this, her devotion was strong enough to make her break into our conversation and engage with us in our own ongoing interpretive efforts. A bond was instantly established. There we sat in the cafe, puzzling over the latent ambiguity of one of our childhood books more than ninety years after Beatrix Potter had first published *The Tale of Peter Rabbit* in 1902.

Apropos culinary habits and their susceptibility to the influence of early cultural experience, there is an unforgettable page in Jean de Brunhoff's *The Story of Babar*, originally published in 1933, on which the old King of the elephants happily consumes an innocent-looking red polka-dotted mushroom. Immediately below this picture, however, he is shown crumpled in pain, his brow furrowed and his crown slipping off. Most arresting of all, his normally gray elephant hide has changed to a bilious shade of green. "[The mushroom] poisoned him and he became ill, so ill that he died. This was a great calamity," reads the text. In my interviews with adults about their early reading, I have found several who were deeply affected by this scene. One woman told me that she avoids eating mushrooms to this very day but nevertheless continues to cherish *The Story of Babar*—a picture book of such extraordinary power that it was able to alter a tiny aspect of her behavior forever.

A recent autobiographical piece in the *New Yorker* by literary editor Robert McCrum reports that, after three months of marriage, he suffered a massive, incapacitating stroke. The bleakness of his convalescence was brightened, however, by moments when his wife read to him from their favorite children's books. The scene he evokes is one of extraordinary tenderness and warmth as the young couple returns to such books as *Alice's Adventures in Wonderland* (1865) and *Charlotte's Web* (1952). "There was something profoundly consoling about these old friends. . . . I found my thoughts returning to childhood . . . and then moving forward through the years," he writes. This unfortunate couple, battered by fate and forced physically apart, were able to reinstate their capacity to be together in other deeply satisfying ways through reencountering, in the form of these old books, a heretofore unexplored common heritage. McCrum's description may remind readers of parallel moments in their own lives.

Each of these anecdotes bears witness to the formative power of early cultural experience and its role in determining the attitudes and behavior of adults. Because of the partnership they require, my choice

From *The Story of Babar* by Jean de Brunhoff. Copyright © 1934
and renewed 1962 by Random House, Inc. Reprinted by
permission of Random House, Inc.

has been to study picture books as opposed to the other representational objects and phenomena available today for children. Adult participation—physical, emotional, and intellectual—is vital in the cultural lives of young people. It matters both for learning and for pleasure, which go hand in hand.

6

I shall take up a selection of picture books and examine them thematically along psychological, ethical, and aesthetic axes—the psychological being paramount. My goals are several. First, to enrich communication between adults and children by demonstrating approaches and posing questions that can be extrapolated from the examples given here and reapplied elsewhere. This goal requires looking closely at pictures, words, and their internal negotiations as well as at their more far-flung associations. The finest picture books, after all, must appeal to the minds and hearts not only of the children to whom they are principally addressed but also of the grown-ups who select, buy, and read them aloud. They must, in short, appeal cross-generationally. To do this, they need to convey meaning on several levels.

Every now and then, I shall point out instances in which the children with whom I have been reading differ from adults in their understanding of a pictorial detail or a narrated event. Interestingly, even when young children correctly discern an author's or artist's intended meaning, they often perceive quite different meanings in the text or image that also make sense to them. Adults, on the other hand, rarely look beyond the intended meaning. One of my purposes here is to sensitize adult readers to the variety of "other" meanings that may be consciously perceived by children but tend to fall outside the purview of artistic choice, intention, and control. If you are curious about this phenomenon, you can readily experiment with it by eliciting alternative readings to pictures in improvised dialogues with the children you know. Such dialogues in the presence of books and in the act of turning pages together constitute a kind of *conversational reading*. To foster it is an important goal of this project.

Another objective is to suggest some partial answers to my own question as to why certain picture books have survived for so long. Some that I will consider have retained their popularity for over half a century; others are more recent. Their publication histories are extraordinary. As of February 1996, for example, well over nine million (9,331,266) hardcover copies of *The Tale of Peter Rabbit* had been sold in the United States alone. Available records of domestic sales of *The Story of Babar* show 788,971 hardcover copies and another 1,166,497 copies of just one paperbound edition had been sold as of the same date. *The Velveteen Rabbit* records show sales of over three and a half million copies in paperbound editions (see "All Time Bestselling Hardcover Children's Books," pp. 27–32). One reason that I have not, in this project, focused a great deal of attention on contemporary books is that I am intrigued by the phenomenon of "staying power" and by what makes certain books irresistible to successive generations. By disclaiming any attempt to be comprehensive, I hope to forestall disappointment on the part of those readers whose favorites have not made it into these pages.

My initial hunch is that the popularity of classic picture books derives from their remarkable capacity to tap ongoing issues of deep emotional significance for children. The picture books that became classics do so, I suspect, because they dare to tackle important and abiding psychological themes, and because they convey these themes with craftsmanship and subtlety. Musicality, rhyming, visual artistry, humor, surreal juxtapositions, elegance, simplicity, and suspense combine in them to construct layers of meaning that reward countless hours of cross-generational reading.

The importance of craft and workmanship deserves emphasis. This is especially clear when we think of the spate of "psychological self-help" books for young children that have recently appeared on the market. These contemporary picture books deal didactically and often quite superficially with difficult real-life situations. My response to them, as a genre, is that although there is surely a place for them, their influence may prove to be short-lived, in part, because so many of them lack the aesthetic qualities necessary to engrave a book on children's hearts and cause it to be passed on to new generations. Artfulness implies subtlety, and subtlety is as important to the success of a children's book as it is to works designed for adults. A book may focus directly and pointedly on a specific emotional and/or social problem, but if it cannot tell a good story, provide visual stimulation, and engage its audience in an imaginary world, it will fall by the wayside. A book that can do all of the above, on the other hand, may teach a child wonderfully rich lessons about life and death, about goodness, sadness, evil, conflict, and so on.

This point of view was corroborated recently at a university bookstore. Near the entrance, an enticing table of children's books had been strategically placed under a sign that read: "GREAT VALUES: CHILDREN'S BOOKS FOR $1.29 OR LESS." These were, however, rejected wares that the store was trying, rather desperately, to unload. With pen in hand, I noted the following titles from the display: *My Big Sister Takes Drugs; I Wish Daddy Didn't Drink So Much; I'll Never Love Anything Again; She's Not My Real Mother; Mommy and Me by Ourselves Again; I Am No Cry Baby; At Daddy's on Saturdays;* and *Our Teacher's in a Wheelchair.* Their quality varied. I noticed, however, that the discount table contained none of the books that are discussed in these pages, and that the sales table, despite its inviting sign and location, was attracting minimal attention from browsers.

Turning away to leave the store, I happened to notice a father holding hands with his little son; tucked under his arm was a copy of *The Little Engine That Could,* first published in 1930, a book that had not been placed on the discount table. I asked him whether his son was already acquainted with this book. The young man smiled and nodded, explaining that it was because *The Little Engine That Could* was such a favorite with his son that they had decided to buy another copy to give as a birthday present to a friend. Why did this nearly seventy-year-old book continue to appeal whereas a whole tableful of newer, more overtly psychological ones did not?

At stressful junctures in a child's life, during certain crises, I believe that self-help books such as the sort I saw on the remainder table might prove useful. By dealing explicitly with painful situations, they might provide the occasion for opening a dialogue between parents and children. By bringing potentially embarrassing, shame-laden, or tragic issues into the open and making them public, they might, at best, give parents and children permission to talk about them with each other. Yet, beyond that beginning, I suspect that genuine psychological power comes from a very different place—from metaphor and symbol rather than from forthright representations of what is near at hand. As child psychoanalyst Selma Fraiberg (1959, p. 23) once put it, "the child's contact with the real world is strengthened by his periodic excursions into fantasy."

A gifted artist searches within and experiments to bring back pictures and stories from some other place. Using all her ingenuity (like Max with his wild things), she emerges with new worlds of signs and wonders. Only from such inventions, from scenes that fascinate in and of themselves but also evoke other times and places and people, can deep psychic work be accomplished. Those who cling to the here and now fail to achieve the desired effect because to remain in the realm of the familiar is to mobilize quick defenses, to bore, to weary, and therefore to constrict rather than expand horizons.

Psychologically explicit (or what I am dubbing "self-help") books for children are not unrelated to other phenomena in our fin-de-siècle culture. In the mental health professions, for example, therapeutic interventions are expected to be brief, simple, straightforward, and quantifiable. These days, institutions and caregivers seem unwilling to reserve the time necessary for richly nuanced interpretative work that involves metaphor. They show little interest in rewarding the slow uneven process toward meaning that can lead to permanent therapeutic gains. Meaning and interpretation, however, remain central to the project of living a human life as well as to the narrower task of consciously altering human behavior. Perhaps this principle, though, to remain true, requires a background of personal freedom—a condition eroded daily in contemporary American culture.

Admittedly a vague term in common parlance, imagination is a word to which I would like to give a very specific meaning in the present context. I take it to mean conjuring up *inner possibilities*—that is to say, the gratification of (sometimes impossible) desires and the provisional working through and mastery of basic fears by means of fantasy, mental adventure, and magical transformations. Picture books, encountered in the presence of adults, can, I propose, stimulate the imagination in this sense and strengthen young children internally for their ongoing discovery of the limitations of the real.

To claim that the books examined in these pages touch on themes that matter *perennially* to young children will seem to fly in the face of contemporary critical voices that espouse pluralistic perspectives and hold that diverse cultures and even periodic changes within a culture may result in corresponding changes in human psychology. My conviction, nonetheless, is that bedrock issues of early childhood *do* remain in place—however disguised—from one generation to the next. If this were not true, we would be hard-pressed to understand how, across the blurred boundaries of time, space, gender, race, class, and age, human beings clearly have the capacity to understand and empathize with one another. Classic picture books remain beloved because wherever children live, and whatever the color of their skin, the shape of their eyes, or the texture of their hair, there is always a given body and mind and an unchosen set of parents to be reckoned with. There are daily separations and reunions to be negotiated; new worlds to be explored; love, jealousy, disappointment and aggression to be expressed; a maze of obstacles and opportunities to be appropriately defined and made peace with; final losses to be mourned.

Engagement with psychological content, however, as I saw in glancing at the table of remaindered items, does not guarantee a favorite children's book. The representation of a significant theme stands the test of time only when it is so skillfully rendered that we come upon it gradually, and it does not diminish in power with each successive reading. Books that slightly hide their themes are not quickly abandoned. One mother told me that she always gave her son books to read that were a little beyond him, not only to stretch him but also to ensure that he would continue to seek them out and, in that way, form a lasting bond with them. In keeping with her sentiment, I have not grouped books into categories according to the ages of child readers. My sense is that the best books grow with their young readers and are rarely cast aside. Furthermore, issues of separation, self-assertion, and so on may be seen as constant throughout the early years of childhood.

With regard to enduring appeal, a Columbia University professor told me that when his daughter came home for her first college vacation, she and a childhood friend spent hours together reading aloud from their favorite children's books. Giggles and exclamations emanated from behind her closed bedroom door. When his daughter described the experience to him afterward, he said he had the feeling that this return served a dual purpose: it was both a comforting reassurance that the past had survived intact and a clear marker of distance on the girls' path away from childhood toward maturity.

Another case confirms the ongoing appeal of books beyond the specific years for which their publisher targeted them. A two-year-old boy habitually searched for the moons in Sendak's *Where the Wild Things Are* (1963). At every reading, he asked for the moon on any page where it is not represented. Later, when he was four years old, loving the book just as much, the same little boy had no interest whatever in the moons but now expressed anxiety during the wild orgy that occurs in the central pages of the book, where there are simply pictures and no words. Although it may seem rash to speculate in the absence of other information about this child, we might hazard a guess that, whereas issues of separation had preoccupied the boy when he first encountered the *Wild Things*, a different psychological issue—namely, the control of impulses—had by age four become a major theme in his young life. What intrigues me is the overarching fact that, in spite of whatever changes had occurred in his development and in the external world between the ages of two and four, this unique work of art was capable of keeping up with him, so to speak, and of symbolizing for him the ongoing major themes in his life—a testament both to *its* psychological resonance and power and to his own and to the match between them.

In selecting what to cover here, I have chosen, with notable exceptions (mainly, Beatrix Potter) American picture books of the twentieth century that are still in print. Although it would have been a fascinating complementary undertaking, I have dealt only minimally with the details of their history. Similarly, my focus has not been on their artists and authors, although I have occasionally referred to them when their lives seemed central to my understanding. Rather, my psychological focus has led me to group these works by motif rather than by chronology or individual creator. Some books are mentioned more than once, and the first reference to each includes its original publication date so that interested readers can place it in historical context. In making choices about specific works, I have relied on criteria of psychological richness, aesthetic value (literary and pictorial), and longevity. Unable to deny the subjectivity of these criteria or of the ensuing selections, I can only beg your indulgence. There are simply too many outstanding picture books to able to squeeze all the good ones between the covers of an interpretive work such as this. Perhaps my work will stimulate further interpretive efforts on the part of others. If so, I shall feel well rewarded.

The best books, because they pipe deeply into the fantasy life of children, interrelate with one another on many levels and, I suggest, can thus serve to establish foundations for future interpretive activity in the arts and culture. To give an example of how this incipient cultural associative processing works, Amy, a three-year-old at Harvard's Peabody Children's Center, was listening to Margaret Wise Brown's *Goodnight Moon* (1947). Thoughtfully, she interrupted the story to remark that the rabbit character looked a lot to her like Peter Rabbit. She then asked if we could please read *that* book to her next.

Goodnight Moon itself begins actually with explicit visual references, both to a favorite nursery rhyme, "The Cow Jumped over the Moon," and to a beloved nursery tale, "The Three Bears." These pictorial quotes are given as framed decorations on the wall of the bunny's bedroom, and we might well regard their frames as the emblematic equivalents of quotation marks. Later on these quotes are anchored in the book with verbal labels. Interestingly, when in the early pages of *Goodnight Moon* the cow is directly addressed ("Goodnight cow jumping over the moon"), the image of the cow is released from its frame and sent flying through the air with a page all to itself. This leaping cow is now free to evoke associations for the child as an image in its own right. Among such associations, whether available to conscious recall or not, might be a child's previous experiences of having heard and repeated the relevant nursery rhyme. The three bears, on the other hand, who are at least potentially frightening at bedtime, are never correspondingly liberated. Unlike the friendly cow, they remain confined within their frame. They are bid "goodnight" while securely contained within clearly bounded limits.

Thus, through such citations, encounters with one picture book may evoke memories of other related cultural objects, and connections among books, imagery, poetry, and shared good feelings may be established and reinforced.

Even when they are not intended to do so, picture books provide children with some of their earliest takes on morality, taste, and basic cultural knowledge, including messages about gender, race, and class. They supply a stock of images for children's mental museums. Read by loving parents and respected adults or older siblings, they stand firm against later experience. Yet they are not, as we shall see, always remembered accurately. From time to time, in these pages, memories of adults' early encounters with picture books will be recounted. For several of these accounts, I am indebted to the interviews conducted with Harvard undergraduates by my Radcliffe research partners, Talia Milgrom-Elcott and Sandra Youngmie Lee, in spring 1996, when I was in residence at the Bunting Institute.

One student reported that she brought with her to college her childhood copy of *Where the Wild Things Are* and stashed it between *Beowulf* and Shakespeare. Another student searched among his chemistry textbooks and computer manuals to find an old copy of *Alexander and the Terrible, Horrible, No Good, Very Bad Day* (1972) by Judith Viorst and Ray Cruz. Asked to explain why he had brought that particular book with him to college, the young man shrugged and said that somehow it just wouldn't have made sense to him *not* to bring it. This book was so much a part of his life that he could not have left it behind. He said that he had reread it in September, upon arriving at college, but hadn't taken it down from the shelf since then. "I think I'll read it before I leave, though," he added. "I haven't had any terrible, horrible days since I've been here, so I haven't needed it, but it was always there just in case." He also remembered with pleasure the special whining voice his mother had used when she portrayed the protagonist of the story, a little boy who complains all the time, and he said the book had always helped him when things went wrong—perhaps because it transported him back to a time when he had been securely cared for.

Memories offer valuable though not unproblematic data concerning the lasting power of these early cultural experiences, which messages get registered, how they are affected by the passage of time, and the relative influence of pictures and words. When I mentioned *Curious George Goes to the Hospital* (1966) and *Corduroy* (1968), one middle-aged scholar was able to recall particular illustrations from these books but had no memory for the details of their plots. An image can simply stick fast in the mind independently of its context. I can still see vividly a page from our family's copy of Walt Disney's *Pinocchio* (1939). Searching on his tiny raft for his father, Geppetto, the little woodenhead is about to be swallowed; Monstro the Whale has just opened his enormous mouth in a terrifying double-page spread that uses up all the available space. I distinctly remember pinching two pages together with my fingers so as to avoid having to stare into that cavernous mouth, it frightened me so. Many years later, when the old book was rediscovered among a collection of family treasures, I found to my amusement that this page, which had caused me so much anguish, was missing.

The reading of picture books can provide the occasion for performance art. This aspect has been alluded to in several anecdotes already, and I would like to underscore it now. Picture books can actually be approached like scripts. In fact, one entirely nonverbal book about bedtime, *Moonlight* (1982), by Jan Ormerod, was "read" to me by three-year-old Haley, who was able to find just the right words with which to express her at times delightfully innovative approaches to each picture.

Normally, picture books do include some printed matter, and children who cannot read them are in a position similar to that of nonmusically trained listeners at a concert. Incapable of deciphering the marks on the score, they are forced to rely on the instrumentalists, vocalists, conductor, and so on to translate these unintelligible marks into audible sound. Furthermore, just as accuracy, timing, and the interpretive skill and knowledge of the listener all affect the reception of the music, so do such factors affect children's responses to picture books. Like musical or other theatrical performers, you, the adult reader, are a mediator between your child and a cultural object. Like a musician, you must be at the same time an attentive listener yourself and affected by the "music." And just as the musician "holds" her audience, so also a picture book reader may hold a child—who may even more concretely be sitting on her lap.

An adult reader can play other roles. He or she can provide a *psychological* embrace as well as a physical one. The adult's presence produces a sense of safety, and this feeling of security is of paramount importance because in the years when picture books are used, representations are not yet fully distinguished from the objects that they represent. This means, in practice, that a frightening illustration of a monster can seem capable of emerging from that page and actually devouring a child or of haunting her dreams. Such lability between fantasy and reality, by the way, is captured brilliantly in a picture book by Chris van Allsberg, *Jumanji* (1981), in which a mischievous girl and boy, while their parents are away, play a "jungle adventure" board game in which the players must roll dice and move pieces along a winding trail of colored squares as they enter the deepest recesses of a make-believe jungle. Suddenly, the children look up in horror from their game. Lying on the top of the piano is an enormous lion who has entered the living room of their house. Fantasy has invaded reality. Another example of that lability is the common belief of small children that people they see on the TV screen actually exist inside the set and can be spoken to. This has been exploited to great effect by *Mister Rogers' Neighborhood*, in which the host, Fred Rogers, engages in "dialogues" with his youthful audience. In a world where make-believe and reality spill over into one another, the presence of a parent is comforting.

Like masterpieces of art created for adults, picture books depend on accepted conventions of narrative style and design to provide meaningful experiences for their readers. In the arts, examples of such conventions or containers might be the frame of a painting; the language, meter, rhyme scheme, and diction of a poem; or the established spatial limits—including the stage, curtain, lights, and fixed temporal range—of a theatrical event. If these physical and psychological containers are unstable or transgressed, uneasiness and displeasure may ensue. As depicted in the music and the libretto of Leoncavallo's *Pagliacci*, life can disrupt art. Therapeutic milieus may, similarly, collapse. Painted monsters may emerge from the pages of a book to terrorize young minds.

Realizing, then, that picture books may elicit anxiety as well as pleasure and laughter—sparks of suspense that are normally resolved into satisfying moments of closure—we can see that, because of the immaturity of their beholders, they may require more containment than their own formal elements provide. This added containment comes ideally from the adult reader. By serving as editor and improviser, a parent can explain vocabulary, point out pictorial details, elaborate themes, and relate stories and images to the child's own daily life and to his own. Above all, by listening carefully to what the child is saying and by noticing nonverbal behavioral responses, parents can create the necessary added context.

The significance of this adult role becomes clear the minute we consider the fate of children who suffer its absence. Left to their own devices, abandoned to experience cultural artifacts on their own, such children miss an important step. They often evince motivational difficulties in learning to read and, in many cases, fail to develop a deep love for books. But each time a small child is helped by an adult or an older child to sense the rising and falling of narrative tension and the stunning immediate effects of color and pictorial representation, his or her pleasure and sense of mastery is a step toward initiation into the realm of art and culture.

When talking to a group of first-time mothers several years ago, I asked them to recall the most frightening image from a book read to them in early childhood. With gentle prodding, a few divulged their memories—the toothy disembodied grin of the Cheshire Cat from *Alice's Adventures in Wonderland*; the huge, gaping mouth of Monstro the Whale from the same widely circulated edition of *Pinocchio* that I had had as a child; the page in *The Story of Babar* where a "wicked hunter" has shot the young elephant's mother. Apropos this last memory, I have found, to the contrary, that many adults fondly recall the Babar of their childhoods but often fail to remember his mother's violent death at the beginning of the story. Nevertheless, in revisiting their own youthful anxieties, quite readily accessible despite the passage of years, many of the mothers in this group were sensitized, at least momentarily, to the powerful effect of pictorial imagery on the psyches of their own children.

Asked to recount the techniques they had invented to cope with scary pictures, several remembered anticipating the page and turning it over quickly. Others reported peeking furtively. In general, avoidance was the most frequently reported strategy. No one could remember, or admit to, tearing out a disturbing page or scribbling over an especially frightening picture. These more extreme measures, when resorted to by children, can be a signal of the conversion of fear into aggression, which is, of course, a common human response. Although negative and destructive on the surface, such actions should be regarded by parents and teachers as also having an important communicative aspect. For, by gaining attention and provoking a response, they bring into the open concerns that had been festering secretly in the dark. As little Max teaches us in *Where the Wild Things Are*, to mess up the house may also be seen, from another perspective, as a creative act, as building himself a private little tent-blanket-space, a kind of refuge. Thus, we must try to stay attuned to children's nonverbal behavior, naughty or not, and remember that it often counts as a potent means of communication.

Just as caregiving adults in their mediating and interpreting roles respond to books according to what is happening in their own lives as well as to what they know of a particular child, so, too, children respond to books from their own perspective and through the lens of what they understand. At different stages of growth and in the wake of specific events, new agendas or altered patterns of response to a well-loved picture book may develop. We noted this earlier with respect to the boy who came up with different "readings" of *Where the Wild Things Are* at ages two and four. Another boy, however, who contracted a severe case of scarlet fever, found that after his recovery he feared and disliked *The Velveteen Rabbit*, which he had formerly loved. He could not bear to think of how the loyal Rabbit had been abandoned by the Boy. Many years later, when he himself became a parent, he refused to read *The Velveteen Rabbit* to his own children, and they had to hear it from their mother's lips. Thus, the abandonment was repeated in a powerful and perhaps not fully understood reenactment.

Another example of a child's own agenda supplying an interpretive perspective comes from three-year-old Ann, who was staring at the distressed-looking caterpillar in *The Very Hungry Caterpillar* (1969), by Eric Carle. This creature has just eaten its way through a piece of chocolate cake, an ice cream cone, a pickle, some slices of Swiss cheese and salami, a lollipop, a wedge of cherry pie, and so on, and has developed an awful stomachache. Contemplating what would seem obviously to be gastric distress as her mother recites the names of all the foods the caterpillar has just consumed, Ann pronounces her own diagnosis: "He is sick," she decides, "because he misses his Mommy." In this book, of course, given that the protagonist is a caterpillar, there is no mother. But when little girls like Ann themselves have upset tummies, *their* first act is to turn for solace to their mommies. Here, Ann reads herself directly into the caterpillar image and thus enriches it for herself and, by sharing her interpretation, also for the adult who is reading to and with her.

Similarly, consider Ludwig Bemelmans's *Madeline* (1939). This canonical text is known verbatim in its entirety by many young children (and adults), and yet, notwithstanding their detailed knowledge of it, many seem to preserve their own unique perspectives and continue to come up with insightful sidelights. One example concerns the page where, after visiting Madeline in the hospital and seeing the shower of gifts she has received subsequent to her appendectomy, all the little girls are shown back at school in their beds, which are arranged in two straight lines. Madeline's bed, of course, is still empty. When Miss Clavel rushes in to ask what is the matter, they all cry " 'Boohoo, / we want to have our appendix out, too!' " The text makes no reference at all to Madeline, but it is clearly intimated that the little girls all feel envious of her trophies and wish they could receive similar presents. What fascinates me is that virtually every three- or four-year-old child to whom I have read this book, when asked why the little girls are crying, offers a different interpretation from the one suggested by the text. Each one invariably tells me, not that the other girls are longing for Madeline's gifts and toys, but that they are crying *because they miss their friend, Madeline.* This despite the fact that they know the story well and fully comprehend the force of the intended interpretation.

These two instances of children's alternative understanding are similar in that distress on the part of characters is attributed not to unpleasant bodily sensations or to wishes for material possessions but to the pain of being separated from another human being, mother or friend, in spite of the fact that perfectly well-known and understood meanings are given by the respective texts. In both cases, the children seem unfettered by any need to subordinate image to text. They give utterance to powerful *other* implicit meanings that also inhere in the contemplated objects. In so doing, they expand our ethical, aesthetic, and psychological takes on these books.

Listening to children's voices can remind us of how limited we ourselves tend to be, how tied to notions of fitness and correctness we are. Three-year-old Haley, for example, was "reading" the wordless picture book *Moonlight* to me just a few days after Halloween. She pointed to a page where a little girl has just emerged from her evening bath. The character is shown wrapped in a fringed golden towel that trails elegantly on the ground behind her with yet another towel draped over her wet head like a turban. Haley exclaimed: "Look! That's a queen!"

It was a stunning perception that I, being somewhat remote from Halloween and dressing up, would not have had, but it fixed the image for me in a compelling and unforgettable new way.

In considering how picture books work to form and play into children's understanding, I think it is worthwhile to acknowledge the ambiguities that lie within our social response to representations in general. On the one hand, there is the view that imaginative works in all media empower viewers to explore a wider range of possibilities, to don a greater diversity of costumes, say, than might be appropriate or even permissible in ordinary life. This perspective gives priority to the notion that cultural experiences serve, at least transiently, to elicit fantasies that fascinate us but are proscribed in the arena of overt behavior. Parenthetically, this view, which assumes a distinction between art and life, wish and fact, fantasy and reality, is one we can take for granted with respect to adults but not when we are dealing with young children. For them, the best works are those that present a shifting universe of unfixed boundaries but in which work is also being done on other levels to differentiate and stabilize these boundaries.

On the other hand, the operative agenda of some works of art is not to extend the range of possibility and give concrete form to vague wishes but rather to promulgate and reinforce prevailing social codes that resist diversity. Understandably, literature for children can blend these opposing aims, and I will look at several books that do.

Illustrations and texts in books for young children therefore both carry *and* challenge prevailing cultural ideologies and stereotypes. To negotiate the ambiguities inherent in them, ambiguities in the meanings of specific images and texts as well as in their relations with one another, the adult reader can serve as an important guide.

To read, to sing, to mediate between a young child's psychic world and the surrounding culture is to experience one of life's great joys. In doing so, we introduce elements of what matters deeply to us to those who will live on after us, we participate in the transmission of culture from one generation to the next. At the same time, to engage in the ways I am advocating here means reopening ourselves to the throb of old wants and wounds. It may mean revisiting inside spaces we think we have left behind and beholding there in blurred focus some of the earliest determinants of our own imaginative lives. Such visits, at best, can result in making better sense of those lives as well as of the lives of our children. But the process must inevitably stretch us. Perhaps, if we can cultivate a flexible mix of robustness and sensitivity, we too may be able to grow, alongside the children.

Chapter 2

It's Time for Bed

Dusk. That delicate time suspended between
wakefulness and slumber, activity and rest,
interaction with others and communion with self.
Suddenly, a rush of anxieties and longings may
appear that were absent during the daylight hours.

Falling asleep for children often means relaxing after an action-packed day. Cozy warm covers, perhaps, and a good night kiss. It means bidding farewell to play, food, and sociability. It means surrendering to the need for rest and peace. Poetry and prayer have related it metaphorically to life's final separation. The *Gates of Repentance*, for example, the Reform Jewish prayerbook for the High Holy Days, contains, in its memorial service, the following lines: "Like children falling asleep over their toys, we relinquish our grip on earthly possessions only when death overtakes us" (1984, p. 480). Many Christian children learn to recite at bedtime a prayer that also relates the two: "Now I lay me down to sleep; I pray the Lord my soul to keep. / If I should die before I wake, I pray the Lord my soul to take." Thus, falling asleep at night is an experience that can be welcomed or feared and that is met normally with a mixture of emotions.

Going safely and calmly to sleep each night prepares a child for the more difficult and final partings that must be faced inevitably later in life. In fact, later on, when we look at books that deal explicitly with death, we will find bedtime scenes included. It is interesting to note that the American middle-class child, unlike children of other social classes and many other countries, is expected to sleep in a room by him- or herself, a practice that is implied in many picture books, even in those written before World War II. To sleep in close quarters with other children and with other members of one's family, however, may significantly alter a child's response to bedtime and to fantasies.

Bedtime is negotiated peacefully by young children and their parents most of the time, but not always. When difficulties arise, many factors may be held responsible, some specific to the individual and his or her unique situation, others more general. In this chapter, I will explore a small number of classic picture books that deal explicitly with bedtime and that have long been read to children to ease the tensions that attend this transition. Each book offers a unique perspective; each speaks subtly to underlying worries that may surface from time to time.

Darkness, by blinding children to the consoling sight of familiar surroundings and objects, may itself become a source of fear. One of the books we will look at, *Goodnight Moon*, by Margaret Wise Brown and Clement Hurd, acknowledges this fact; it conveys the comforting knowledge that, despite a little bunny's gradually diminishing power to see the beloved possessions in his room, he can nonetheless count on all of them to survive the night intact, as will he and the love of those who care for him.

Wait till the Moon Is Full (originally published in 1948), by Margaret Wise Brown and Garth Williams, takes a different approach to bedtime by taming darkness itself. This gentle picture book turns the night into a scene of friendly merriment for children.

Bedtime is the point when parents actively separate themselves from their offspring, and under some circumstances and from time to time, this routine parting may be perceived as an abandonment. When parents withdraw physically, they take with them, temporarily, their attention and affection, which, as children quickly perceive, they can refocus on one another or on other individuals or interests. Children left alone in their beds may understandably feel neglected and long to continue being the primary objects of their parents' love and solicitude. (A classic statement of this longing occurs in *Where the Wild Things Are*, when Max, banished to his room, sits exhausted after his orgiastic romp with the monsters, his head resting dejectedly on his hand, and "was lonely and wanted to be where someone loved him best of all.") Enterprising young persons, finding themselves in this unwanted state, invent, as we all know well, a variety of ingenious schemes to delay the inevitable nighttime parting.

Both *Bedtime for Frances* (1960), by Russell Hoban and Garth Williams, and *Moonlight*, by Jan Ormerod, treat this phenomenon from the perspective of a little girl. And I want to interject here that there have been, over the years, far fewer classic picture books with starring roles for girls than for boys. As a result, large numbers of American women have grown up reading stories about boys whereas most American boys rarely encounter comparable stories about girls. This imbalance may contribute in a not inconsiderable way to difficulties the genders experience later on in relating to one another. Here, therefore, in the context of bedtime stories, I want to make a strong plea for cross-gendered reading—for boys hearing stories about girls as well as the reverse. I advocate this practice in the hope that it may help boys to feel as comfortable identifying with little girls as girls of necessity have had to feel for generations about identifying with boys and, later on, with masculine heroes in drama and literature more generally.

Maurice Sendak's *In the Night Kitchen* (1970) also thematizes bedtime as exclusion from parental intimacy, but here the point of view, unlike that of the previously mentioned books, is distinctly masculine. Gender accounts for important differences between the way Mickey, the protagonist of *In the Night Kitchen*, and Frances, the protagonist of *Bedtime for Frances*, choose to cope with and master their respective situations. Bedtime is portrayed in strikingly contrasting terms in these two classic examples. Mickey creates a heroic fantasy in order to triumph over his noisy parents and prove that he can fend for himself in their absence. Frances, on the other hand, in her "abandoned" state, bends all her cleverness not toward establishing her independence of her parents but rather toward reinserting herself into the coveted parental nest. Thus, the two books both separately and together comment on our different modes of socializing boys and girls.

The former are pushed in the direction of autonomy and self-reliance; the latter, toward uninterrupted human contact and interaction.

Fear of bad dreams is the subject of Mercer Mayer's *There's a Nightmare in My Closet* (1968), which may resonate especially with children who are familiar with the Frances books and with *Where the Wild Things Are*, both of which are quoted pictorially in it. Like several of the others, this book models the creation of a scary fantasy: a monster (the dreaded nightmare), which can be tamed and which is even treated by its protagonist, an unnamed little boy, with the ambivalence toddlers usually reserve for their baby brothers and sisters.

Finally, children of four, five, and six have the capacity to be quite independent when left alone in the dark. They may actually revel in the uninterrupted opportunity bedtime brings for exercising their imaginations and for making up nighttime adventures in which they are free to face dangers, rescue themselves, and triumph gloriously over distressful events that occurred during the day. A. A. Milne's marvelous poem "In the Dark" springs to mind:

> Here I am in the dark alone,
> What is it going to be?
> I can think whatever I like to think,
> I can play whatever I like to play,
> I can laugh whatever I like to laugh,
> There's nobody here but me.
> I'm talking to a rabbit . . .
> I'm talking to the sun
> I think I am a hundred—
> I'm one   (*Now We Are Six*, 1927, pp. 100, 101).

Similar imaginative bedtime adventures are given visual form in Crockett Johnson's inimitable picture book, *Harold and the Purple Crayon* (1955). In works such as these, bedtime is portrayed as an ideal occasion for mental experimentation. Little Harold savors the pleasures of his solitude as, utterly uncensored, he "draws" freely and wildly upon the powers of his imagination.

Bedtime is also the time when parents are most likely to read to their children. In this sense, no matter what the overt subject of the book chosen for an evening's reading may be, its fundamental message will have to do with its being the last human contact before sleep. Accordingly, every book discussed in these pages may be interpreted as a bedtime story, and some of what is said here can be applied to other books as well. We will begin, however, with books that explicitly address this theme.

Goodnight Moon

When Clement Hurd, the illustrator of *Goodnight Moon*, died several years ago, he was honored on Valentine's Day on the editorial page of the *New York Times* (Feb. 14, 1988). Declaring that "some things are inexplicably magical," the *Times* article went on to evoke hundreds of freshly scrubbed small children in pajamas falling peacefully to sleep in the world created by this artist. By the time of his death, *Goodnight Moon* had been in print for four decades, and over two million copies had been sold. The *Times* writer's imaginary vision of children actually going to sleep in the world of *Goodnight Moon* takes on even greater specificity when we read it in the context of an anecdote reported by Clement Hurd himself.

Apparently, at bedtime one evening, a little boy of eighteen months had heard *Goodnight Moon* five times and after the final rendition was contemplating the book as it lay open before him, its last pages revealed. These pages are the ones in which the "great green room" has grown dark and quiet and the little bunny has closed his eyes. The words read: "Goodnight noises everywhere." The small boy in question stared at the open book before him and then deliberately placed one of his feet on the left-hand page and struggled to get his other foot on to the right-hand page; thereupon, he burst into tears. His mother, watching this behavior, took only a second to realize what he was doing: he was trying with all his might to transport his whole small body into the cozy, loving world of *Goodnight Moon* (Marcus 1987, p. 22).

From *Goodnight Moon*. Copyright © 1947 by Harper & Row, Publishers, Incorporated. Text copyright renewed 1975 by Roberta Brown Rauch. Illustrations copyright renewed 1975 by Clement Hurd. Printed in the U.S.A. All rights reserved. Used by permission of HarperCollins Publishers.

Who can presume to account for the love inspired by a work of art? The best we can do is offer clues. In the case of picture books, the value of such clues is that they may find their way, subtly, into our subsequent readings to children—not only of the book at hand but also of other books and even of other cultural objects. Clues as to why certain cultural objects are loved may thus enrich our ongoing dialogues with children. As we gain insight into the factors that seem to matter most, we can search for them and attempt to discover and recreate them elsewhere.

Let's start with a key factor: rhythm. What I mean by rhythm are both auditory and pictorial patterns of flow and forward movement.

Goodnight Moon is structured by its rhythms. If you listen to the regular beats of the accented words in its simple text and note how soothing they sound, together with their alliteration ("great green room") and their internal rhymes ("little bears sitting on chairs" and "brush" and "mush" and "hush"), you will perceive the subtle power of this crucial element and begin to look for it in other places. *Goodnight Moon* provides an auditory counterpart and complement for a child's heartbeat as it calms down in the moments before she falls asleep. Parenthetically, its rhythmic structures are common to many of Margaret Wise Brown's less well known but equally fine books, such as *The Runaway Bunny* (1942) and *The Golden Egg Book* (1947), as well as to many books by other authors and artists. I am thinking of Helen Bannerman's *The Story of Little Black Sambo* (1899), a book that has just been updated and reillustrated in two quite different and fascinating versions, that I will consider in my final chapter. In that book, the two repeated refrains, "Little Black Sambo, I'm going to eat you up," and "Now *I'm* the grandest Tiger in the Jungle," serve a complex dual role: they create suspense *and* calm fear. They set up expectations that can be fulfilled—rhythmic repetition that arouses anxiety and simultaneously soothes by means of its predictability. Thus, as in *Goodnight Moon*, the formal structure creates ideal conditions under which children can play out themes concerning the mastery of fears. In *Goodnight Moon*, these fears are mainly of darkness, abandonment, loss of love and of control; in Helen Bannerman's book, the fears are preeminently oral in nature—fears of being eaten, destroyed, engulfed, lost. In each work, rhythm establishes a holding pattern for the emotions. Rhythm and recurrence, therefore, are elements we might watch and listen for when selecting books for young children. I shall have more comments later about *Little Black Sambo* itself and about the psychological value of repetition, both auditory and pictorial.

Two clocks in the bunny's room are set at seven when *Goodnight Moon* begins. As measured by the hands on these clocks, the time has progressed to ten past eight by the time the last page is reached; thus, an entire imaginary hour has elapsed between the book's first and final moments. This slowing down is exquisitely appropriate to its theme: the transition between day and night, activity and repose.

This prolongation of time in *Goodnight Moon* symbolizes and concretizes an antidote for conditions even more poignant today than when the book was originally published some fifty years ago. Today's American children are, of necessity, clamped squirming in the vise of our rapidly paced, technologically driven culture. Paradoxically, they are being held down while being speeded up at an ever-accelerating rate. Given little space for the growth of their own imaginations and little time for the gradual acquisition of mastery, today's children are bombarded with prefabricated stimuli—images, sensations, impressions that occur fast and furiously. As the media disseminate "information" in visual terms and pictures fly past, we understand little about the long- or short-term effects of the speed and volume of communication. What might be *its* psychological consequences? Might, for instance, the rapid processing of imagery, particularly imagery that is exciting and frightening, curtail rather than nurture human capacities for reflection, containment, and nuanced emotional response? Could it be that the cherished ancient metaphor "to see is to know" might collapse if exposure to visual material is too rapid? Could speed decrease rather than increase the virtues of delay and deliberation, not to mention empathy? What serious human losses are implied in the shift we are witnessing from a slower paced narrative-verbal culture to a faster paced image-based culture? And especially, what are the effects of this shift on the very youngest children, whose first mission is to find and construct for themselves a meaningful and safe world?

Goodnight Moon absolutely refuses speed. It cannot be hurried through. In this sense it works as a welcome antidote to the pressures we impose on our children. Children who have been rushed through the day can relax into it. Confidently, they know what will come next; and yet, as they trace the antics of the little mouse or encounter a new word or observe a new form, they are learning as well. They can feel, in this imaginary space, the pleasures of satisfied expectations, the meeting of hope with fulfillment. Thus, never static, *Goodnight Moon* is also a site of exploration. It creates a world that reminds me of an artist's studio, where familiarity becomes the locus for growth. Think, for example, of Matisse's painting *The Red Studio* (1911), with its similar electric Chinese red; its touches of green and flecks of gold; its wine glass, chair, and chest; its framed and unframed pictures; and its possible clock and window. How like an artist's studio is the bedroom of a small child? Filled with highly invested possessions, this room is also a dual locus of security and discovery, of work and of rest.

To return now to rhythm and recurrence, I want to note that these aesthetic features work pictorially as well as auditorily in *Goodnight Moon*. The repetition of imagery here is patent and wise—wise because it is reassuring. When we understand that young children are engaged in the ongoing process of forging and strengthening their nascent sense of identity and of boundaries, we can see that, as Selma Fraiberg points out in *The Magic Years* (1959, pp. 174–75), they may resist falling asleep precisely because the loss of consciousness seems to threaten their newly developing sense of identity, their concept of who they are. If this idea seems strange to you, consider for a moment your own intermittent adult fears of falling asleep. Often these fears have to do with anxiety over giving up control and over the temporary loss of consciousness, anxiety fueled by the symbolic alliance of sleep and death, which we have already remarked. In the presence of such dysphoria, *Goodnight Moon* works on many levels, psychologically and aesthetically, to allay fear. Its pictures shore up the child's sense of intactness just at the moment when that cohesion seems to be slipping away. By picturing all the familiar objects of daily life, and by repeating them and naming them, its pages convey a clear message that life and self are whole and can be counted on to continue being there, even as darkness descends.

Françoise Gilot, in her memoir *Life with Picasso* (1989), describes how, in the village of Vallauris in southern France, women known as "weepers" traditionally go to the bedside of a dying person and re-evoke with that person all the events they can recall of his or her ebbing life, such as the time his hair was pulled by another child on the day of First Communion; thus the "weepers," with a series of word-pictures, reinforce the dying individual's sense of identity at a time when that intactness is on the verge of vanishing forever. Villagers, through this tradition, are given the opportunity to pass away in peace after being affirmed and witnessed and after having gathered together, in a sense, all the memories that gave them a sense of completeness. Gilot says that, hearing about this practice, she protested to her housekeeper, a weeper, that she found it cruel and grotesque. The weeper replied: "Just the contrary. . . . If he can recall everything of importance that happened to him on earth, happy *or* sad, he can start his new life on the other side happy and free" (p. 294).

By analogy, in *Goodnight Moon*, the catalogue of items pictured are just those that matter to children. The room is filled with objects that intimately connect each small boy and girl to the routines of ongoing daily life. I have already noted the framed pictures on the wall and their resonances. The red balloon might suggest birthday parties and other celebrations and prefigure, for some children, their experiences with another well-known picture book, *The Red Balloon* (1956) by Albert Lamorisse. The bowl of cereal, brush and comb, slippers, telephone, clocks, dollhouse, books, mittens, socks, animals, and doll—all serve as reminders of elements of a child's own personal life and function as reassurances of the ongoing nature of the self. Just as the catalogue of the weeper helps an old person to die in peace, so too the collection of objects in *Goodnight Moon* enables small children to fall asleep in peace.

Another picture book fits in here. *I'm Suzy* (1966), by Dorotha Ruthstrom and Alice Schesinger, is not ostensibly about bedtime but performs exactly the same sort of psychological work to which the anecdote from Gilot's memoir refers. Each page of *I'm Suzy*, picturesque and detailed, portrays a little girl's engagement with the various activities of her daily life. The format of the text differentiates her as "Suzy" from everything and everyone else around her—from the animals, objects, and other persons in her surroundings. Thus, the first-person voice of the text states: if Suzy were a "pretty surprise present," she would wrap a red ribbon all around herself and tie it in the middle, whereas if she were a kitten, she would wear the same red ribbon around her neck; but because she is not a present and not a kitten but rather a little girl called Suzy, she wears the red ribbon in her hair. In this fashion, text and pictures proceed to distinguish the child from her environment while affirming her embeddedness in it and its crucial importance for her. The refrain emphasizes that the child is *not* all the other things with which she is connected but uniquely herself, and the book ends with two psychologically related images: on its penultimate page, Suzy is shown being embraced by her mother, and on the last page, she is seen hugging herself, while an earlier-mentioned puppy and kitten climb around her. The words beneath this final picture express her pleasure in selfhood: "I'm so glad I'm Suzy."

A book of this sort—and there are many of this genre, featuring boys as well as girls—read just before bedtime, can provide the sort of strong support for self that is given by *Goodnight Moon*. My hunch concerning this point was informally tested and confirmed during a reading one day to four-year-old Alexandra, who, never having encountered the book before, chimed in each time I read the words of the refrain, "I'm Suzy." She continued to join in wherever the phrase occurs until the very last page of the book when, instead of saying "I'm so glad I'm Suzy," Alex said spontaneously: "I'm so glad I'm *me!*"

Returning now to *Goodnight Moon*, color is also important. Green and red are complementary colors—strong opposites that rivet the eye. I think now, with *Goodnight Moon* in front of me, of Van Gogh and of two stunningly related paintings— the *Night Café* and *Bedroom at Arles*, both painted in 1888, and both eerily evoked here somehow by *Goodnight Moon*. Van Gogh himself struggled mightily all his life with separation and identity, the very issues that are at stake for young children when they go to sleep. In *Goodnight Moon*, that glaring red, green, and gold palette is tamed by Clement Hurd, but the book is not without undertones of wildness.

This visual analysis brings up another point concerning the layers of meaning in such a book. *Goodnight Moon* is not *merely* soothing, not simply saccharine. It admits the possibilities of something vaguely sinister and *then* proceeds to soothe. Look at that tiger rug. Notice the bunny turned expectantly toward a phone; the two cats facing each other with a little mouse behind them; the pictorial reference to Goldilocks, who trespassed and barely escaped the wrath of the grizzly bears, and the little bunny actually climbing out of his covers to look up at it, for the picture hangs right over his head—and above all, the impending darkness. I do not mean to overemphasize these factors but merely to observe that implicit struggles with what is difficult ground this book and lend it some of its richness. Bold, highly saturated colors—green and red—speak volumes: this is not a pastel book.

The psychological function of the surviving objects in *Goodnight Moon* is profound. They teach young children that life can be trusted, that life has stability, reliability, and durability. The youngest children live, as it were, in a world of vanishing objects. A baby cries when mother leaves because her absence is experienced as threatening to the child's very existence. A crucial step in early development is therefore the establishment of what has been called "object permanence," "object constancy," or "basic trust." Essentially, these related ideas simply mean a secure knowledge that just because something cannot be seen at a particular moment it has not disappeared forever. One's loved ones are a permanent acquisition, even when lost to view; one's self is ongoing as well. Games of hide-and-seek and peek-a-boo are founded on the need for such learning. Here, the issue is patent: each object in *Goodnight Moon* can be recognized and named, and each one persists from the beginning to the end. Darkness may envelop the world, but love and self endure. On the very last page, to make this point explicit, the grandmother has left for the night, and little bunny is alone. Clement Hurd, for the second time, quotes from another book he and Margaret Wise Brown made together, *The Runaway Bunny*, in which a child and his mother are continually reunited after multiple separations. *Goodnight Moon* thus metaphorically pledges enduring love.

Like alphabet books, which are introduced a bit later in children's lives (when mastery of verbal language begins to skyrocket), *Good-*

night Moon affords opportunities for pointing and naming. It can be a jumping-off place for games in which children say the name of, and bid goodnight to, all the toys and paraphernalia in their own rooms. Spoofs abound. The *New Yorker* cartoonist Stevenson did a marvelous one (*New Yorker,* Jan. 8, 1990, p. 42) in which a balding, middle-aged tycoon, reading in bed, looks up from his book to say "Goodnight room. Goodnight moon!" And Charles Shultz depicted Lucy under a striped blanket in bed while Charlie Brown reads to her beside a darkened window. Lucy, as usual, complains testily to Charlie Brown: "Why would anyone want to say 'Goodnight' to the moon?"

Why, indeed? Over and over again, we encounter this image depicted in children's books. It plays a central role, as we will see, in *Harold and the Purple Crayon*, where a little boy's memory of the moon shining in through his bedroom window finally enables him, after much searching, to find his way home. It figures in *Where the Wild Things Are* and also in *In the Night Kitchen*. It appears, of course, in James Thurber's *Many Moons* (1943), Sadie Rose Weilerstein's *What the Moon Brought* (1942), Brown's *Wait till the Moon Is Full,* Tomi Ungerer's *Moon Man* (1967), Mercer Mayer's *There's a Nightmare in My Closet,* and in the more recent Caldecott winner *Owl Moon* by Jane Yolen and John Schoenherr (1987), where it is mentioned in the title and depicted on the cover but nowhere else, and in countless other books, where frequently it takes the form of an orb or crescent shining in through a window.

Because of the multiplicity of these images, their referents are complex. In other words, because children exposed to picture books associate each depiction with a host of prior experiences, the referent for each is never simply the natural moon in the sky. Instead, it is all the *pictured moons* a child has known and loved, *Goodnight Moon* being the paradigmatic one and in all likelihood the first encountered.

What does this symbol evoke? One obvious answer, because of its roundness, is the mother—her face, her breast. Like a mother from the perspective of a small child, the moon appears in repetitive cycles, disappearing and always predictably returning, changing its appearance but always identifiable. Just as a mother may don different costumes, express diverse moods, assume a variety of facial expressions and yet still be mother, so too the moon alters its shape and size and look but is nonetheless unmistakably the moon. Illuminating the darkness, it, again like a mother, serves as a beacon in the frightening realm of the unknown. Associated by children with bedtime, its predictable presence is a constant bulwark against the strangeness and boundlessness that darkness brings. In this sense, the moon shining in through a window seems a pictorial equivalent for the stable environment created for children by their mothers but also, analogously, by any adult reader of the picture book.

Furthermore, the moon shining in through the window, pictured on the page of a book, can be thought of as mirroring the child's own face as he or she contemplates the scene. A fine example of this is in *Moon Man*, where the beholder is clearly expected to identify with the soft, round-faced title character, whose longing for another planet, where men and women dance all night with one another, ends in a happy return to his own familiar surroundings. Unlike *Bedtime for Frances*, where a little girl tries to rejoin her parents in reality and finally gives up, or *In the Night Kitchen* where Mickey triumphs over his "rejecting" parents by creating a fantasy in which he manages without them, the Moon Man child creates a *fantasy* of joining his parents and participating in their adult activities—but then, after a while, finds that it is not so much fun after all and that it is simply more comfortable going back to his own space.

In keeping with psychological studies (Kernberg 1987) showing that young children tend to conflate mirror images of themselves with their mothers, we could interpret some of these pictured moons as representing a kind of combined self and mother. This idea jibes with the notion that the young child's reluctance to part with his or her mother has to do with the deep sense that, through her caregiving and other ministrations, she is in fact a part of the child, and losing her is tantamount to losing an aspect of his or her own being. If that idea seems strange to you, you might turn it around and consider examples from your own experience in which mothers have described their children as parts of themselves. My point here is not to make any strong claims about the meaning of the moon to any particular child but simply to underscore the richness of the lunar symbol and suggest some possible associations to it. As for the window frame through which the orb or crescent appears, this seems to me a possible figure for the door frame through which a mother often enters and vanishes, and, likewise, for the frame of a mirror.

Goodnight Moon is, in short, an amazing work. It lies there, spine-ripped, scotch-taped and smudged, pages coming unsewn, tenderly defying all those scholars who want to historicize everything. It says: But look at me! I was made fifty years ago, before the mothers and fathers of today's young children were born, yet I am loved more than ever. Despite the changes wrought by the past half-century—McCarthyism, Sputnik, the civil rights movement, Haight-Ashbury, Vietnam, the women's movement, Watergate, gay rights, the internet, cyberspace, and the advent of a new millennium—I am still taken to bed every night by thousands of American children, to whom I belong and who still need me.

Wait till the Moon Is Full

This Margaret Wise Brown classic, illustrated by Garth Williams, came out in the postwar period just a year after *Goodnight Moon*, and, although it has been reissued and is available today, it has never possessed the stamina of the latter. (Few books do.) I believe that this lack of staying power is only partly due to its leisurely and measured pace. It is a book about taming the night, but it is also about the unpopular childhood task of learning to wait. Children listening to it must do just that. Moreover, the parent reading it must have a high patience quotient, for the story recaps precisely the trajectory of parent-child reactions when tolerance for frustration is at a premium.

For toddlers, waiting is an extremely difficult task because it means controlling desire and the powerful impulse to do something right now.

From *Wait till the Moon Is Full*. Copyright © 1948 by Margaret Wise Brown. Printed in the U.S.A. All rights reserved. Used by permission of HarperCollins Publishers.

The demand to wait sets up within a young child an inner struggle between the part of the self that wants to push forward and another part that is willing to comply with the request and hold back. Today, in a world filled with gadgets—for example, ones that click to make pictures appear on a screen—the tolerance for delay is less prized than in 1948, when the world was recovering from devastating war (that is, from the effects of rampant impulsivity and uncontrolled aggression). Waiting seemed an important lesson to teach. And yet, all education and civilization depend on the human capacity to anticipate and to delay.

Throughout *Wait till the Moon Is Full*, except for the first and last pages, which are in full color, Garth Williams uses a lithographic technique that gives texture and softness to each illustration so that the fuzzy fur of the raccoon mother and her inquisitive child seems almost palpable. The warmth and coziness of their rough wooden furniture and the details of their simple dwelling lend an aura of comfort and serenity to each page and provide a secure visual context for the difficult task of postponing gratification. Williams quotes visually and with uncanny power from the works of his great predecessor Beatrix Potter, and his quotations are symbolic as well as pictorial.

On the book's cover and frontispiece and on several other pages, including the final joyful climax, we see an owl who cannot but refer to Beatrix Potter's terrifying and inscrutable "Old Brown," from *The Tale of Squirrel Nutkin* (1903). Irritated by a naughty squirrel's antics, Old Brown nearly skins him alive and ends by breaking off the poor little fellow's tail, leaving him with merely a stump and so traumatized that he loses the power of speech forever. (I will return later to this story.) Night is a fearful place, therefore, where predatory owls hold sway.

Likewise, Garth Williams's frontispiece, showing the mother raccoon in kerchief and shawl, basket over her arm and treading through a meadow, refers unmistakably to the title character, a hedgehog, of Beatrix Potter's *Tale of Mrs. Tiggy-winkle* (1905). Note the raccoon's kerchief, white with polka-dots all over, a visual analogue for the prickles that poke out of Mrs. Tiggy-winkle's white bonnet. Throughout the book, Garth Williams's raccoon mother recalls Beatrix Potter's hedgehog, whose maternal qualities, though patent, are fraught with bristling ambiguity. We shall return to Mrs. Tiggy-winkle, but suffice it to say that Williams's visual sources deepen and complicate Margaret Wise Brown's poetic text, adding psychological richness to what might seem superficially to be a saccharine tale.

A little raccoon, who has seen the day, wants to see the night, and his mother tells him to wait till the moon is full. On each successive page, he questions her as she performs familiar household tasks—washing, ironing, marketing, sewing. Little raccoon, like all young children who are told to wait, asks questions not only about how long he must wait ("Will I see it soon?") but also about what he is waiting for ("How big is the night?" "How big is big?") and about whether others are like himself ("Does everyone sleep at night?"). When his mother gets tired of answering his questions, she sings songs to him, which are actually answers in themselves. For, as we know, a child's manifest question is only the topmost layer of his mental state. By singing to him, the little raccoon's mother is addressing a deeper layer: she is allaying his concern, soothing and distracting him. She is enabling him to wait more peacefully. In doing so, she is answering, in effect, not only the asked but also the unasked question he is posing.

As we saw in *Goodnight Moon*, there is an underbelly of anxiety that fuels this book, so that it treats the night as an element that needs to be gentled. And, as in *Goodnight Moon*, the elements of rhythm and repetition soothe. Each time little raccoon questions his mother, the child listening to the story hears the words: " 'Wait,' said his mother. 'Wait till the moon is full.' " And on the page just before he is finally allowed to go out into the night because at last the moon *is* full, we hear the refrain repeated twice. Reading it to three-year-old Haley, I began by reciting the important line *with* her but ended by simply nodding and letting her fill it in all by herself. It seemed to me that the principal source of pleasure for her, unlike for the main character of the book, lay in the act of repetition rather than in our arrival at the final page of fulfillment, where raccoons and bunnies are depicted cavorting under a pale yellow orb while their mothers sit close by, knitting, chatting, and keeping a watchful eye from their perch on a log. For Haley, I sensed, this idyll seemed anticlimactic. She was expecting something more dramatic after such a long buildup, and perhaps this is where cultural history and changing times do enter and alter our experiences with works of art. *Wait till the Moon Is Full* works wonders in cultivating frustration tolerance, but its ending can be a letdown to today's TV-fed child. Darkness *is* incrementally tamed throughout the book—that is clearly the source of its psychological strength—but its failure to attract a wider readership today may have to do as much with its weak finale as with its intrinsically difficult theme.

Why is the ending so insipid? Is it only because today's children are used to a diet of stronger stuff? I think not. If we ask ourselves what it is that goes on at night about which children are intensely curious, we may find a clue. Both *Bedtime for Frances* and *In the Night Kitchen* acknowledge that a persistent object of children's curiosity, whether explicitly stated or implied, has to do with the nocturnal relations between their parents. This possibility is simply absent from *Wait till the Moon Is Full.* Here, although we have a story all about a little boy's curiosity concerning what goes on when he is asleep, there is no father at all, even at the end. The only remotely adult male character who is introduced visually is the owl, who himself is actually quite radically tamed on the final page. Whereas on the frontispiece the owl is portrayed as large and potentially menacing, perched on the branch of a dead tree, by the final image he has been reduced to the tiniest figure on the page. He rests, hors de combat on the branch of a far milder tree, green and living. Thus, I am proposing, the final page of *Wait till the Moon Is Full* may fail to satisfy today's children not only because it presents a benignly familiar playground scene but also because, after having carefully elevated their suspense, mobilized their anxiety, sensitively recorded their intense curiosity about the night, it culminates in a vision that bypasses two of their most central issues, sexuality and aggression, and thus leaves them still wondering, still guessing, still— despite the promise of its title—*waiting.*

One practical solution to this lack of satisfaction might be to redo the ending with the child to whom you are reading the book. One mother told me that, whenever she and her little son get to the pages in *Where the Wild Things Are* on which there are no more words and Max is having his orgy with the monsters, they simply put the book down and perform their own noisy little hoot-n'-holler. I have not tried this technique myself during readings of *Wait till the Moon Is Full.* It may seem inappropriate, given the soothing spirit of the text, for some children, but it might be a perfect way to capitalize on the book's great strengths without allowing it to peter out in the end. And if a father could be involved in the moon-rumpus, so much the better.

To return to the power of rhythm and repetition here—the literary and pictorial device that structures so many favorite children's books—one interesting function of it became clearer to me when I was reflecting on Haley's reaction to *Wait till the Moon Is Full.* As noted earlier, part of the difficulty of waiting, for children, comes from being blocked in their wish to "do something now." As I was noticing Haley's pleasure in repeating the refrain in this book, I realized that this act of repetition was in fact affording her the opportunity to do precisely what she craved: to *do* something in the present, to act, even though it was a substitute for the desired act—namely, to be let in on the secrets of the night.

This insight about the active valence of repetition in the context of reading picture books with children caused me to recall two other particularly stunning instances in which it functions similarly. One is the story of *The Three Bears* (1967). Of all the versions I have encountered so far, my unrivaled favorite is the one illustrated by Feodor Rojankowsky. The pictures in this edition are full-color watercolor paintings with brushstrokes visible, the three bears' fur so thickly textured, so warm and brown, that you can almost smell it and hear the bears making growling noises. On one page, their massive heads loom so large, zoom in so close, that you feel the wetness of Father Bear's nose, the roughness of his gray-pink tongue, the sharpness of his teeth and of Mother Bear's black curving claws. Rojankowsky paints it all into pulsating life for children: the three porridge bowls steaming, the lush forest deep with evergreens and white birch, and Baby Bear's bedroom wall adorned with a painted picture straight out of *Der Blaue Reiter,* an equine symbol for energy and uncontrolled wildness. Here, the repetition really counts: "Someone's been sitting in my chair! Someone's been sitting in *my* chair! Someone's been sitting in *MY* chair!" And, with the change of voice implied in each recurrence, the picture book metamorphoses into a performance piece, Rojankowsky turning magically from illustrator into set designer, costumier, choreographer, and director. Actually, as I conjure this transformation, I wonder whether it was not just such an underlying impulse that drove Maurice Sendak away from the making of picture books into the realm of opera first and then, later, into children's theater. The links are surely there.

My other association, which comes directly from the repeated line in *Wait till the Moon Is Full*, involves a mother-son pair as well, but this time of painted jaguars, not raccoons. I am referring to Rudyard Kipling's *Just So Stories* (1902) and in particular to "The Beginning of the Armadillos," in which a mother jaguar, giving advice to her predatory little son, speaks to him "ever so many times, graciously waving her tail." This phrase, like a Homeric epithet, is repeated a half-dozen times in the course of the tale and, like "Wait till the moon is full," provides both a musical refrain and emotional ballast for the narrative. Kipling, throughout the *Just So Stories* (a title that, by the way, I am certain refers to this very device of rhythm and repetition and to children's demands to hear the words of each story repeated in *exactly* the same way each time) ceaselessly invents such flourishes. His repeats, however, unlike those in most of the other texts we have been considering, serve more purely as ornaments than as actual elements of plot. In the story of "How the Elephant Got His Trunk," for example, we meet an important character always referred to as the "Bi-Colored-Python-Rock-Snake," and the action of that story takes place on the banks of "the great gray-green greasy Limpopo River all set about with fever trees." Similarly, in the ticklish tale of "How the Rhinoceros Got His Wrinkly Skin," the Parsee, who is innocent, wronged, but well-avenged against a plundering rhino, is mentioned only and always as "the Parsee from whose hat the rays of the sun were reflected in more-than-oriental splendor." Each of these epithets, then, as in the case of *Wait till the Moon Is Full*, serves, with its imagery, rhythm, and alliteration, powerful psychological as well as aesthetic functions. In so doing, I suggest, it lives on in memory long after the details of plot, character, or even explicit illustrations are forgotten.

Bedtime for Frances and *In the Night Kitchen*

Clearly, these two books, so different from one another and each so fine in its own way, merit separate treatment. I have allowed them to coexist here for, as I have come to realize, they dwell together in my own mind. Furthermore, to write about them together permits me to make a few general observations on the topic of gender difference in picture books.

Bedtime for Frances is another book illustrated by Garth Williams, and to come to it next is to feel a warm sense of familiarity. Its title page reveals a little girl badger, who, with her paw in her mouth, peeks out from behind a partly open door into a room where, we can imagine, her parents are still sitting up together enjoying each other's company. She looks a bit sheepish, knowing full well that she ought not to be there, but a tiny ray of hope flickers: perhaps this time they will let her stay up and join them. The image captures those paradigm moments in childhood when, even though they know perfectly well that you are going to say "no" to them, children go on hoping that, just this once, you will be softhearted and give in. In the same way perhaps, every time I have ever seen a truly affecting performance of *Macbeth* and begun to pity the tormented murderous thane, I hope against hope that just *this time* great Birnam wood to high Dunsinane hill will not repair.

Bedtime is hard, this picture hints, because in many American households it signifies the young child's separation from the company of loved ones. Not only that, but the parents themselves get to go on being with one another, possibly doing pleasurable things, secret things, night things. Frances, peeking in through the doorway, expresses a poignant sense of exclusion: bedtime means being left out.

This poignancy becomes all the sharper when we see the first illustration in which the triad of mother, father, and child are portrayed in cozy proximity—the fur of one touching the next, their ears forming a nearly equilateral triangle. This is what bedtime means relinquishing! And this warm closeness is repeated on the page where mother and father badger are shown kissing Frances goodnight. In fact, on the page after the goodnight scene, we see Frances lying in bed with a

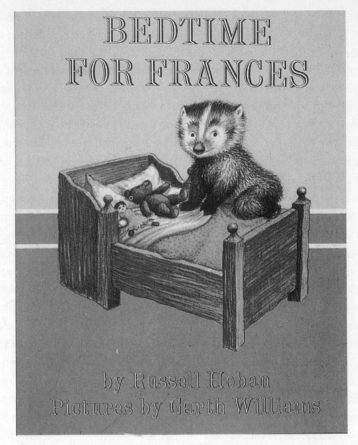

BEDTIME FOR FRANCES

by Russell Hoban
Pictures by Garth Williams

small doll, but the opposite page, where an illustration would normally
be, has been left blank. This blankness dramatizes the contrast between child-with-parents and child-all-alone. It is the only blankness
in the book, and it figures pictorially the silence that also accompanies bedtime. The quiet. No more talking. Frances, however, *does* talk.
She talks to herself, as do many children at night—to fill in the silence

and to repopulate their now-empty worlds. Like little Nick Bottoms in Shakespeare's *A Midsummer Night's Dream*, who, when plunked down in the forest, begin to sing lest they be frightened in their solitude.

Another picture book that touches on this exclusionary element of bedtime is Maurice Sendak's *In the Night Kitchen*, where little Mickey, tucked into his bed at night, hears thumping noises in the dark and shouts "QUIET DOWN THERE!" in the direction of his parents' bedroom. Mickey is angry at hearing uninterpretable sounds that imply a parental scene to which he has not been invited, and this ire sets in motion an entire nocturnal adventure that, just as in *Bedtime for Frances*, involves food, milk, and imaginary danger. As is the case with Frances, Mickey's exclusion from his parents' intimacy precipitates the story (literally, in this case, because Mickey falls out of his bed).

Focusing on this theme, then, let us take a closer look at the striking gender differences portrayed in these two books. Both Frances and Mickey are unhappy about being left out and temporarily abandoned, as it were, by their parents. Mickey, true to acceptable masculine behavior, directly unleashes his anger over this fact. He protests loudly. The high volume of his voice is indicated pictorially by the size of the letters drawn to represent his words. Large enough to fill the entire frame of the picture top to bottom, the three words, QUIET DOWN THERE!, are formed of thick black lines followed by an emphatic exclamation point. They are also command words, appropriated directly from adults. Interestingly, although he is provided with a frightening fantasy adventure in which he is nearly baked in an oven, Mickey never expresses anxiety or dread. Instead, he literally surmounts (rises, airborne, above) his difficulties and becomes a smiling solo hero who, at the end, triumphs over his parents by abandoning them, just as they have, in his mind, temporarily abandoned him. The expression on his face throughout the book is a nearly continuous smile (except for the brief moment at the very beginning when he is angry). Rather than dealing with being left out by trying to get back in, Mickey literally bypasses his parents altogether (passes by their bedroom) and shows that he can survive without and despite them. His story partakes in the adventure genre—a typical tale of male autonomy and derring-do.

In the Night Kitchen, not without significance, frames itself as a fantasy. Unlike *Bedtime for Frances*, where the protagonist's imaginings interweave her experiences in the real world, Sendak's frame (adapted from the *Little Nemo* comics by Winsor McCay, in particular "Little Nemo in Slumberland," 1908 [see Robinson, 1974]) reveals that, although Mickey's fantasy does star himself as survivor and rescue pilot, he begins and ends tucked safely under the covers of his own child-sized bed—in other words, being cared for implicitly by loving parents (as is also the case with little Max, his alter ego in *Where the Wild Things Are*). This notion—that self-saving, self-creating, and self-sustaining elements constitute the preferred bedtime fantasy of little boys—perpetuates a longstanding male myth. In so doing, it also reminds us of an important aspect of picture books: namely, that while they are representing and recapitulating, they are also generating and perpetuating. In other words, when an old myth is reworked and appears on stage, even in modern dress, it may continue to have its habitual effect and to drag along with it its old baggage, including a sometimes problematic ideology. Children imbibe deeply. Picture books, encountered when the world is new, inform them that things are or were, or could be or should be, as depicted.

Bedtime for Frances sets things up differently. It is not by any means devoid of fantasy, but its fantasy elements are more solidly embedded in reality than are those in the Sendak book. I offer this observation without value judgment, but recognize its importance from the point of view of gender. Boys seem to be allowed to stray unrestrainedly into realms of pure unreality, whereas girls are precluded from these realms and required to remain closer to the here-and-now. For a split second, I was going to invoke Lewis Carroll's Alice here as a counterexample, but I decided immediately against it, for in fact her chronic dysphoria, her anxiety, her perpetual confusion, and her discomfort in Wonderland make her instead a case in point. A little girl's behavior, although motivated initially by similar feelings, may turn out to be quite unlike that of a boy's. Think of Peter Pan versus Wendy. Or again of Frances, who never gets openly angry at being put to bed. She never raises her voice to her parents. Instead, she projects whatever hostile feelings she may be harboring into imaginary beings and then, interestingly, turns them not against her parents but back against herself. There is always some scary animal or creature who is out to attack *her*. Rather than shouting at her mother and father, as Mickey does, thereby expressing her feelings directly to their proper objects, she conjures up wrathful tigers, giants, and spiders that are out to get her. Her feeling of being temporarily forsaken by her parents leads to no open manifestation of protest or rebellious independent triumph either within or outside her relationship with them. Instead, she works diligently, ingeniously, and singlemindedly to prevent the exclusion. Like Mickey of *In the Night Kitchen*, she bends her efforts toward avoiding the pain of being left alone, but not by means of fantasizing marvelous adventures for herself. Frances manages her temporary misfortune by trying to undo the separation. Striving to reconnect, she dreams up a series of creative solutions to the problem as she implicitly constructs it. Her construction is very different from Mickey's: namely, how to stay with them—how to enter, rather than bypass, the parental bedroom.

Over and over in picture books for young children, we encounter these gender differences. Little girls turn anger against themselves, whereas little boys send it outward. Boy characters set off on adventures and try to become heroes by learning to fend for themselves; girls are expected to hold on tight and solve their problems within, not outside of, their primary relationships. Later I will look at such issues more closely through a consideration of *Madeline* and *Angry Arthur* (1982). It is worthwhile pointing out, moreover, that these differences in attitude and behavior characterize not only male and female *child* characters but fictional *parental* characters as well.

In Margaret Wise Brown's *The Runaway Bunny* we see the contrast in pure culture. This longlived book presents the gender drama in terms of relations between a male and a female character of different genera-

tions. A male bunny announces that he wants to run away, to which his mother responds, "If you run away . . . I will run after you. For you are my little bunny." Throughout the narrative, the bunny tries to go off on his own, but he cannot escape his mother, for she manages cleverly and magically to remain with him. When he says he will become a rock on a high mountain, she responds immediately that she will become a mountain climber; when he tells her he will become a sailboat and float away, she answers that she will then be the wind and blow him wherever she wants him to go. In the end, the child capitulates and returns to the safety of her arms, which have been waiting for him all along. Thus, the boy child, setting off on his own, comes back finally to accept love and nourishment (depicted here as a carrot) from his mother.

" 'Shucks,' he says, 'I might just as well stay where I am and be your little bunny.' " Both characters, therefore, pursue their gender-coded ideals but, because mothers are more powerful than little boys, and possibly because the author is a woman, in this case feminine desire prevails. To note this, however, is in no way to ignore the supremely important and reassuring message of *The Runaway Bunny*, which concerns loyalty and dependability. It is crucial for toddlers of both sexes to know that their mothers are permanent fixtures in their lives who can be relied upon to be there, no matter what. This message, however, although it takes clear precedence over that of gender, does not supersede it.

A recently published book about a mother and son takes *The Runaway Bunny*'s position to extremes. *Love You Forever* by Robert Munsch and Sheila McGraw appeared in 1986 and last year reached its fourth paperbound printing. I mention it here not by way of recommendation but by way of concern.

On its cover, an appealing small boy in diapers sits on the bathroom floor in front of a large open toilet. This is anomalous because, of all the rooms in an ordinary house, the bathroom, and especially the bathroom as equipped explicitly with a toilet, is the least frequently pictured indoor space in books for young children—despite its relevance to one of the major tasks of early childhood. So already, on its cover, the book presents us with an exception. And because the book's cover seems so strange, it raises an interesting artistic problem—namely that of how an artist can in fact change an existing convention and remedy the longstanding omission of toilets depicted in children's books without offending beholders. How might an artist avoid reactivating the very stereotype she is trying to supersede? For a picture book artist, such a task is especially interesting because the address is to both children and adults. The dilemma is similar to that of parody, where one wants to invoke a familiar object but set up the conditions for an altered response to it. Indeed, *Love You Forever* occasionally brings parodic notions to mind. And, as I have noted, neither artist nor author, while programmatically attempting to tell one story, can prevent other stories from being told as well.

So, having the toilet there seems like a good idea from the point of view of redressing an omission and filling in an important pictorial gap in children's literature. Certainly, it functions as an eye-catcher on the cover. Yet, seeing something pictured that has been systematically excluded from depiction may merely evoke all the prejudices and psychological issues that caused it to be excluded in the first place. On the part of some viewers, it may simply need to be excluded again. Thus, the (adult) beholder's initial reaction to this cover may be negative.

The little boy seated on the blue-tiled bathroom floor smiles and seems about to let an adult wristwatch drop backwards into the toilet bowl. Toilet paper is strewn about everywhere, a ribbon of toothpaste oozes snakelike across the tiles, upon which an open bottle of baby oil is likewise spilling, and powder has "found its way" on to his shirt, the wall, and the floor. This scene of bathroom wreckage recalls to mind a simpler but delightfully wry line drawing of a so-called bathroom wrecker in Munro Leaf's *Manners Can Be Fun* (1936), in which a naked little boy drips puddles across the floor and leaves dirt rings in the tub, while hairs poke out of his brush and his toothpaste tube is similarly uncapped. That earlier bathroom scene, however, contains no visible toilet. Here, the pastel-colored scene of disarray is surmounted by the book's title writ large: LOVE YOU FOREVER. A seemingly odd juxtaposition. Yet the background of the image offers a clue: consisting of wallpaper in a conspicuously feminine-coded floral pattern, it signifies a ubiquitous maternal presence. Even before opening it, we can figure out that "love you forever" will probably mean just that: Mommy will love you forever, no matter how messy (or shitty) you may be.

That the little boy is holding a watch and seems to be on the verge of letting it drop into the toilet seems telling. Time, in this book, is going to be cavalierly disregarded. This mother and son, despite the passage of time as measured by minutes, hours, and years, are going to adhere with absolute rigidity to their stereotypically gendered roles. Whereas, in *The Runaway Bunny*, the mother's attachment and availability seem understandable both on account of her child's age and also on account of the age of the child who is, putatively, listening to the story, here, on the other hand, the boy character is going to pass rapidly through successive stages from infancy to adulthood. But despite his developmental progress, his mother will remain invariant in her behavior toward him. She ages as well, her hair turning from brown to gray and her size diminishing vis-à-vis his as he matures physically. Nevertheless, with no modifications, she repeats, throughout the book, the four-line refrain:

> I'll love you forever,
> I'll like you for always,
> As long as I'm living
> my baby you'll be.

The boy, throughout, is shown to be as disconnected and unresponsive to her as she is to the changes taking place in him. To portray the successive stages of his growth, the artist shows him messing up different rooms of the house in distinctive ways. First, as we have seen, as a toddler, he wreaks havoc in the bathroom. Next, as a schoolboy, he leaves footprints and fingermarks in the kitchen. As a teenager, he is shown knocking over vases in the living room, unplugging the lamp, spilling food on the carpet, and making a loud racket. He has, apparently, only a two-mode repertoire: messing and sleeping, for his scenes of disruption alternate with bedroom scenes of total passivity. It is in these latter scenes, while he is asleep, that his gradually aging mother literally creeps in on hands and knees and, lifting him into her arms while he is unconscious (this is depicted as happening even when he has reached his twenties), she reaffirms her love for him as "a baby." Thus, despite his developmental progress, recorded only through pictures of transgressive behavior, the mother continues to treat him exactly like an infant.

The Runaway Bunny features a charming and clever dialogue between the mother-son couple, one in which the child's inventiveness is matched by the mother's riposte, so that the story becomes one of an affectionate battle of wits between the two and models imaginative play for those who encounter it. Here in *Love You Forever*, on the con-

From *Manners Can Be Fun* by Munro Leaf. Copyright © 1958 by
Munro Leaf. Copyright © 1936 by Munro Leaf. All rights reserved.
Used by permission of HarperCollins Publishers.

trary, there is no dialogue whatsoever. The boy disregards the mother
entirely and finally moves away. The mother, correspondingly solipsistic, engages in one-way reiterations of her four-line mantra, uttering
it only, however, when he is fast asleep, oblivious, unable to respond.

Entering stealthily like a spy or an animal on all fours to stare at him
and repeat her mantra, this mother is a terrifying spectacle, a trauma-
tizing icon of perpetual surveillance. Indeed, a man I know told me
of a recurrent nightmare he had for years in which, no matter how
far away he went or where he ended up, when he turned around, his

mother would be there—smiling, waving at him, and trying desperately to attract his attention. He simply could not shake her.

Most bizarre of all, in *Love You Forever* there is a page that it took me a few moments to grasp. The son has grown up and moved to a house of his own. On the moving day, we see uniformed men and a truck, but the mother is conspicuously absent. On the next page, however, a car is shown traveling at night with a wooden ladder strapped to its roof. This loving mother, so it seems, "sometimes on dark nights," actually drives across town to her adult son's house with a ladder, climbs up said ladder, enters his bedroom through the window, crawls across the floor, picks the "great big man" up in her arms, and rocks him exactly as she did when he was an infant, repeating her four-line refrain.

Taking up the gender-coded "I'll-always-be-near-you" message of *The Runaway Bunny*, this book turns it into something oppressive, if not horrifying. The son, toward the end, seems to be living alone in a bachelor pad with a single bed and few ornaments. Yet suddenly, on the last page, he metamorphoses into a father and is shown in a reverse-repeat image with a baby daughter in his arms, singing his mother's old refrain to her. What I find intriguing and somewhat perverse in all this is that, just as the boy, growing up, is given no visible father, so likewise, in the end, the deus ex machina baby girl is given no mother. Thus, the facts of procreation are entirely bypassed. Primary relations occur not between adults but between cross-generational heterosexual partners—mother with son, father with daughter. A confusing message for young children. Yet the book has been selling, and its jacket proclaims that it is "about the enduring nature of parents' love and how it crosses generations." I would argue against this claim. This book portrays no authentic dialogue between its characters; it makes a travesty of growing up by reducing it to alternating scenes of negative behavior and complete inactivity; it distorts a mother's love by making it seem unilateral, pathologically static, and insatiable. The mother here, unlike Margaret Wise Brown's fuzzy white rabbit, is frightening. In support of interpreting her as a witch, I would adduce the presence of a cat on virtually every page of *Love You Forever*. Her son, unlike the plucky bunny child who engages on every page with his mother, seems a dunce.

Returning now, with this background, to *Bedtime for Frances*, we can perhaps be especially sensitive to the depiction of parental behavior. We can note the fact that each time in the opening pages a parent announces "time for bed," whatever he or she said is echoed by the other. (" 'Yes,' said Father. 'Yes,' said Mother. [and later] 'No,' said Mother. 'No,' said Father) This repetition creates a united front of stability for the child. It is important to remark also that the parents alternate in answering, so that neither predominates, although, as the book unfolds, we will see that Frances, like many little girls of her age, prefers to approach her father, as though he might prove to be the softer touch and/or the final authority. The parents' united front is portrayed graphically as well as textually. Moreover, this united front is carefully preserved throughout the series of Frances books in any instance where both parents are present. I believe this is a source of great strength, whether or not it is an accurate reflection of a particular child's real life. The representation of the paradigm itself can exert a powerful influence, molding attitudes and aspirations alike.

In particular, we might note the cozy scene where Frances, after having been put to bed, comes into the living room to find her parents nestled snugly on the couch together, eating pieces of cake in front of the TV set. The love and closeness of the parental couple are experienced by most young children as the foundation of their security, a psychological fact that explains, parenthetically, the destabilizing effects on them of divorce. The bond between her parents is the structure that supports Frances's emotional life and serves as her model for adult love relations. This is beautifully conveyed by the scene of mother and father badger sitting side by side, manifesting physical warmth, eating sweets together, an activity associated in children's minds with love, and enjoying a pleasurable experience (the television show) with each other. At the same time, the child, although cherished by her parents, is not welcome as a part of their intimate twosome.

Frances wants to be a part of their scene (she asks for a piece of cake), and she also wants to disrupt their closeness. She manages to do this effectively by getting out of her bed four times in a row to seek their attention on a variety of pretexts. In addition, she seeks to interfere with their coupling in a particular way—namely, by distracting her father—again, a typical behavior of many little girls from three to five years of age, who often wish to monopolize their father's affection while constructing their mothers as formidable rivals.

Here, we should note the role assigned to Frances's mother. She is the parent who initially announces bedtime and then, when Frances immediately asks for milk, pours the drink for her. She, true to maternal type, gives nourishment and sustenance. She also sets the rules and makes the boundaries; to signal this, her picture appears on both the very first and last pages of the book. She is the parent with whom the child starts and finishes, the one who proclaims bedtime and wakes Frances up the next morning. This tallies with the reality of many young children, for whom it is, early on, a woman, not a man, who sets up the perimeters of their daily routine.

Frances's mother, in addition to limit-setting and feeding, is also the one shown hugging and kissing her in the goodnight scene while Father stands nearby in the doorway smoking his pipe. The drawing wonderfully evokes a baby's earliest relation to its mother in pregnancy because Frances, shown from the back, appears to be just a furry ovoid, positioned right in front of her mother's abdomen. Primary physical closeness of young child to mother rather than father is common to the imagery of many picture books. A particularly noteworthy example is Richard Scarry's *Is This the House of Mistress Mouse?* (1964). The cover of this tactile book has a hole through which the reader is invited to insert her finger repeatedly in order to touch a furry substance. The fur turns out to be the hide of several frightening animals before it can be interpreted as belonging to the baby mouse of the maternal title character. On its final page, the scene resembles that in *Bedtime for Frances*. The baby mouse in its cradle wears pale blue like its mother, who rushes toward it with her arms outstretched, and the two color-matched figures gaze adoringly at each another. Meanwhile, Father mouse, dressed in red, yellow, and green, his hands behind his back, admires the baby from a distance. In both books, gender difference is conveyed through pictures alone—by means of gesture, spatial relations, and color. The text accompanying these pictures just says, three times: "Good night."

Returning to the bedtime scene in *Frances*, I would like to point out the presence of a window. Nearly all children's books with bedroom scenes portray a window. This ubiquitous symbol opens a space from the inside, which feels familiar and safe, to the outside, which seems unfamiliar and potentially unsafe. Through the window, a child can see the night. To relieve the anxiety of the window, many picture books supply a bright-faced moon, but here there is no moon in the window. Frances becomes frightened, first by wind blowing in at her curtains, and later by noises made by a moth's wings smacking the glass of her window. These noises are described, significantly, with precisely the same words ("bump" and "thump") that Sendak chooses for the sounds that so upset Mickey in *In the Night Kitchen*. Mickey, incidentally, when falling from his bed, glides past a window through which both moon and stars are visible, the stars in this case being allegorical in a special way that I will explore below.

In addition to separation from their parents, bedtime leaves children with other transitions for which the window makes an ideal signifier. Left alone, lying in her bed, the normally active Frances transfers her daytime physical energy to her mind, and, as her muscles relax, her imagination flourishes. She withdraws, although not entirely, from the external to an internal world, two realms symbolized, again, by the window.

Leaving Frances alone in bed with her doll and teddy bear, let's turn for a moment to a fascinating painting by the Belgian surrealist artist René Magritte. Magritte was intrigued by windows and painted many of them. One in particular, *La condition humaine* (The human condition, 1933) is extraordinary. I have written elsewhere (1994b) about this picture; it depicts an easel set up in front of a window in such a way that the edges of both easel and window coincide, so that the scene portrayed on the canvas overlaps precisely its counterpart in the world outside the window. Clearly, Magritte is playing on many themes with this image; one of them, however, is supremely relevant to the windows as symbols that appear ubiquitously in books for young children. This theme is, simply put, that of the overlap, the confusion between notions of what we take to be located inside ourselves and what we take to be external. What, in other words, is me versus not me? For example, have I just imagined or dreamed this, or did it actually happen? In calling his picture "The Human Condition," Magritte points out to his adult beholders, who may think that such matters are largely solved, that indeed they are *not* solved and that, furthermore, there was a time in our lives when we felt such questions to be wide open, a time when painted bears and devouring whales, dinosaurs on movie screens, and screeching TV witches were enough to cause shivers, tears, and nightmares—and when, likewise, wishes made on stars or four-leaf-clovers could come true. The window, therefore, Magritte intimates, is a translucent membrane suspended between fantasy and reality, a membrane that thickens and darkens as we grow older but never becomes entirely opaque.

In *Bedtime for Frances*, the window functions in exactly this way. Frances, throughout the story, has used her imagination to invent creatures—a tiger, a giant, bugs, spiders—who frighten her and serve as a pretext for her to reactivate the concern of her tired but protective parents. Finally, in the end, it is the moth smacking its wings against the window that causes her to realize, paradoxically, that because it is real and therefore cannot get through the window, she need not be afraid of it. The window exists to keep out what is real, but, as in the story of Peter Pan, it can keep out *only* what is real, not what is unreal. To have the book end this way, with the moth bumping against the window pane, is thus philosophically brilliant, an exquisitely apt gesture.

Let's turn now to *In the Night Kitchen*. First, we should note that this book was something of a shocker when it first appeared in print, in 1970. Many American librarians were so stunned by the sight of a little

From *In the Night Kitchen*. Copyright © 1970 by Maurice Sendak.
All rights reserved. Printed in the U.S.A. Lettering by Diana Blair.
Used by permission of HarperCollins Publishers.

boy's penis in a children's book that they insisted on coloring it over, as if Mickey were wearing a diaper (see Lanes 1980). Of course, similar ruses have been applied for centuries to the genitals in painted images of the infant Christ (see Steinberg 1984), so perhaps we should not be entirely surprised. In their zeal to vanquish the specter of male nudity, however, these librarians may have overlooked some interesting interpretive possibilities. And their act was certainly an overreaction. Sendak's work started no trend; child nudity is still a rare sight in picture books.

The context of nudity here strikes me as fully as important as the bare fact. I am remembering a moment in one of my college art history classes. The course was on Italian Renaissance painting, and the professor had projected an image on the screen of Titian's allegorical *Sacred and Profane Love*. Two equally beautiful women are portrayed, one robed lavishly in white with a jeweled circlet and gloves, the other virtually nude with merely a piece of cloth draped over her thighs. As we students gazed at the scene, our teacher asked us to say which of these women represents profane and which sacred love. We, of course, got it wrong. It is not the woman in white but the nude who stands for sacred love. Nudity in this setting is a symbol of truth and honesty, whereas the sumptuously dressed woman symbolizes vanity and a love for the things of this world.

I mention this anecdote to indicate that Mickey's nakedness requires some interpretation. What may have seemed unsettling and perverse about it to some has perhaps less to do with prudishness than with the implicit juxtaposition of sexuality, aggression, and self-centeredness. Mickey, after hearing disturbing noises and falling out of his bed— past his parents' bedroom and then on down into the night kitchen— lands naked in the middle of a bowl of dough that is being gleefully mixed by three identical chefs. Although they resemble Oliver Hardy, of the slapstick Laurel and Hardy movies of the 1930s and 1940s, these chefs are not merely funny. They have unmistakably Hitler-like mustaches, and the middle one is carrying a container of salt embellished with a black, yellow-bordered star of David. On the next pages, this now-naked child is mixed into the batter and is taken, inside it, to a waiting oven. Trellises showing trains appear in the background of several scenes. There are cylinders, towers, and exhaust fumes. The whole idea of something uncanny and terrifying happening in the middle of the night overdetermines the nakedness here, linking it to scenes of humiliation and indignity, to pages of never-to-be-forgotten history, to trauma—in fact, to Holocaust.

Two details are noteworthy in these images. On successive pages we find containers of "Phoenix Baking Soda" placed before a cracked eggshell. Clearly, these are clues to the theme of survival, allusions to the myth of the amazing Arabian bird that, after being consumed by fire and reduced to ashes, regenerates itself, only to repeat the process indefinitely. In addition, the sky is filled with stars, another reference to survival, for in the twenty-second chapter of Genesis, just after Abraham has offered up his son Isaac to the sacrificial fire, we come upon the following words, the Lord speaking now to Abraham: "Because you have done this and not withheld your son, your favored one, I will bestow my blessing upon you and make your descendants as numerous as the stars of heaven" (Gen. 22:16–17). Thus, this strange scene of a naked child about to be baked in an oven takes on in context complex cultural significance. In corroboration, we find, on double-spread pages where the event is actually being portrayed, repeated images of containers of salt on which the star of David is imprinted. *Eat bread and salt and speak the truth.* And, as the story goes on, the importance of food—the stealing of food, the hoarding and sharing and dying for lack of food during the Holocaust—becomes an insistent never-stated theme that beats steadily beneath the melody that can be heard.

Suddenly, after the third appearance of the Phoenix canister, we are surprised by billows of gray smoke that pour out of the oven. Consternation appears on the bakers' faces, and the child reappears, his naked body now covered with brown dough. One glob sticks to the top of his head forming a cap of dough, a cap with an uncanny resemblance to a kepah or yarmulke, the traditional head covering worn by Orthodox Jewish boys and men.

At this point, the child escapes and by pounding and pulling, fashions the dough around himself into something resembling a one-seater World War I fighter plane. In the final frame on this page, the dough forms a propeller by means of a gesture frankly masturbatory in connotation, and Mickey then flies off with a contented expression, leaving the bakers stunned and angry. They howl for "MILK," but Mickey flies up over their heads into the sky of the night kitchen, which is Sendak's ingenious transformation of the New York City skyline—tall buildings replaced by bottles, pitchers, corkscrews, egg beaters, even a nutcracker.

Leaving Mickey soaring over their heads, I want to consider the meaning of this cry for milk. Milk is, of course, every human child's first food; it is necessary for survival. In the literature of the Holocaust, it forms the most powerful metaphor in the great poem "Todesfuge" by Paul Celan:

> Black milk of daybreak we drink it at evening
> we drink it at midday and morning we drink it at night
> we drink and we drink
>
> (see Felstiner 1995)

Prominently figuring in cultural works for children in all media, milk appears often, as it does in Sendak's book, as a feature of narratives that turn the tables. In other words, instead of parents giving milk to their children (as we saw in *Bedtime for Frances*, where on the very first page she is given milk by her mother), in these narratives children display their nascent maturity and independence by supplying it for themselves and for their parents as well. *Hansel and Gretel* is a paradigm text for this turnabout: when their angry, selfish, and incapacitated stepmother breaks a pitcher and spills milk, the small boy and girl go forth to seek nourishment for themselves and are meant to supply it to the household as well. Similarly, Aninka and Pepíček, brother and sister characters in the Czech children's opera *Brundibár* by Krása and Hoffmeister (1938) (see Spitz 1994b) must seek milk for their ailing mother, a quest that gives rise to the drama of the libretto. Absolute dependence on mothers (and fathers) as prime sources of nourishment (milk being also a metaphor for love) must therefore be modified as children grow toward self-reliance and develop the capacity to nurture others.

It could be argued that Mickey's journey into the night kitchen incorporates both of these goals. He clearly demonstrates his capacity for self-sustenance and rejects the position of victim. He refuses to be just a lump of dough that can be molded and baked by others: he breaks out of the oven, enjoys his triumph and the pleasures of his own body, his nakedness, his flight in the fighter plane (with its sexual overtones), his immersion in milk ("GOD BLESS MILK AND GOD BLESS ME!"). But perhaps, in the end, his journey is not entirely solipsistic, for he remembers to supply milk to the bakers for their bread. Thus, he crows happily "COCK A DOODLE DOO!" and lands fulfilled under the covers of his bed, smiling "yum."

Another book that employs milk as a metaphor is *Yen-Foh: A Chinese Boy* (1946), a superb collection of Chinese tales about a boy exemplary for his wisdom and kindness, illustrated by softly colored lithographs by Kurt Wiese and written by Ethel Eldridge. Yen-foh's parents, in one of these tales, become ill with a disease that induces blindness and that can be cured only by drinking milk that comes from deer. Yen-foh, eager to save them, goes into the nearby forest and, cleverly placing a deer hide over his body, manages to obtain the milk they need and thus to cure them. I cite this story because its theme is related, but its emphasis is quite different from that of the Sendak work. Although children need to learn to fend for themselves, the accent can be placed on altruism, as in the Yen-foh stories, or on autonomy, as in the case of *In the Night Kitchen* (and Sendak's other works), which feature child characters who are radically alone. That state of aloneness, I suggest, contextualizes the nakedness and lends it an additional aura of unease. Mickey is a solo figure. And although he gives milk to the bakers, this is an act of dubious altruism, given the layers of meaning in the story. "Pure" is a word that recurs on the last pages where nudity is represented. Mickey, smiling throughout his ordeal, is stripped and solitary. Is he truly free, or is he coerced—by history, by gender, by fate? Pain, I feel, is an undercurrent here, complicating the manifest message of this apparently triumphant text.

To return to the topic of gender, women, who are generally associated with kitchens, have no role to play here. And their exclusion from *In the Night Kitchen* is an element that, whether explicitly noticed or not, cannot help but have an effect. It creates, I suggest, an emotional hiatus, a deep lacuna in this book, which is filled by a kind of androgynous self-sufficiency that for some children and adults fails to be entirely satisfying. A small detail on the book's cover, easily overlooked, prefigures this agenda. Centered at the bottom of the page, on what appears to be a milk carton, a horned bovine animal appears. Over this creature the word "cream" is written. This animal suggests both a destructive bull and a nurturing cow. Apparently insignificant, it foretells the presence of an abiding strand of psychological complexity in this text.

In the Night Kitchen, a favorite of some children, is feared by others. As with the remaining books in Sendak's so-called trilogy, *Where the Wild Things Are* and *Outside Over There* (1981), some part of each child's response will depend on the parents' level of comfort with these books, for they all reach into murky wells of inner experience and attempt to bring up handfuls of what lies hidden there. As Sendak remarked, "They are all variations on the same theme: how children master various feelings—anger, boredom, fear, frustration, jealousy—and manage to come to grips with the realities of their lives" (as quoted in Lanes 1980, p. 227). When asked whether he thought children have the maturity to understand the meanings implicit in these books, Sendak answered: "I think children read the internal meanings of *everything*. It's only adults who read the top layer most of the time" (p. 205). But children's sensitivities and experiences differ, and such differences deserve to be valorized. Reading picture books to young children allows us to do just that—to try to ascertain the match between a child and a particular cultural object. Although I do claim that certain themes are universal, I do not wish to underplay the protean variety of form and expression by which such themes have been and can be represented. *In the Night Kitchen* is indisputably a fascinating work, but it is clearly not the right bedtime story for all children.

There's a Nightmare in My Closet

On the first double-page spread of this popular Mercer Mayer book, we come upon imagery that will seem familiar to children who know *Goodnight Moon* (the little boy's bed is in the same position on the page as the bunny's) and *Bedtime for Frances* (the curtain blowing in at the window will recall its final pages). As the story progresses, children may even recall the well-known territory of the wild things, as well as the lands where Dr. Seuss's fanciful hybrid creatures roam. Such associations, even when not fully conscious, work to tame a new story and its pictures and lend them an aura of underlying comfort, especially when, as here, the content may be disturbing.

Rendered in a line-driven cartoon style similar to that of Sendak and Seuss, the pictures in *There's a Nightmare in My Closet* illuminate the text so fully that the plotline can be read straight off the images themselves. This may be due in part to the fact that its author and illustrator are the same person; yet that factor does not always produce this result. We have only to consider de Brunhoff's *Babar,* Bemelmans's *Madeline,* and Sendak's *Where the Wild Things Are,* all of which have image-texts that interact in more complex and somewhat less interdependent ways.

There's a Nightmare in My Closet tells the first-person story of a little boy who determines to rid himself of his nighttime fears, which have taken the form of a Nightmare that lurks in his closet. Armed with a helmet and toy gun, he threatens to shoot the beast when it emerges. When it finally appears, however, the beast turns out to be a huge, goofy monster who looks contrite and fearful rather than threatening. The little boy shoots anyway. At this, the enormous Nightmare begins to cry. With its finger in its mouth, it resembles a giant baby and in that guise manages to mobilize the identification, pity, and scorn of children listening to the story. Interestingly, the boy protagonist's initial reaction is not contrition or empathy but anger. And, as we know, many parents in fact feel a rush of anger when their punished children cry. So the boy's reaction here actually mirrors a parental position, albeit a not

very enlightened one. He tells the bawling Nightmare to be quiet and then, his heart softening, takes him comfortingly into his own bed — thus acting out in fantasy (from the parental side as well as his own) exactly the goal that Frances was trying to achieve with her shenanigans and Mickey was trying to deny with his flight into the night kitchen.

Closing the closet door and lying in bed under the covers with his

Nightmare, the boy says he knows that another Nightmare may yet come but adds hopefully, with a smile, that his bed is not big enough for three. Nevertheless, on the last pages of the book, when the boy and his tamed monster have gone to sleep in the darkened bedroom, an enormous head pokes out of the closet door. Another monster has suddenly appeared. There are no words, and the book ends.

On thinking it over, I realized that my own reaction to this ending was somewhat mixed. On the one hand, *There's a Nightmare in My Closet* attempts to convey a highly sophisticated idea. By introducing the second monster at the end, it points out to children something they need to know, and indeed *do* know—that fears, even those that have been dealt with successfully, tend to recur. A similar message is conveyed in Sendak's *Pierre*, the fourth book of his *Nutshell Library* of 1962. *Pierre*, a prototypical little ethics primer, to which I will return in a later chapter on mischief and disobedience, tells the story of an oppositional toddler who brags "I don't care" so often that he is actually eaten by a lion. Just to give a sense of the psychological and aesthetic sophistication implicit in this classic story, I want to mention that Sendak places an identical border at the start and end of his text, in which the child's verbal "no" is translated pictorially into the form "upside down," so that the little boy is depicted turning a somersault. Pierre's parents cajole him in vain. They command and implore and finally depart, thereby abandoning the child who, left to his own negativism, is eaten up by a lion to whom he has also responded, "I don't care." When at length the parents return, they find the lion in Pierre's bed and vent their wrath now on him (on the child's and their own projected aggression). Finally, in a recap of the upside-down motif (Pierre had stood on his head to defy his father), the lion is turned upside down and spits Pierre out. The whole family rides home astride the lion, who is thereby not banished but accepted as part of the family. Aggression is in this way valorized and accepted as an ongoing issue for both parents and children. What is relevant to *There's a Nightmare in My Closet* is the last page of Sendak's story. As the family rides triumphantly home on its back, a deliciously furtive smile adorns the face of the lion. The beast gazes up mischievously at Pierre, as if to say "So, you really think you are finished with me, do you? Well, you just wait and see. . . ."

This book is a highly sophisticated lesson about open-endedness that is similar to, although more benign than, the lesson of the second monster in *There's a Nightmare in My Closet*. Some young children, however, especially at bedtime, may require greater closure, more security. Indeed, one of the most satisfying aspects of picture books at bedtime is that they possess a finite quality. Their covers open and, importantly, close. Each story has a clear beginning and a fixed end. These limits add an important dimension of order to the child's world, and children usually prefer books that have well-defined endings. For this reason, *There's a Nightmare in My Closet* worries me a bit. By introducing a scary new monster on the last page, I think this book deprives some children of the closure they crave and leaves them in a state of apprehension, wondering and concerned about what might happen next. If so, instead of teaching a lesson about the normal recurrence of anxieties and bad dreams, this book might actually contribute to a child's already present stock of worries.

In order to test my hypothesis, I decided to read *There's a Nightmare in My Closet* to three-year-old Haley. When I showed her the book and asked whether she had ever seen it before, she replied "Yes" promptly. Then, immediately, she added: "There's *another* monster." This spontaneous unsolicited bit of information seemed a wonderfully timed and ingenious counterphobic remark—rather as though she were trying, by invoking the second monster in advance, to arm herself against it. We began the story. Haley sat quietly while I turned the pages, reading. Every now and then, she interpolated something verbal, but it was I who physically held the book and flipped each successive page—until we neared the end. Haley began to look more serious as the boy closed his closet door and then lay down in bed with his tamed Nightmare to go to sleep. At the final, wordless page on which the new monster emerges from the closet, Haley looked at it for a split second and then, with a rapid gesture, took the corner of the page in her own right hand

and turned it over quickly, looking hard—as if to see what would happen next. But the page, of course, was completely blank.

This small incident felt significant to me. It corroborated my hunch that, on some level, for at least some children, the ending provided by this book is inconclusive and unsatisfying. It underscores the *individuality* of children's responses to picture books and the need for parents to notice, respect, and cherish it. Haley, who had hopefully turned the last page over to see what would come next, even though she knew that the end had already been reached, did not, on the other hand, refuse to hear this book again. To the contrary, the very openness of its ending may be appealing to some children and serve as a spur toward repetition and mastery. It may incline them to want to reexperience it, to pit themselves against it, as it were—their knowledge and courage versus the anxiety it evokes.

Parents reading this book may choose to pose a question or two at the end, such as: "What do you think will happen now?" or "If you were that little boy, what would you do now?" thus inducing an imaginative discussion in which the child might be inspired to invent his own personally more satisfying ending. It might turn out to be another violent solution, such as shooting the second monster, or, more mildly, ordering it to go away, or, benevolently, squeezing it into bed with himself and the first monster. What matters with stories like this, which leave unwoven threads, is that they can become spurs to imaginative creation—story-telling, drawing, acting, singing, dancing—an untold variety of collaborative adventures between the generations. As regards those children for whom the book does feel satisfying, I think it is the little boy's identification with his parents vis-à-vis the monster, his courage and eventual compassion, and his calm, that make it possible for him to tame his fears and for the child experiencing the story to participate vicariously in that project with him.

Harold and the Purple Crayon

This discussion of participation and identification is a perfect segue into *Harold and the Purple Crayon*. Written and illustrated by Crockett Johnson in 1955, this delightful story, made up entirely of purple line drawings, transforms every toddler into an artist. It calls on children to identify with its creator and become, as it were, the artists and authors of their own invented worlds. *Harold and the Purple Crayon* valorizes the realm of make-believe and models the creation of a bedtime fantasy. Little Harold draws one himself before our eyes with his purple crayon. As he gives it form, he projects into it his private wishes and danger situations. Young children are absolutely mesmerized by this book. When four-year-old Rachel heard the story, she exclaimed in wonder: "He can draw on *nothing!* Like *this!*" and she pretended to draw on the air. "He can draw on nothing and then go on it!" she continued, referring to Harold's ability to create lines that support him, his ability to construct a world in two dimensions that is endowed with the properties of a three-dimensional world.

Harold decides to make an apple tree for himself, for example, and places a frightening dragon nearby to guard it. But then, backing away from the dragon, he realizes that his purple crayon has been shaking and that he is now over his head in water. He comes up "thinking fast," makes himself a little boat and sails to a sandy shore, where he creates a picnic lunch consisting of every kind of pie he likes best. When a group of four-year-olds was asked what they would do about the problem of the water, each one came up with a different response. One said, "I would get an inner tube!" Another shouted: "I would call out to someone to help me!" Thus, the ingenuity depicted in the story called forth corresponding inventiveness in the children listening to it.

After pleasing, exciting, scaring, and rescuing himself, Harold ingeniously finds his way back to the safety of his bedroom. In the last picture, he lies snugly in his bed with the moon shining in through his window. After he literally draws the covers up, his purple crayon drops to the floor, and Harold drops off to sleep—these verbal puns serving

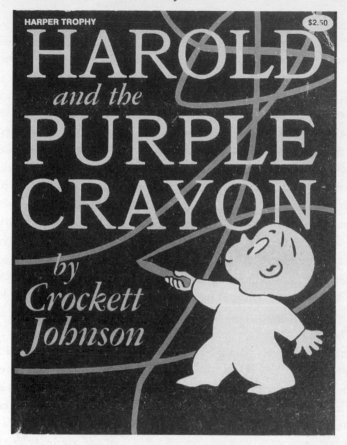

From *Harold and the Purple Crayon* by Crockett Johnson.
Copyright © 1955 by Crockett Johnson. All rights reserved.
Used by permission of HarperCollins Publishers.

as analogues for the visual puns that have carried the story along from
page to page in a witty and wonderful elaboration of the unpredictable
associative links that go on all the time in the minds of children.

Again in this book, the moon plays a central role. It is Harold's
memory of the moon shining in through his bedroom window that en-

71

ables him, when he is lost, to find his way back to familiar surroundings. The effect of quotation is especially potent here. Children listening to *Harold* often smile at the repeated words, "And the moon went along with him." As we have seen, this symbol seems linked for them with home and mother and with their prior experiences with other picture books such as, of course, the paradigmatic *Goodnight Moon*.

When Harold does find his way home and realizes that the window frame surrounds the moon, the notions of inside and outside, which young children are learning to sort out, become complex. We are reminded of Magritte's painting *La condition humaine*. A group of four-year-olds, when asked how Harold could be *inside* when he was walking around *outside*, came up with a marvelous set of hypotheses: "He's inside now, but he was outside before"; "He was inside the whole time, but he was walking around outside"; and "He was inside and outside at the SAME TIME!" When challenged as to how someone could be both inside and outside in reality, one little girl had a brainstorm: "You could stand in a door," she said, "and be half in and half out."

Picture books, as we've noted, live on in the psyche far beyond early childhood. At Yale University, for example, undergraduates traditionally entertain their parents at graduation with improvisional performances. The young actors accept cues from the audience as well as prompts from one another and then elaborate on them by hatching instant characters and plots. Because of their warm childhood memories of this picture book and because its visual wit parallels their own inventive work, one group of students honored *Harold and the Purple Crayon* by naming their company "The Purple Crayon of Yale."

Time for Bed

Before leaving our chapter on night, I want to mention a book that came to my attention and appeared in print only a few years ago. *Time for Bed* (1993), by Mem Fox and Jane Dyer, is a lovely and gentle bedtime book, incandescent with delicately colored close-ups of mother-child animal pairs on each double-spread page. Each image has been rendered in gossamer, translucent watercolors with unobliterated pen-cil lines, soft brushstrokes, and limpid washes. The book starts with a human mother reading to a sleepy child whose eyes are closing as she holds an open book adorned with stars and a crescent moon. Then, on each double-spread page, a different species of animal comes tenderly to life: mouse, goose, cat, cow, horse, fish, sheep, bird, bee, snake, dog, deer. Two-line rhymes accompany these images, couplets that in-clude the name of the animal and also something significant about the experience of going to sleep. For example, one rhyme acknowledges darkness, whereas the next points to the stars; another invites the child listening to snuggle, yet another to think of something funny that hap-pened during the day, listen to a whispered secret, make a wish—to withdraw peacefully into rest and relinquish the outside world. These couplets remind the child that others too are falling asleep, that the process takes time, that reciprocal love exists, that sleep is necessary, and, finally, that the last kiss is about to be bestowed and that stars will shine throughout the night.

In studying this beautiful book, I was struck by a paradox: the continuity—but also an undercurrent of troubling contrast—between its representation of the one human mother-child pair and the vari-ous animal mother-child pairs. What struck me in particular was the juxtaposition of the baby animals with the human child—a canoni-cal *white-skinned, blond*-haired *blue*-eyed child of indeterminate gender with whom all child readers can presumably be expected to identify. Or can they?

Anthropologist Judith Goldstein (1995), in a fascinating article, raises the questions of what sort of pictorial conventions enable us to care about others, and why it is that the displacement of human experi-ence onto *animal forms* works so well. Her answer in part is that "chil-dren's books . . . use animals to encourage empathy, to permit children to identify without being blocked, presumably, by the particulars of race or sex or ethnicity. The logic of this universalization/abstraction," as she explains, "has it that making all the characters animals is an ad-vance over making them all white. The logic also implies, however, that it would be impossible to ask children to identify with individuals culturally defined as visibly different from themselves."

In other words, when we look at a human face, we immediately register its similarity or dissimilarity to our own and supposedly we respond accordingly. When it comes to animals, however, this factor is removed. Art Speigelman, in his book *Maus* (1973), for example, portrays the history of his father's experiences during the Holocaust, but rather than rendering an actual likeness of his father's countenance on each page, he uses the generic head of a mouse. Strangely and disturbingly, by giving mouse faces to all the Jews in his pictorial narrative, Spiegelman is able to elicit *more* sympathy for them than if they had been given ethnically identifiable human countenances. Why should this be so? What does it say about human beings that we must put ourselves into nonhuman form in order to seem more "human" to one another? I am thinking of the bunny in *Goodnight Moon*, and of the fact that the "little girl" in *Bedtime for Frances* is a badger. As you read through the coming chapters, you will meet little boys and girls in the guise of elephants, dogs, bears, ducks, rabbits, cats, and so on. Why is it that, with animals, a universalizing can take place and identifications occur that break down when human characters are introduced?

That *Time for Bed* portrays its human child as gender-neutral—presumably to enable children of both sexes to identify with him/her—betrays the fact that, whereas gender is seen as a problem that needs self-conscious address, race and ethnicity are not. Blond, blue-eyed children have a well-documented symbolic status in our culture (see Morrison 1970; Warner 1994). Despite its gender inspecificity, then, the little child in this book is not a neutral image. I want to underscore this point because it occurs in a book that is otherwise aesthetically superior, tender, and wise. The issues of race, gender, ethnicity, and their representation—which I will address head-on when I consider *Little Black Sambo*—are a dilemma in children's literature. They are issues we should be aware of because we will encounter them continually as we read to our children.

Before leaving the topic of night, one final point deserves emphasis: when love is felt to be secure, children can allow themselves to be curious about the world, to explore mentally, to learn, and to grow. When, on the other hand, love is contingent and the world unpredictable, anxiety gains the upper hand, and children's energies must be deployed elsewhere. We see, under those unfortunate conditions, a waning of the lust for adventure. In choosing books to read to young children at bedtime, then, this principle may serve as a guide—modified always according to the individual, because children differ so, and by the particular circumstances of any given evening.

⟾ Chapter 3 ⟾

Please Don't Cry

When we take an old picture book down from the shelf, we are reminded that children are shaped not only by the circumstances of their individual lives but also by the historical moment into which they are born. For some, it is a time of peace; for others, an epoch of war, when family life may be invaded by terror, devastation, imprisonment, and exile. Even in times of relative social calm, however, most children's lives brush up against death, occasionally death that is sudden and tragic. For a child, the stage is narrow: what she or he knows and feels *is* the world. Therefore, in this chapter we will look at several kinds of books that may seem, perhaps, more unlike one another to adults than to children. They are books about catastrophic loss. First, we will look at books that deal with the death of cherished animals; next at books that deal with the loss of grandparents, not just to death but to changes caused by aging that may alter the ability of elderly relatives to relate to the children they love; and finally at just one book that deals with death in the context of war. I present the material in this order because it seems to follow the progression of losses as they are frequently encountered by children in this country, where war has been kept at a distance and grandparents often live far away.

First, however, I want to address a related issue, namely the question of reading books that deal with sober topics to young children at all. After all, reading to children is meant to be a pleasurable activity, and it cannot be fun to read about sadness and loss. Books that survive for many years are often those that are high-spirited. Yet, as authors on fairy tales have pointed out (see Bettelheim 1976; Tatar 1992), long-lasting stories frequently deal with highly disturbing themes. Just as we adults go to the theater to watch plays and hear operas that bring tears to our eyes, so children should be permitted to have experiences with art objects that are not all sugar and spice. Although children cannot be protected from loss, they can be exposed to it in ways that range from the sensitive to the callous, the inquiring to the hushed, the slow and careful to the swift, sudden, and overwhelming. With a beautifully crafted picture book and a measure of unhurried time, an attentive child and an engaged adult can accomplish important psychic work that may not involve gaiety but that can, in its own way, be considered to include other deep forms of pleasure. That is, if we count the communication of shared and meaningful experience as a form of pleasure.

The Death of a Pet

The demise of an animal may be a child's first exposure to death and one that will be re-evoked later under altered circumstances. Thus, a twenty-year-old book like *The Accident* (1976), by Carol Carrick and Donald Carrick, can serve as a source of solace in the present as well as of deep understanding to be drawn from in the future. But, as noted earlier, books about animals are never limited by their ostensible subject matter. They can lay a foundation for dealing with many issues, including the succession of griefs from which no human life is exempt. *The Accident*, in particular, differs from the "self-help" books mentioned in chapter 1 in that it works on many levels and opens the way to further reflection. It offers a scene to which other scenes can be referred.

Children and animals form unique dyads. Among portrayals of these special unions, I know of no work that rivals a tender tale by Isaac Bashevis Singer called "Zlateh the Goat" (1966). This story, written originally in Yiddish, is available in English translation with black-

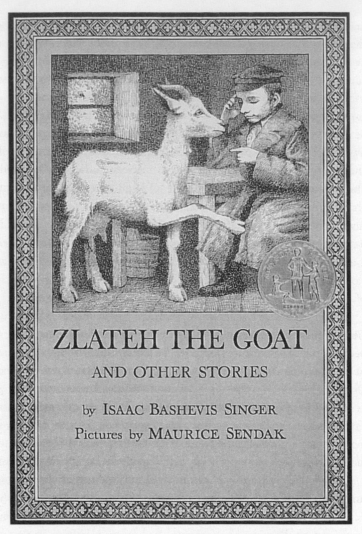

ZLATEH THE GOAT

AND OTHER STORIES

by ISAAC BASHEVIS SINGER

Pictures by MAURICE SENDAK

and-white illustrations by Maurice Sendak. Unlike most of the stories discussed in this chapter, it is not about death per se but about tragedy averted.

Of course, with a writer of Singer's stature, the telling counts as much as the tale; yet, in order to set the stage, I will render it in my own words. I do so in order to evoke, before we begin, what some of us adults may have lost, namely, the atavistic bond that exists between children and animals. For non-Jewish readers, I would like to explain that Hanukkah is a nonreligious winter holiday especially beloved by children. Its traditions include lighting candles, frying potato pancakes (latkes), exchanging presents, singing, and playing a game of chance involving spinning tops (dreidles) imprinted with Hebrew letters that determine how much can be won or lost. The holiday commemorates a miracle that occurred during the second century, after the destruction of the Temple in Jerusalem, when the eternal lamp was deprived of oil yet remained unextinguished for eight days.

"Zlateh the Goat" takes place at Hanukkah time in Poland. A furrier's family is under considerable economic duress because there has been no snow, no cold weather, and therefore no business. The father, in order to buy holiday supplies, decides to sell the old family goat, Zlateh, who can no longer give much milk. Aaron, the oldest boy, is delegated to take her to the town butcher. His sisters cry as he leaves with the rope around Zlateh's neck, and Zlateh trustingly licks her master's hand, for she knows that human beings are kind and that the family has always given her food and cared for her.

On their way to the village, a whirling snowstorm arises. Icicles form on the goat's fur. Frozen and lost, the boy fears for their lives but makes out a mound of snow under which he realizes there must be a haystack. Burrowing in, he and the goat find shelter. Zlateh feeds on the dried hay; Aaron cuddles against her warm animal body and drinks her milk after finishing his bread and cheese. He bores a passage through the hay to let in air, and they both sleep. For three days and nights, the snow and wind and cold continue. Aaron talks to Zlateh and tells her stories; she answers only "Maaaa" and licks him with her tongue. Aaron dreams he never had a father, mother, or sisters and that he and Zlateh had been born in the snow.

On the fourth day, Zlateh and Aaron hear sleigh bells. The storm ends, and the family, having given up hope, are overjoyed to see the boy and goat reappear. Aaron's sisters hug and kiss Zlateh. The cold weather sends villagers back to their father the furrier for warm coats. Latkes sizzle every night of Hanukkah, and Zlateh is welcomed into the house to observe the shimmering holiday candles. She shakes her head and makes her one sound, "Maaaa"—"which," Singer says, "expressed all her thoughts and all her love" (Singer 1966, p. 90).

Readers of this simple story, especially with the accompaniment of Sendak's delicate black-and-white drawings, can hardly fail to succumb to its spell; reading it, we can almost smell the warmth and closeness that fasten children to their animal friends.

With this tale in mind, let us turn now to two picture books of the 1970s that deal with the deaths of beloved animals. In both cases the protagonists are boys. During the 1970s in the United States, coping with the death of young men had an immediacy that found voice in popular songs and in American culture at large. During the long war years, field success in Vietnam was measured by body count, and the average age of American recruits was only nineteen years. With this in the forefront of the nation's consciousness, the topic of death finally found its way into mainstream literature for even the youngest children, though displaced, as we see here.

The Accident

The Accident (1976), by Carol Carrick and Donald Carrick, is a small masterpiece. It manages, through a counterpoint of pictures and words, to give in slow motion and with great delicacy an extraordinarily complete representation of the distinct phases a child may pass through in response to tragedy, loss, and bereavement. Each separate moment is given verbal and/or pictorial expression.

What happens on the actual pages of this book, however, is gentle

From *The Accident* by Carol Carrick. Jacket © 1976 by Donald Carrick.
Reprinted by permission of Clarion Books/Houghton Mifflin
Company. All rights reserved.

and, superficially, easy for every child to grasp. Looked at psychologically, it possesses a profundity missing from many apparently more sophisticated treatments of its subject.

There are no pure hues here—no bright, highly saturated pigments. Everything is toned down: muted shades of brown, orange, yellow, and gray. These colors signify fall, or late summer perhaps, a season symbolic of waning time. The cover image, with its conspicuous border, signifies, I venture, that death is a finality. Yet this border also gives comfort, for children feel safest, we know, when boundaries are clear and endings explicitly defined. The border frames a peaceful scene. Center stage, a big-boned tawny retriever wades in a shallow stream, all four paws underwater. He looks offstage, alert, while behind him, peering down into the river, a barefoot boy in rolled-up jeans is fishing. The dog's tail overlaps the figure of the boy, so that their bodies are, from the viewer's perspective, contiguous. An overall mood of serenity and expectation are created to which even the letters of the title contribute: clear but not sensational or obtrusive, they are slanted, falling—as in "accidere" (Latin for "to fall")—which is what the dog will do and what the letters themselves denote and the colors suggest. But notwithstanding the hushed tones of the cover, the dog seems vibrantly alive, attuned to his canine modes of smelling and watching and listening in a world that will suddenly vanish for him.

Like the cover, the title page resembles a stage set: an indistinct landscape with watery trees and no people or animals, just misty, vegetative life. Here, before the story begins, the weather conditions—rain, perhaps slippery roads—create an aura, an underlying mood and sense of anticipation.

Coziness characterizes the first double-page spread, where we meet the boy, Christopher, and his dog, Bodger, in their summer-cottage kitchen. Foregrounded again, the dog lies on floor, slightly anthropomorphized; cuddly and friendly, he nuzzles a bone but looks almost as though he is reading the paper on which it rests. What matters here is the closeness between boy and dog. Artist and writer have each striven to give us a strong grip on that relationship so that, when it ends, that ending can be sharply felt.

Christopher's parents have gone off canoeing after dinner; he and Bodger have stayed behind so he can watch his favorite TV show. When the show is over, they go out to meet the returning parents. Dusk falls as they trudge through the woods on dirt paths and finally reach a paved road where cars whiz by. A warning sentence alerts the reader: "The faster cars and trucks made so much noise and wind when they passed that Christopher thought the blast might knock him over." Double-spread pictures with integrated texts offer wide-angle views throughout the book—a design format exquisitely well suited to the breadth of psychological perspective here.

In the penultimate page before the accident, Christopher, on the opposite side of the highway from Bodger, calls the dog over to him as they approach the lake (which is pictured on the right-hand page). In a dynamically composed image, Bodger bounds across the street to be with Christopher just as a truck with headlights ablaze emerges, as it were, from the lower corner of the left-hand page.

Before we *see* what happens, we know. Words tell us that tires screeched and that the little boy's "shoulders hunched and his eyes squeezed shut." His body responds as if he himself had been hit. His muscles tense; his vision closes off. He calls out the dog's name. Children hearing the story may here feel their own bodily sensations. We brace ourselves, and we also do not yet see.

On the next page a pale yellow stream flows from the truck's headlights, and a strange man bends over Bodger, who lies inert on the road against a darkening sky. Christopher stands with his hands still nearly covering his eyes. In an exquisitely sensitive gesture, the man who killed the dog "raised his hand as if to hold Christopher back." What does this gesture, which is both named and pictured, mean? Why does this adult ward the child off, wave him away, keep him from coming closer, prevent him from seeing death? It is clearly an instinctive reaction—a gesture of protection—and one that will be repeated metaphorically by Christopher's father later on, when he makes the decision to bury Bodger alone, without his son being there.

Adults are forced to make hard and fast decisions at such times. Should young children be allowed to witness death? Taken to a funeral, brought to the cemetery? Should they be permitted to visit a dying person, or a memorial for the dead? (I will soon discuss a book devoted to this theme.) In raising his arm, the stranger is expressing a tenderness and concern for Christopher. Even when adults err at such times, either because they cannot read a child's needs clearly or because they are temporarily blinded by their own intense feelings, their *desire* to do the right thing may eventually, as in this story, be accepted by the child as overriding any misconception or mistake. What works here is the spontaneity of the man's two gestures: with one hand, he touches the animal's body, and with the other he wards Christopher away. The language of the arms speak: don't come over here, son; I don't want you to have to see this.

Furthermore, because the child encountering the picture book *is* seeing it, the image of death presented by the artist could not be more benign. Bodger lies inert, but with no visible blood or disfigurement. What matters is that a life has ended. Nothing sensational or morbid distracts us from that knowledge. The child encountering the picture book is protected just as Christopher is.

The text at this critical moment tells us that Christopher knows what has happened but asks anyway. *He needs words to make it real.* Just as in the final page of *Where the Wild Things Are*, words bring us into the realm of consensually validated reality. He asks:

"Is he dead?"
The man shook his head sadly.
"I'm sorry, sonny."

The "I'm sorry" matters. Here on the page of death are words that acknowledge adult responsibility, words that accept guilt and express regret. Think of the power of these "magic words," as they are called in *Bartholomew and the Oobleck* (1949) by Dr. Seuss, where a grownup king must learn to say them. True, in this case, the child hearing them is not ready for them. He probably does not even hear them. But *we* hear them, and *we speak* them, and the child listening to the story hears them. There is no denial. There are no excuses. The stranger acknowledges his deed in two simple words that every child can recognize.

Another set of headlights signals the arrival of Christopher's parents. He rushes toward them, betraying his hope that now things will be all right, that "somehow his Dad would take care of things." This page speaks to children's deeply rooted trust in the omnipotence of their parents, a trust on which their sense of safety in the world depends.

But when the driver of the truck explains that the dog ran unexpectedly in front of his vehicle, Christopher's father nods to him and in so doing bitterly disappoints his son, who "wanted his father to get mad at this man and tell him he would be punished for what he did." Betrayed, Christopher sees his father's lack of anger as meaning that his father is sorrier for the stranger than for Bodger. To convey this, the text shifts abruptly to the child's point of view. Christopher's perspective is clear and unidirectional. Right and wrong are unclouded. Adult vision, however, is many sided, a notion adumbrated by the graded tonalities of each page, as if the artist too were seeking to record notions of multiplicity and mixes of feelings. Christopher's father comprehends the stranger's horror and guilt, his son's loss, *and* the tragedy of the animal's death. These multiple identifications of adult sensibility are acquired only gradually, however, and are not readily available to children.

In the darkness now, Christopher's mother kneels and puts her arm around the boy. The stranger squats down. He says that he has puppies at home and offers a puppy to Christopher.

" 'I don't want a puppy. I want Bodger,' wail[s] Christopher. 'And you killed him!' "

When his mother repeats that the driver of the truck did not mean to do any harm, Chris suddenly gets it: the whole thing is not a dream. But why does he grasp the reality of the situation just at this moment? I think it is because now not just one but *both* of his parents are united in their helplessness to change the situation. When his mother, as well as his father, takes pity on the man who killed Bodger, Chris comes out of his dream and ceases to hope for a miracle. Instead, he gets angry. Again the text shifts from the adult's to the child's perspective. It is unfair. Christopher calls the man "dumb." He wants to get even. In the biblical spirit of an eye for an eye, he declares: "I ought to run *him* over with a truck." In trying to palliate his rage, his mother presents a moral position that makes no sense to him, flooded as he is by loss, disbelief, and the feeling that he has been betrayed by those in whom he had trusted.

That night, Christopher lies in his bed under a comforter. A drawing of a Chinese philosopher hangs on the wall overhead. His mother sits on the bed with him. Looking into his eyes, both her hands on the comforter, she makes no attempt to speak. Adult words had proved ineffective; now, therefore, she allows her presence alone to console him. Christopher relives the accident in his mind and tries out different endings, but "the bad dream always rolled on out of his control until the moment when Bodger was lying in the road."

The next morning Christopher comes downstairs into the breakfast room and confronts the first tangible change wrought by death: Bodger's bowls are gone. His father calls him by his baby name, "Chrisso," and asks him if he'd like to go fishing. Here, we see the father trying somehow to restore a sense of confidence and love and to give something to him when what was so precious has been taken away. But Christopher, realizing that he is being offered a substitute, refuses. To accept his dad's offer would mean, from his point of view, betraying Bodger. It feels forbidden to do something pleasurable when one is in mourning. Interestingly, when he answers his father, however, he does not say simply "no"; he says "No thanks." This constitutes, in this delicate moment, a significant touch, revealing that, despite hurt and disappointment, this child knows on a deeper level that his father loves him and is trying to help.

Mothers traditionally offer food, and Christopher's mother is no exception; likewise, his refusal of her French toast follows a common pattern of first reaction to death: bereaved persons, in identifying with the deceased, may decline to do anything initially to prolong their own lives as well as to experience pleasure. Christopher feels that, with Bodger, some part of himself has also died. This is conveyed in a well-wrought scene, where the picture forms a kind of shell for the words: Christopher's dad sits with him outdoors on the porch steps of their cottage in silence. Christopher leans away from him and refuses to look at him, but their bodies touch. The words accompanying this picture convey Christopher's point of view: sour grapes—everyone complained about Bodger; well, now they won't have to do that any more. Using reversal as a bitter defense, he turns the bad event into an ironic good.

At length, Christopher finds the courage to ask his father, "What did you do with Bodger?" His dad says that he buried the dog near the brook, and with this information, the boy explodes in new burst of anger. He is furious and hurt that this was done without him. His father explains that he thought Christopher would not want to be there. And here, I think, we can see the parent protecting himself a little bit too, not wanting to face the child's overwhelming grief.

Christopher, at this point, separates himself from his father. He runs off into the woods muttering angry words. "You didn't care about him. You don't care about me either."

This is a key moment. It is absolutely true to life. Parents, no matter how well-intentioned, cannot bring the dead back to life, and they must inevitably disappoint children because life eventually brings situations that the most devoted parents cannot solve, heal, control, or even understand. Children, who idealize, respect, and love their parents, may have moments of rage and disappointment when this occurs.

Also, children sometimes feel misunderstood when parents act to protect both them and themselves. The call is not easy. Remember the warding-off gesture of the man when Bodger was killed? He, too, was trying to protect the boy. He did not want Chris to have to see the animal in death. Yet adults, instinctively wishing to shield children, may fail to recognize that some children need the right to choose for themselves. On the other hand, there are circumstances when an experienced parent may know better than her child and be able to imagine consequences that a child would be unable to predict. In such cases, parents may behave in such a way as to prevent a second disaster (emotional and/or physical) and brave their child's wrath at being excluded from the decision-making process. Each case is different, but the beauty of this book is that it evokes the possibilities and causes us to reflect on them.

What we see next are father and son reunited and paddling across a river in their canoe. This is a fast-forward, for, of course, in real life, this stage takes far longer to negotiate than a one-page-turn of a picture book. We are told that, when Christopher came back from the woods, he found his father still sitting on steps. *This is terribly important.* It indicates the father's wisdom. He knows that his job is to demonstrate beyond the shadow of a doubt that he can survive any aggression directed against him. Bodger has died, but Christopher's father is still living. Worried already that maybe the accident was his fault, that if he hadn't gone out or hadn't called Bodger across the road at that particular moment the tragedy might have been averted, Christopher now feels guilty that he has been unkind to his dad as well. The text says: "Christopher felt embarrassed. He was afraid to see his father's face."

What matters most is that *his father has waited for him*. He has remained in exactly the same place. He has manifested his faith in Christopher's return; he has withstood the boy's anger. Furthermore, *he* is not angry. He has not taken offense at his son's behavior. Weathering it, sitting still, he has permitted it to occur and to run its course. In so doing, he demonstrates his confidence in his son. Importantly, he does *not*, under these circumstances, run after the child, does not follow him into the woods or call him back. Christopher's father registers no anxiety that the boy is out of control from grief or that he will do something foolish. He trusts him, and this trust is a powerfully sustaining force for a child.

We can make an analogy here to a different situation but to comparable parental wisdom by turning to a page in *The Story of Ferdinand* (1936), by Munro Leaf and Robert Lawson. There, the mother cow, seeing her son behave differently from the other young bulls and worried about those differences, nonetheless refrains from badgering him. She permits him to sit by himself under a cork tree, quietly smelling the flowers. Her trust in Ferdinand is what enables him eventually to withstand the trials he must face. Similarly, Christopher's father, by sitting quietly and allowing his son to vent angry words after his pet dies, gives the boy strength to move on.

Christopher's father now, at this well-timed juncture, recommends something positive to do: he suggests that they find a beautiful gravestone to mark the dog's burial spot. Together, they sally forth in a canoe. Christopher, unenthusiastic at first, gradually feels excited about the prospects of choosing just the right stone to mark the place. This emotional shift is perfectly timed and takes place in his father's presence. It is a shift from loss and pain, and the mustering of anger to mask those unbearable feelings, to a positive act in the present. To mark and commemorate the dead is to turn from a preoccupation with the fact of death to a celebration of a particular life. It is a move from sorrow to solace, a change in focus from losing to keeping.

Together, father and son dig up a stone and place it over the spot. The landscapes on these pages are soft, limpid, and luminous. As Christopher kneels beside the stone, his father bends over it, and the text reads: "Christopher didn't know what to say. But his father did." This is another wonderful moment. What matters now are the good memories of Bodger's short life. No young child would know precisely what words to use at such a time because he would not yet have experienced enough such moments. In using words now, therefore, his father not only comforts Christopher but also models for him an appropriate verbal response to death, a response that may be long remembered. Christopher is finally at a point when he can listen. What his father does is reminisce. He picks out the retriever's funny way of playing in the water, trying to catch a fish and then looking surprised when all the fish swim smartly away from him. Christopher giggles, and then the giggle turns into a sob. The little boy finally begins to cry: "Oh, Dad!"

Grieving at last, he turns to his father to allow himself to be comforted. Thus, by reminiscing, the parent provides an occasion on which to relive a precious moment from the past, to face the fact that it will never come again, and to let go of it. Chris, by exclaiming, expresses his awareness now that his feelings are shared and that he is not alone with his sorrow.

"His father put an arm around Christopher's shoulders. Christopher turned and let the strong arms enfold him. He didn't feel angry with his father any more." This is the last page. We see only the little boy with his arms dangling by his sides, the dad with his arm resting on the boy's right shoulder, and a striated stone marking the dog's grave.

This deceptively simple book, which condenses tomes of psychological wisdom, is not easily read without a catch in the throat. It is also, by virtue of its measured pace, a book that lends itself to conversational reading, to frequent interruptions, to the interpolation of children's questions, and to the recounting of relevant memories.

The Tenth Good Thing about Barney

Another book from the same period, *The Tenth Good Thing About Barney*, by Judith Viorst and Erik Blegvad, was published in 1971. Widely circulated and frequently reprinted, this book, about a little boy's reaction to the death of his cat, Barney, differs from *The Accident* aesthetically, psychologically, and perhaps even ethically. It teaches that death is not final and irrevocable but is part of a cyclical process: death is a biological phenomenon that involves decay but eventual re-generation in some altered form. Clearly this message has a different emphasis from that of the previous book.

Only the cover is in color. On it, a horizontal oval encloses a gentle scene rendered in pen and ink with watercolor washes of softly graded blues and golds. At the center, a small group—a boy, a girl, and a set of parents—huddles together with their backs to us. They stand under a tree, and the father's shovel is an obvious clue that we are witness-ing a burial site. As in *The Accident*, there are other intimations as well: the season again appears to be fall. A white orb in the sky might easily be read as an autumn moon; the mood is calm and pensive. Inside the book, black-and-white pen-and-ink drawings illustrate the text, and they are rendered in a whimsical style not unlike that of many *New Yorker* cartoons. The whole tone of this book is lighter than that of *The Accident*. Death is made palatable. Its sting has been removed. Death has been turned into something less momentous, less devastating than in *The Accident*. In so doing, this book raises important questions that it does not attempt to resolve.

Let me draw your attention first to the frontispiece. A predatory-looking cat is perched in the branches of a tree and seems to be clawing at something. At first glance, that something seems to be a baby bird, but it is actually only a leaf, the last leaf of summer. The sun (or moon) hangs low in the sky. Overall, the picture has a strangely disturbing

From *The Tenth Good Thing About Barney* by Judith Viorst. Illustrated by
Erik Blegvad. Illustrations copyright © 1971 Erik Blegvad. Reprinted
with the permission of Atheneum Books for Young Readers, an
imprint of Simon & Schuster Children's Publishing Division.

effect, not only because of the cat's furtively aggressive gesture, but
also because the image itself is unmistakably a visual quotation. It derives from, or at any rate evokes, John Tenniel's famous drawing of
that peculiarly sinister feline character, the Cheshire Cat in *Alice's Adventures in Wonderland*, a picture that forever stamps that creature on
every reader's mind.

What should we make of this reference? The Cheshire Cat, of
course, disappears in *Alice* just as Barney the cat does in this book,
but through dematerialization rather than death. Yet, perhaps this is
precisely the point. Rather than seeing death as a termination, *Barney*

presents it as a temporary disappearance. (Children are asked to believe that, when flowers sprout in the springtime after Barney's burial, they will actually *be* Barney in an altered form.) Perhaps, therefore, the Cheshire Cat is an appropriate symbol. Yet I feel uneasy. The Cheshire Cat is, after all, a character who frightens and confuses Alice. Its claws and teeth are what she notices when first encountering the creature, who seems to be a sort of nightmarish equivalent of her own cat, Dinah. And Tenniel's illustration is hardly friendly. Members of lecture audiences have actually told me that Tenniel's image is for them one of the most terrifying pictures they remember from childhood—especially the second drawing, in which the cat disappears among the tree branches, leaving behind only its sharp-toothed grin. This image, some have said, haunted their childhood dreams and could not be exorcised. On the other hand, in support of the reference, the scary image at the start of *Barney* might be read as intimating the loss of self that follows death as well as the rage and helplessness that are associated with it—and even possibly its phantasmic aura, especially when death is thought of, the way it is here, as a transient state of being.

Particularly unsettling is the fact that this strange frontispiece is virtually the only visual clue we ever have as to Barney's appearance, because the cat is already dead when the story begins. About midway through the book, a cartoon appears in which two cats with halos sit among the clouds while another plays a lyre, a picture meant to illustrate a debate in the text about whether or not cats go to heaven. On the final page, a cat we can assume to be Barney is seen from the rear, its tail raised. This is all. There are no other visualizations of the title character. In these circumstances, the frontispiece assumes a strong establishing valence. In the last image in the book, where Barney is observed from the rear walking proudly away after his burial has taken place, we are invited, presumably, to take the cocky figure as emblematic. It epitomizes, after all, the message that death is not final. Also, like its continually reappearing feline prototype in *Alice*, it may be taken as referring humorously to the old adage that a cat has nine lives.

A well-known song from the 1960s may hover in the background of this 1970s children's book. "Where Have All the Flowers Gone?" its lyrics composed by Pete Seeger in 1956, thematizes and idealizes a cyclical view of death. Over the years, this song has acquired a canonical status in American culture and become a paradigm vocal expression of waves of yearning, first for the soldiers who died in World War II (it was sung by Marlene Dietrich), then for those who perished in the Korean War, and finally for the men killed in Vietnam. It was recorded by the Kingston Trio and by Peter, Paul, and Mary and became so popular that it reached the Hit Parade. It is a song that, both in its subject matter and in its own history of being recycled, might remind us of an even earlier cultural icon with a similar message—James Thurber's anti-war fable, *The Last Flower* (1939), a brilliant little book in which the human alternation of building and destroying, love and hatred, growth and decay is immortalized in line drawings of unique delicacy and eloquence.

In *Barney*, as we have noted, all the action takes place after Barney has died. We never find out what color he was or whether he had long or short fur. We do not know what caused his death or whether he perished suddenly or slowly, in youth, midlife, or old age. In mulling over the frontispiece in this context, the depiction of a cat in the branches of a tree makes good sense, for the character of Barney is so undeveloped, so lacking in individuality, that he seems to be nothing more than a part of some undifferentiated animal-vegetable kingdom. Bodger, on the other hand, is anthropomorphized from the start. It may be significant to note that cats *are* different from dogs, and that the ties children form with them may be correspondingly different, but on this point I have lingering doubts.

Barney, then, introduces death to children in different terms from those in *The Accident*. Its potential effectiveness in preparing young people for subsequent experiences with human deaths may be moot. In any case, its implicit message requires serious deliberation. Either animals cannot be mourned in the same way people can or, if they can, then human deaths must likewise be considered "good" in sense that they too help to grow flowers—a limited message at best.

The meaning of death is thus radically altered here. The bereaved boy's parents in *Barney*, unlike Chris's parents in *The Accident*, give their son tasks to perform, prescribe his behavior, and expect him to get over his grief quickly. His father tells him that he will feel better soon and teaches him to feel comfortable rather than uncomfortable about the death of his pet. Planting seeds in the garden and eating sandwiches, father and son effect a magical reversal of death into life.

What interests me psychologically here is that I believe the reversal works only and precisely because of what is missing: namely, our actually getting to know Barney before his death. The solution makes sense only because we never have a chance to encounter the animal's uniqueness, his special qualities, whatever they might have been, or his relationship to the unnamed boy. This is not "Zlateh the Goat." In the context of *that* story, no child would be willing to accept Zlateh's death as "good" on the basis that her body would decompose and cause plants to grow. She is simply too real, too lovable, too important. My point is that we can go along with a cyclical view of death only when, as in *Barney*, there is no differentiated character, or when, as in "Where Have All the Flowers Gone?" there are so many deaths to mourn that individuality no longer counts. The deceased becomes a phantasm. Which makes the reference to Wonderland all the more appropriate.

On the first page of *Barney*, a boy in profile, his head in his hand, sits at a table and weeps. The text is written in the first person, with the author assuming the child's voice. I normally resist this narrative style; unless handled with special sensitivity, it courts the dangers of appropriation. Think about it this way: the picture book is being read *to* a child *by* an adult who is assuming the voice *of* a child. Distinctions are blurred, therefore, between the voices of adults and children. In general, I prefer to maintain these distinctions so as to keep the psychological space more open and free. Oddly, despite this conceit, or perhaps perversely because of it, *Barney* penetrates far less deeply into the recesses of a child's mind than does *The Accident*, which is written from the perspective of an adult narrator. Here, what the child says (which is the entire text) describes only what can be observed from the outside. We never find out anything about what is going on within.

After telling us that his cat died, the unnamed boy says:

"I was very sad.
I cried, and I didn't watch television.
I cried, and I didn't eat my chicken or even the chocolate pudding.
I went to bed, and I cried."

Interestingly, as in *The Accident*, television crops up immediately. Children's attachment to it is taken for granted; giving it up is seen as a major sign of distress. In *The Accident*, it is Christopher's attachment to television that prevents him from going canoeing with his parents and thus precipitates the events that lead to the death of his pet. In *Barney*, in the wake of the death of a pet, the first pleasure the child relinquishes is television. The second is food. This is also true in *The Accident*, where Christopher refuses the French toast his mother offers.

With this abrupt beginning and no stage-setting, we are plunged into the middle of things. We are called upon to try to share the boy's sadness even though, except for the frontispiece, we have no experience of the object of his grief or of the child either. And we learn little more.

This lack of knowledge, as I have noted elsewhere in these pages, has the potential to function positively, to elicit projection and force the child to draw upon his or her own resources in order to become emotionally engaged with the book. By withholding information and starting where it does, *Barney* creates an open scene where a space is made available for us to enter and participate, if we can. We see little of the child's face. We never meet his pet. His parents are cartoonish, abstract figures. Thus, the situation presented can be invested with whatever the child encountering it needs it to be, and this could be an asset.

By the next page, however, the openness shuts down. The boy's mother is portrayed as leaning over him in his bed, grasping him so tightly that there is no air left between them. Unlike Christopher's mother, who provides a clear distance between herself and her son, a boundary that is demarcated and emphasized by a strong vertical line, and who sits in silence, the mother in *Barney* encroaches both physically and psychically. She makes detailed suggestions: she proposes a funeral; she instructs her son to think of "ten good things" about his deceased cat. In her proactive stance, she differs from Christopher's mother, who senses that her child needs space and gives it to him while remaining close by to provide the comfort of her ongoing presence. These two mother-son pictures speak volumes, and it is worthwhile to compare them. In *The Accident*, we can observe a fascinating internal distinction between the picture and the text, for the words merely describe Christopher's obsessive recycling of the traumatic events and never mention his mother at all. Only in the accompanying picture does she appear, a silent witness and psychological container for his worrisome thoughts. She does not speak because she knows that, although she is needed, any words she might utter would be intrusive.

In *Barney*, the corresponding illustration has, as I have noted, a cartoon-like air: as she leans over her child's bed, the mother's raised, rounded rear end forms the centerpoint of the image. Her smothering hug seems a visual analogue of her intrusive verbiage. Why "ten good things"? Why "ten"? Why only "good" things? Why "things" at all? Why not, for example, emphasize relationship over characteristics? Surely relationship is what matters in the story of Zlateh. Better yet, why not let whatever comes out of the child simply emerge? Why attempt to control it?

One must acknowledge diverse styles of parenting, however, as well as differences among personalities and ethnic groups. I remember being pained and confused as a little girl when grown-ups laughed and joshed boisterously during the period after a funeral and during the week of intense mourning observed by Jews after a death in the family. It did not help at all to hear my mother explain that this behavior afforded some people a much-needed sense of relief. *Barney* creates distance between its readers and the events it portrays. Never completely disengaging our emotions, it likewise never fully draws us in. It asks us to *think* about death with our children as well as to feel it. *The Accident*, on the other hand, can hardly be read without emotion.

Curiously, when the boy who owned Barney tries to think of "ten good things," as his mother bids him, he can only come up with nine, and they are general and abstract: Barney was brave, smart, funny, clean, handsome, and so forth. The only specific act he mentions is that Barney "only once ate a bird." This line, however, enables us to return to the frontispiece with added insight. After a death, as some have noted, there may well be particular negative memories that float to the surface and supersede all others for a brief time. Here, it is the cat's naughtiness, his aggression, his specifically oral greed, which the child selectively remembers. Why? How can we explain the staying power of such a memory, which in this case seems to be visually quoted in the frontispiece? It is literally the only act of Barney's to which the book ever alludes.

In trying to make sense of this centrality of the negative memory, I remembered that, after my own father died, one particular incident from my earliest years kept replaying itself in my mind. It involved a blinding snowstorm, a whirling blizzard that had darkened the sky and thickened the frosty air with those extra-large wet crystals that children love to pack into igloos and snowmen. My younger sister, father, and I, zipped into our heaviest winter garb, trudged outdoors with snow shovels and sleds. Night fell early, due to the season, and the temperature rapidly descended. My father asked us to go indoors. My sister complied with his request, but I, having a more rebellious temperament and being unable to bear the thought of missing the still-falling snow, begged permission to remain outside a little longer. My father agreed. Time passed as I played by myself in the fairyland that was forming all about me when, glancing up at one of the illuminated leaded windows of our house, I saw a spectral face. It was my father's. Knocking insistently against the pane, he signaled me to come inside at once. All tingly, happy, and covered with melting whiteness, I did so. Standing there in the doorway before him, I looked up at his face with pleasure and gratitude and was stunned to hear him raise his voice and angrily rebuke me for my disobedience. Mortified, I shrank before him, smarting with shame and with what I perceived to be his injustice, for I had believed he had given me his permission.

I recount this story because for a week or so after his death it kept recurring and seemed to me the most intense memory I had of him—the single instance I could recall of unfairness from a parent deeply loved and to whom I had had the warmest ties throughout my life. Why a negative memory at such a time as this? And why, by analogy, the memory that Barney once ate a bird? Perhaps we remember such things at such times because, in the aftermath of death, with the first pangs of loss, we need to project the rage we feel on to the very object of that loss. In a world turned upside-down, the dead become angry and fearsome. Only later on, when the pain subsides, can we reclaim the anger as our own and realize it is death, not our loved ones, that has robbed us, that it is *we* who are angry at having been left alone. Also, with bereavement there comes a radical sense of disempowerment. Thus, the cat's naughtiness and his ability to get what he wanted and actually eat it up was not only horrible but also consoling to the child. Likewise, my evocation of my father's power over me represented a kind of security; it was based on my knowledge that his ultimate concern was for my well-being and safety.

In *Barney*, unlike in *The Accident*, the father buries the pet in the child's presence. Immediately thereafter, food is both mentioned and portrayed. This conjunction is in compliance with numerous ethnic traditions—in particular, with Jewish observance, where food is an important aspect of the shivah ritual. In *Barney*, friends come to the home of the bereaved, and a little girl named Annie appears with flowers. The mourners eat, drink, and speak generally of the deceased. The children's discussion escalates into a conflict over whether or not Barney is in heaven. The little boy yanks Annie's pigtail in a psychologically well-timed moment of displaced rage.

In the children's debate, gender stereotypes are preserved intact: the girl insists that the cat is in heaven eating tuna and cream, the boy maintains the rational-scientific position that the cat is merely in the ground. Called upon to adjudicate this dispute, the father neither comforts nor explains. He eats a cookie himself but offers none to the children. He equivocates with a succession of "maybes," whereupon the children begin to fight. Separating them and ending their aggression by fiat, he neither satisfies their curiosity nor clarifies anything for them (or for the child hearing the story). Instead of giving emotional, physical, or intellectual sustenance, he stops them and then leaves. The text reads: "My father told me he had to work in the garden." Life simply goes on. Adult readers may be reminded of Pieter Brueghel's ironic portrayal of death in his *Landscape with the Fall of Icarus* (ca. 1558), and of the Netherlandish proverb that went with it: "Not a plow stops when a man dies." Not a father stops when a pet dies.

Next, on an imageless page, the bereaved boy offers to help his father in the garden and then expresses his regret that Barney is dead. Affirming matter-of-factly that it is sad, the father says: "It might not feel so sad tomorrow." The child listening to the story might wonder why. *Why* will it not feel so sad tomorrow? And what might be the long-term ethical consequences of such a position?

While the little boy watches, his father plants seeds in their garden. Here, in an unsettling reversal, the child, dressed like his father, towers strangely over him. The older figure kneels in the earth, closer to his own final resting place, while the young one stands tall, hands on hips, surveying the scene. The image recaps precisely the turnabout they are enacting—transforming death into life.

But when the boy examines the seeds and complains that he cannot see leaves or flowers yet, his father explains that all things change in the earth. Barney will "change until he's part of the ground in the garden," and his corpse will help create the leaves and flowers of plants. That's the cat's job now: "a pretty nice job for a cat."

A "job" is a particularly powerful concept for young children. A job is what Mommy and Daddy go to when they are not at home. It is what makes life possible. In *Bedtime for Frances*, little Frances's father finally gets her into bed by telling her that he has a job, the wind has a job, and *she* has a job: namely, going to school in the morning. Parenthetically, another classic picture book, Richard Scarry's *What Do People Do All Day?* (1968), begins with the statement "Everyone is a worker" and goes on to describe a variety of jobs: building a home, sailing an ocean liner, and so on. And the title character of the recent movie *Babe* (1996), wildly popular with American children, is a pig who survives only by learning to do a job, a sheepdog's job; by doing the job, the pig avoids death. In *Barney*, this important notion paradoxically and confusingly extends to death. A dead cat has a job.

On the next to last page, the boy's mother sits on his bed and all the "good things" about Barney are reviewed. A tenth one is now added: namely, that Barney is in the ground helping flowers to grow.

On the final page, the cat, as we have noted, walks away. In doing so, he leaves the book's message behind: namely, that some kind of life continues after death. Death is therefore something of an illusion. Because this is so, we have less need than in *The Accident* for strong emotion. *The Tenth Good Thing about Barney*, while appropriating a child's voice, eschews highly individualized portrayals of either life or death and creates a world in which feeling is muted and intensity is out of place. Whether comforting or disquieting—an effect that will vary from reader to reader—such a book cannot but elicit challenging questions from both adults and children. And this is, of course, as it should be.

Grandmas and Grandpas

In the United States today, men and women are living longer than ever before, but because young families are more mobile than ever, children may actually see less of their grandparents than was the case in former decades. This is lamentable because intergenerational bonds are among the strongest anchors we have in the turbulence of our lives. Oddly, in past times, when children had more opportunities to interact informally with grandparents, fewer picture books were devoted to the subject; today, the theme has achieved popular status. The flood of new books about grandparents could perhaps be interpreted as participating in a kind of cultural nostalgia. In some cases, these books may even serve as a substitute for what once was or might have been — a kind of compensatory experience, in other words — a providing of imaginary grandparenting when in fact those important kin are missing from children's everyday lives. In any case, the oldest book we will highlight here was published just under a quarter of a century ago in the early 1970s, and the most recent one appeared in 1988.

Tomie de Paola, author of *Now One Foot, Now the Other* (1980), produced two other picture books that should be mentioned in passing even though they do not involve loss. *Strega Nona* (1975) and *Pancakes for Breakfast* (1978) deal in warm and whimsical ways with grandmotherly characters in the context of two of American children's favorite foods — pasta and pancakes. These books, I suggest, contribute to the landscape against which the ones we are going to look at in detail may be seen. In general, the portrayal of old people in western art and literature deserves a sharp critique, for age is all too often ridiculed: cruel witches and envious crones are the prototype for aged women, and doddering fools the stereotypical representations of old men. Tomie de Paola, however, in his tender and understated way, undercuts these stereotypes by placing sympathetic images into circulation. Strega Nona and the unnamed hungry lady in *Pancakes for Breakfast* are delightful characters with whom children can readily bond and in whose triumphs they can share.

With regard to some very long-lived grandmother figures, there is one who trots immediately into view. She appears with an iron in her hand and "a nice hot singey smell" around her. She is stout and short. She wears a large apron over her petticoat, and her nose goes "sniffle, sniffle, snuffle" while her eyes go "twinkle, twinkle." Poking through her cap are "PRICKLES!" She is, of course, the title character of Beatrix Potter's *Tale of Mrs. Tiggy-winkle*, an unforgettable personage who, although her hat is full of hairpins stuck in backwards, makes cozy tea for her visitor, Lucie, and provides for her by washing and ironing her "pocket-handkins." Instantiating an image of maternal ambivalence from a child's perspective, Mrs. Tiggy-winkle is portrayed as helping Lucie and feeding her but at the same time making the little girl feel that she doesn't want to get too close. Mrs. Tiggy-winkle's equivocal status vis-à-vis Lucie may have to do not only with her age and gender but also with issues of race and class. "[Her] hand," we are told, "was very very brown, and very very wrinkly with the soap suds." Lucie, by contrast, is described as fair-skinned and blond. Thus, the distance between them may be ascribed not only to Mrs. Tiggy-winkle's being grandmotherly but also to her valence as a worker, a servant from the implicitly lower classes and *with a darker skin*. The class distinction is also signified by the human/animal dichotomy that Beatrix Potter employs elsewhere in her tales (see my discussion of her *Tale of Peter Rabbit* in chapter 4), where distrust among species is the order of the day, and animals and humans are pitted against one another. In any case, once met, Mrs. Tiggy-winkle, with all her pins, sticks fast in our memories — demonstrating brilliantly the artist's gift for an apparently simple invention that, on second glance, proves richly evocative and ideologically complex.

Another grandmotherly figure must also be mentioned: the Old Lady in *The Story of Babar.* She too is not, strictly speaking, a grandmother but has for many decades assumed that role in children's minds. Admittedly, we can see the Old Lady as grandmotherly only by bracketing the contemporary academic discourse on colonialism, which would emphasize her whiteness, her wealth, and her cultured social status vis-à-vis Babar, who, from that perspective, is remarkable principally for being dark (gray), naked, and untutored. Elegant and bountiful, the Old Lady showers the young elephant with gifts. She buys him new clothes, teaches him to do his morning exercises, gives him a splendid red car so that he can drive into the countryside, hires a private tutor for him, and includes him in grown-up, human parties, where she shows him off to her distinguished guests. When at length he grows homesick and longs to return to the great forest, she does not cling to him but graciously relinquishes him. In a charming scene, we see her laden with bonbons and other gifts for him to take along with his clothing and red bedroom slippers as he packs in preparation for leaving her—possibly forever.

On the day of Babar's departure, the Old Lady, garbed in her emblematic high-necked black dress, stands alone on the balcony of her townhouse and watches as he grows small in the distance. "Sadly, she wonders: 'When shall I see my little Babar again?'" These words and the image itself evoke in the reader a feeling of sympathy for her. We feel *her* loss and sadness, and this is the last we see of her in the book. Its sequel, however, *The Travels of Babar* (1934), recalls her; she is summoned to rescue Babar once again. From the vantage point of adulthood, I wonder now why Jean de Brunhoff did not arrange to have the Old Lady reappear at the end of the first book. Babar and Celeste get married, after all, and their wedding constitutes the culminating event of that narrative; surely, through a simple turn of plot, the Old Lady might have been invited to the festivities. Curiously, her absence did not disturb me as a child, nor, for that matter, did her not reappearing concern me; the Old Lady had simply dropped out of the story. She was there when she was needed, and she was forgotten when she was not. My little girl self, needing her no longer, simply let go of her. It is only through adult eyes that I am able to perceive the story otherwise. For after all, in the sequel, when she is again needed, she reappears. The perfect grandmother: there when you want her help; not there when you don't. Not surprisingly, of course, the Old Lady is, symbolically, a grand*mother*; I suspect that the gendering here is not without significance.

Before leaving *Babar*, I want briefly to mention the death of the little elephant's mother, which occurs at the beginning of the story and catalyzes the action of the plot. It is an extremely disturbing moment. I have mentioned earlier that this death is forgotten or repressed by many adults who can vividly recall other images and details from the book. Yet in the context of the story, it plays a symbolic role. Clearly the loss of grandparents does not have the same meaning to children as does the loss of parents, except possibly in cases where the grandpar-

From *The Travels of Babar* by Jean de Brunhoff. Copyright © 1934 and renewed by Random House, Inc. Reprinted by permission of Random House, Inc.

ents have assumed the role of primary caretakers. Yet, in the imagination, all mothers, stepmothers, grandmothers, fairy godmothers, and witches can be symbolic of one another.

The Story of Babar opens on a scene rendered in close detail. The forest floor, carpeted in yellow, sprouts tiny red flowers that bloom against clumps of green grass, and a waving line of pink hills marks the horizon. Two red bird-shapes adorn the sky, and a little elephant rests in a hammock suspended between two palm trees as his mother "rocks him to sleep with her trunk while singing softly to him." It is a page of bright serenity. Every young child's mother, it seems to be saying, is an ongoing wellspring of life.

In order for children to grow, however, this blissful state of tranquillity must be disrupted. There must somehow be a "death" of this idyll of unity, peace, and comfort. In *Babar*, that disruption comes about not by means of the child's expectable maturation or by the mother's gradual alteration of her care but by a violent act from outside that affects them both. This violent act—"The hunter has killed Babar's mother!"—may be seen from a purely psychological viewpoint as a plot device to precipitate the little elephant out of infancy toward self-reliance and maturity. He must flee in order to survive. He must begin all by himself to seek his fortune, to pursue his own life, his own adventures. But, because of the early love he had received from his mother, as revealed in the beautiful image with which the book begins, he is able to adapt to the changed conditions and to make the best of the new life that awaits him. When he grows up, he becomes, eventually, King of the Elephants, but he never forgets his mother. "He often stands at the window, thinking sadly of his childhood, and cries when he remembers his mother." Grief is allowed here to run its course. We are not asked to let it go.

Now One Foot, Now the Other

Now One Foot, Now the Other (1980) is a tale of heroism set in the context of a little boy's relationship to his grandfather. Bobby becomes a hero in this story not by inventing ingenious fantasies, braving dangers, conquering villains, or going off on his own to seek his fortune—all time-honored routes to male glory. Instead, this small boy achieves success in the arena of human affairs by persevering in repeated acts of nurturing. By creating him in these terms, Tomie de Paola again does more than tell a good story; he demonstrates ways in which children can help others and adapt to illness and loss. He also challenges conventional stereotypes of gender role behavior and gives young people of both sexes a model of the ways *boys* can act, a model that has had too few advocates—in literature for young children, in popular culture, or, more dramatically, in education. By making both of his principal characters male, de Paola works to extend and transmit important ethical values. We can think back in this context to the stories of Yen-foh, mentioned earlier, where a similar masculine ideal was valorized.

Little Bobby, named after his grandfather, Bob, and thus identified deeply with him from the start, learns to walk by holding onto the old man's hands. In each successive image, a visual parallelism unites the two figures. As they build tall towers of blocks together, the child's and the older man's gestures and expressions mirror one another. In telling and retelling Bobby the favorite story of how he learned to walk, the grandfather uses the expression "Now one foot, now the other," the book's title, which becomes a metaphor for the entire narrative.

The dyad of Bobby and Bob, grandchild and grandparent, also replicates in print and picture the current sharing that each child and adult reader are experiencing with the book, a doubling that further enriches the moment for both of them.

The two characters enjoy exciting, scary, appropriately masculine activities together. On Bobby's fifth birthday, they visit an amusement park, ride a roller coaster, eat hot dogs and ice cream, and attend a fireworks display. On the way home in the dark, Bobby asks his grandfather to retell the story of how he learned to walk. White, crescent-shaped, but drawn as a slice cut from a darkened orb against a gray-blue sky, the moon on this page resonates with all the waxing moons we have come to associate with *Where the Wild Things Are*, before Max eventually gets to the island of monsters. It is thus a premonitory moon.

On the very next page, tragedy strikes. Bobby is told by his parents that his grandfather has had a stroke. This image is beautifully wrought. We see the family in profile: the father's hand rests on the mother's shoulder, while she places both of her hands tenderly on Bobby's face; he, staring into their eyes, lets his own hands fall helplessly by his sides. On the next page, we have a bedtime scene. Bobby sits in pajamas, his knees drawn up; he looks away from us out of his window at the moon, which is now full. The visual source here (and perhaps deliberately quoted) is unmistakably *Goodnight Moon*, a symbol of solace and continuity. Just as all the cherished objects in the little bunny's room survive the darkness of night, so, this image implies, will Bobby's grandfather and his love for Bobby survive the illness that has cast a pall over his life and their good times together.

The grandfather cannot remember Bobby, and the child is both bereft and frightened. Under a picture of the boy sitting pensively with boots and muffler in the snow, we learn that many months have passed since his grandfather went into the hospital: "Bobby missed his grandfather." When he is told, finally, that the doctors have given up hope that Bob will ever be able to walk or talk again, the facing picture portrays father and son in the kitchen. The doctors' dire and hopeless message is conveyed to Bobby while he is holding a glass of milk and sitting with a plate of cookies before him. This comforting image adds context to the unwelcome words. The text makes no mention of food; the words are pessimistic, hopeless. The warmth and coziness of the accompanying picture, however, enable the words to be contained, as it were, and to be calmly heard.

The two pictures that follow portray a parallel progress, physical and emotional. Bob has returned from the hospital, and as he slowly regains a little strength, he moves from lying down in bed to sitting up in a chair. Bobby, meanwhile, ventures closer and closer to him. These two pages manage, by their titration of the old man's position and the boy's parallel movement and bodily gestures, to convey all the fear and uncertainty and longing of the child as he confronts this altered person with whom he had formerly been so intimate.

Convinced against his parents' pessimistic predictions that he *can* make a difference and reestablish the cherished relationship he has had with his grandfather, Bobby repeats their old games. He builds a tower of blocks. He helps Bob hold a spoon. Finally, he retells their shared story of learning to walk. In the last picture, the reversal is complete: the child helps the old man learn once again to take one step after another.

Having internalized over time the experience of being nurtured by an older person (*Now One Foot*), this young person has been able to tap his own creative capacities and return that nurturance in kind (*Now the Other*). An added touch concerns the symbolism of the elephant-who-never-forgets. Bob and Bobby have a special game in which, when a tower of wooden blocks is built, the last to be put on top is always the elephant block. Each time that particular block is in place, Bob pretends to sneeze, the whole structure collapses, and they both laugh. This block, adorned with its picture and the letter *B* (for Bob and Bobby), is the image we come upon at the very end of the book, printed on the lefthand corner of the final page. It seems a perfect emblem for the power of memory to bring about healing and for attempts to restore what has been good in our lives. Parents reading this book might, however, want to explain to children that not all such efforts can be as successful as Bobby's.

Always Gramma

Closely related to *Now One Foot, Now the Other* is *Always Gramma* (1988), which features a girl and her grandmother. Written and illustrated by two women, Vaunda Micheaux Nelson and Kimianne Uhler, it too portrays a situation in which an older person suffers disabling illness—in this case not a stroke but a form of Alzheimer's disease or senile dementia—and the child in the story must face the disruption this causes in their relationship. Visually, the book is highly distinctive. All of its illustrations are watercolor wash paintings that blend realism with an aura of indistinctness.

Like *Now One Foot, Now the Other*, and, perhaps one could even say, like *Barney*, this book has a cyclical structure. Like *Barney*, it assumes the child's voice as narrator: "I remember every song Gramma ever taught me." Unlike *Barney*, however, this book paints a rich picture of relationship before it portrays loss. In its opening sentence, memory is declared as focal, and it is of course precisely the lack of memory that becomes the book's tragedy.

Pictures and words convey the special relationship that obtains between this unnamed little girl and her Gramma: they sing and imagine together, go wading, bury a pet canary, plant violets, skinny-dip in a mountain creek, bake a special yellow cake with creamy icing. Most striking of all, stimulated to use her own imagination, the little girl makes wings from two kites and hurts herself trying to fly; her Gramma, at this point, instead of chastizing her, hugs her and applauds her courage and inventiveness. Rather than being angry, she tells the child that someday she "might do something to change the world."

This presentation is very different from that shown in the book about Bob and Bobby, where the relationship between grandfather and grandson is companionable but conventional. Grandfather Bob doesn't actually do anything with his grandson that a father would not do. In fact, as one reads *Now One Foot, Now the Other*, one wonders why the grandfather and not the father is so close to the boy, or why all three are never shown doing things together. Putting this to one side, in *Always Gramma*, the grandmother's relations with her granddaughter are portrayed as *different* from what we might expect to exist between a little girl and her mother. Gramma is thus established not only as a unique character but also as a model for how grandparents in general— precisely because they are a generation older, come from a somewhat different culture, are *not* the children's parents, and are not therefore primarily responsible for their safety and welfare—can offer delightfully eccentric, unusual, and inspiring experiences in and perspectives on the world.

When the girl becomes aware that her Gramma has begun to "act different," as she puts it, she is shown sitting on the floor hugging her Raggedy Ann doll with a bunny beside her that looks a great deal like the Velveteen Rabbit. Kimianne Uhler, the artist, possesses a special gift for conveying facial expressions. Over and again, she captures in paint that poignant mix of worry, perplexity, sadness, and suspicion that adorn a child's face in circumstances that are troubling but beyond understanding. When the girl's mother tries to explain that Gramma's forgetting is not like her own, the little girl makes an effort to palliate this news by pointing out that she does not always remember her school lunch. Here, we see a child trying to identify with an older person, trying to encompass the grandmother's experience within the range of her own. We see, in other words, the working of empathy.

The artist's use of empty space here in the double-spread images of this book is especially important because it is a marker of the space that is opening up gradually between the child and her grandmother. Empty space also creates a visual oasis where the eye of the beholder can rest and reflect.

We see the grandmother bring her husband a cup of coffee although he already has one; she leaves the cake in the oven so long that it burns; she absentmindedly puts a lighted cigarette in her pocket; she takes the child for a walk in the woods but forgets how to get home. When her husband, who is portrayed with exquisite tenderness, finally has to put new locks on the doors, Gramma becomes uncharacteristically angry. Eventually she is taken to a nursing home, where she can be cared for in safety.

Just before this happens, we have a canonical bedtime scene. On a left-hand page, the little girl sits alone, propped up against her pillows with her Raggedy on one side and a teddy bear on the other. Her serious expression and the tilt of her head express what words cannot. The painting gives a wide-angle view of her coverlet. The image invites quiet contemplation. It affords an amplitude of space that symbolizes the expanse of time and space necessary to assimilate change rather than be terrified or overwhelmed by it. The next time we see the little girl, she is peering pensively over the top of a bureau at a framed black-and-white photograph of her Gramma. Then, on the next page, she is in the nursing home, sitting face to face with the grandmother herself. Like Bobby, she reminds her Gramma of their shared times together and catches her up on the current events of her life. "When I hold her hand, she squeezes mine. I know Gramma knows I'm here."

On the final page of the book, we see the child alone but smiling. Splashing barefoot in the same mountain stream in which she skinny-dipped with her grandmother, she is singing the song they always sang together and remembering their joy.

Nana Upstairs and Nana Downstairs

This 1973 picture book, again by Tomie de Paola, features a little boy named Tommy who visits his grandmother and great-grandmother every Sunday. The younger of these women lives downstairs and, clad in an apron, bustles about beside her wrought iron stove. Upstairs in bed lies the frail, elderly great-grandmother, who invites Tommy to stand on his tiptoes and take candy mints out of the sewing box on her bureau. As Tommy watches his grandmother tie his great-grandmother into a chair because she is ninety-four years old and is too frail to sit unassisted, he asks to be tied into his chair too, because, he says, he is four years old. What matters here, as we noted above, is the portrayal of *identification* between the young child and the aged grandparent. In de Paola's illustration, the point is unmistakably made: Tommy and the old lady sit side by side, strapped to their respective chairs, while they chat and nibble their peppermints. Nana even holds Tommy's stuffed rabbit, a symbol, via *The Velveteen Rabbit*, of love that not only survives wear and tear but grows greater through time and use and age.

These moments of identification lay a foundation for empathy and thus for care, responsibility, and, in general, ethical action. Like the grandmother in *Always Gramma*, Tommy's "Nana Upstairs" (the name he gives his great-grandmother) presents him with her own eccentric view of life; she tells him stories about the so-called Little People and enables him to visualize them for himself. Furthermore, contra the portrayal of old women as unattractive, Tommy in this book watches admiringly as his grandmothers comb out their long gray tresses, winding and braiding them, and the text speaks of their "beautiful" and "silver-white" hair. Again, the artist Tomie de Paola strives in his work to reverse derogatory stereotypes and to place more positive and kindly images into circulation.

When Tommy is told that his Nana Upstairs has died, he asks what that means. At this point he is sitting on his mother's lap, and her response, unlike the mother's in *Barney*, involves a finality: his Nana won't be there any more. On the next page, this idea is given visual form. Tommy, in a beanie hat and jacket, his hands hanging limply by his sides, stands with his back toward us facing the now empty bed in his great-grandmother's vacant room. It is a strong image.

In each book we have studied so far, a little boy, confronted with loss or death, either looks away or is not portrayed fully facing the beholder. In the case of *Always Gramma*, however, in which the protagonist is a girl and both author and artist are women, the child is drawn full-face; her gaze is powerful and intense. We cannot avoid her troubled eyes as she grapples with the complex emotions that rage within her. Looking into her face, we can see her pain. Are there gender differences here that have been captured and are being perpetuated by these picture books? I must leave this as an open question.

Tommy cries, and, in the bedroom scene we have come to expect by now, we see him kneeling on the covers with his "velveteen" rabbit. He gazes away from us out the window into a starry night. This picture contrasts dramatically with the bedroom scene in *Always Gramma*, where, as just mentioned, the little girl faces us under her coverlet, in an enclosed space, and we are drawn in, frontally, to her grief. Here, on the following page, a falling star appears through Tommy's window.

A falling star. When Tommy goes to his parents' bedroom to tell them about it, his mother suggests that perhaps the star is "a kiss from Nana Upstairs." Stars and death have a long pictorial association, and I want apropos to consider two relevant picture books, nearly a century apart.

Charles Dickens's "A Child's Dream of a Star," which appeared in an illustrated edition a year after the author's death in 1871, epitomizes a tradition of associating stars and death at a time when death was not a taboo subject for children; so many infant, child, and childbirth losses occurred that the topic could not be avoided. Dickens's sentimentally sweet tale, accompanied by subtly ominous line engravings, portrays an idealized, intimate, eternal love bond between two small children, a brother and sister. This love, which persists beyond the grave (the little girl dies), occurs in the context of their mutual adoration of nature and in particular of one unique star, to which they bid farewell each night before lying down in their beds to sleep. When the sister dies (and it is perhaps unnecessary to comment that, if one of the two must die, it clearly needs to be the girl rather than the boy), the brother dreams that their star opens up. Shining trails of angels create sparkling roads from sky to earth and earth to sky, which is where his sister now awaits him. Every time a new death occurs, and there are many in the story, the dead sister searches the radiant trail that ascends to the sky to see whether her brother is yet among those who are ascending. Other people mount the starry route to the heavens, but never he. At length, though, he becomes an old man, and, on his death bed, he feels age slipping from him like a garment; at last he too rises "towards the star as a child."

Many of the illustrations for Dickens's story are bedroom scenes. We see the little boy in his bed in a room with a window (just as we do in the twentieth-century books—the stories of Christopher, Bobby, and Tommy), and an iridescent, spiritual bridge of light filled with crowds of winged angels reaches from earth to sky. This trail of light is similar to the shooting star in Tomie de Paola's book, which, I am suggesting, partakes in a pictorial tradition that includes but does not begin with the Dickens story.

This same tradition informs a postwar picture book, *What Miranda Knew* (1944), by Gladys Adshead and Elizabeth Orton Jones, a book that frightened me when I was a little girl. Not knowing anything of the pictorial tradition that symbolizes death by means of stars and clouds and angels, I found this book eerie, bizarre, and vaguely sinister—even though it never once refers textually to death (which is to me now its obvious theme). It frightened me because I *knew* it had to be about something other than what it seemed to be about, but I could not form a clear idea from its sentimental illustrations and incomprehensible plot as to what that something was—namely, the death of grandparents. As I think about it now, perhaps the problem was that I *did* sense that the story was about death, and this terrified me all the more because it made death seem lovely and graceful when I knew from my own experience that death was sad, painful, lonely, and irrevocable. By treating death as a topic that could not be mentioned by name, *What Miranda Knew* made it all the more disquieting.

Miranda is a fuzzy gray Persian cat who lives with two old people in a fairytale cottage surrounded by well-kept beds of hollyhocks, geraniums, petunias, and other gaily colored flowers. As the old people putter about their garden, they yearn for their children, who have long since grown up, and for their grandchildren, who live far away. One day Miranda discovers a basket with two human babies in it. Out of the blue (literally), a bevy of angels, all winged little girls approximately three to seven years old, arrive to tend these babies. The old people are depicted sitting with them in newfound bliss, surrounded once again by youth and joy.

Shortly, the angels tell the old couple that they must take the babies back where they came from (a place that is unnamed) and that they, the old folks, must come along too. Diapers, washcloths, rattles, and all are packed up in a wicker basket, and the group ascends as an ensemble into the sky holding hands, the old folks supported by the angels. Left alone in the garden, Miranda twitches her tail as she watches them fly up in a stream reminiscent of the one in the Dickens story and of the shooting star in *Nana Upstairs*. The littlest angel returns to fetch the almost forsaken cat, and in the end they are all in the sky together, smiling at us from a bank of clouds.

The book is called *What Miranda Knew*. But what *did* Miranda know? Throughout my childhood, *I* certainly never knew. Secretly scared, I both wanted and yet did not want to know. The whole book, with its apparent innocence and sweetness, its honeyed hues and rosy settings, seemed to be covering something that, until my own adulthood, I could not fully fathom. What matters is that experiences such as this are not unique. They are not even uncommon. Children are exposed to a variety of pictorial traditions, and it behooves us to realize that images are not transparent. Just as children need to learn the alphabet and Arabic numerals and punctuation, so they must learn our pictorial codes; we really cannot take them for granted.

Both "A Child's Dream of a Star" and *What Miranda Knew* associate death pictorially to stars, clouds, and angels, as well as to the notion that age and youth come together in death. They thus invite a cyclical interpretation that relates them to the message we deciphered in *Barney*. Furthermore, because stars, like flowers, are part of the non-human world, these stories all participate in the tradition of interpreting death not principally in terms of personal loss but in terms of its valence as one of the ongoing phenomena of the natural world.

In *Nana Upstairs*, Tommy, when he grows older, learns that his "Nana Downstairs" has died, too. As before, peering out into the night, again through what seems to be a bedroom window, he observes another falling star. As we saw in Dickens's story, the symbols are repeated, and with their recurrence, there is comfort and a sense of mastery rather than the helplessness that so often accompanies loss. A detail worth noting is that on Tommy's bureau, as on that of the girl in *Always Gramma*, we find a small framed photograph of both grandmothers, a beautiful way of conserving memory.

War and Death

I would like to turn now to a recently published book that deals with war and death and that also involves a grandparent. Picture books on the subject of war do not seem to be survivors. This may be because the saga of any particular war, while engrossing to the generations who witnessed it and were directly affected by it, seems to hold less interest for succeeding generations who, sadly, have fresher scars of their own to attend to.

The Wall

Eve Bunting and Ronald Himler (1990) have collaborated to create a small gem of a book about the Vietnam Veterans' Memorial in Washington, D.C. On the title page, a handwritten message by the art-

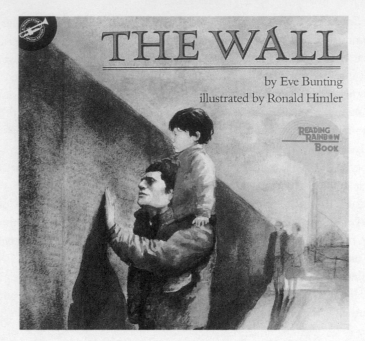

From *The Wall* by Eve Bunting. Jacket © 1990 by Ronald Himler.
Reprinted by permission of Clarion Books/Houghton Mifflin Company.
All rights reserved.

ist, Himler, proclaims its antiwar message in bold uppercase letters: "CHILDREN, LIVE IN SUCH A WAY THAT WE WILL NEVER NEED ANOTHER WALL LIKE THIS ONE."

Visually, this book reminds me of two other books I have described in this chapter, *The Accident* and *Always Gramma*, for it utilizes the same watercolor wash technique, with blurred contours and hushed tonalities occasionally interrupted by splashes of bright red or blue. As in those books, this artist has favored double-spread pages with plenty of open space. Although I am never fully comfortable with an adult's appropriation of the child's voice, which occurs again here, in this case it is used with rare sensitivity.

In the cold of winter, a father and son pay a visit to Maya Lin's justly famous monument to find the boy's grandfather's name on the Wall and to honor him. The grandfather had died in 1969, before the little boy was born. Gazing at the seemingly immense expanse of dark gray with its multitude of names, they cannot immediately locate the one they are looking for, and their waiting turns out to be important. First, the waiting gives us time to feel the chill of the air on this dull, sunless afternoon. In addition, we can see how the Wall reflects its onlookers so that they must confront their own faces, their own mortality, super-imposed upon the names of the dead. Finally, a legless stranger in a wheelchair appears and greets the little boy with the friendly words, "Hi, son," thus closing the gap between himself with his mutilated soldier's body and both the narrator and the child listening to the story: *we are all in this together.*

A man and woman of grandparent age stand before the Wall; as the woman weeps for their lost child, her husband comforts her. The little boy observes their grief. On the next page, he bends over to examine the assortment of mementos left by mourners at the base of the monument: a teddy bear, some miniature American flags, handwritten letters held in place by stones, photographs, a propped-up cross, a bouquet of flowers on a stick. These treasures interest him because he can name them and touch them and make sense of them. They are on his level at the bottom of the Wall; he can stoop and inspect them.

Father and son run their fingers over the Wall. They touch it in the way children always long to touch sculpture and architecture but are generally forbidden to do. When the father finds his father's name, he keeps touching it and then lifts the boy up so that his hands can make contact with it, too. After taking a rubbing of the grandfather's name, they see another pair of visitors—a grandfather with his grandson. The older man is telling the boy to button up his jacket against the cold. Cold. The chill of loss is mollified by care and kindness.

While the mourning father in our story stands with his head bowed against the Wall, a group of uniformed schoolgirls approach carrying small American flags. One asks loudly whether the Wall is for dead soldiers. A teacher replies with sensitivity: "The names are the names of the dead. But the Wall is for all of us."

Memorials *are* precisely for us, to help us not to forget. The girls deposit their flags and leave, and then the boy places a photograph of himself at the base of the Wall beneath his grandfather's name. To protect it from the wind, he secures it with a pile of stones. Suddenly, he worries about something: How will this grandfather, who died before he was born, recognize the photograph? How will he know who he is? "I think he will [know]," his father reassures him, placing a hand on his shoulder, and, as they stand together with a whole page of blurred gray facing them, the little boy says, "It's sad here." This time, unlike the father in *Barney*, who suggests that his child will feel better the next day, the reply is one of simple assent: "I know." Then comes an effort to idealize the military death: "But it's a place of honor. I'm proud that your grandfather's name is on this Wall." The child agrees. He says he feels proud too.

What happens on the next and final page is worth the whole book, for it rings out as forthrightly and undeniably as does the small child's voice in "The Emperor's New Clothes." Walking slowly away, father and son leave the memorial, and a vast expanse of steely gray opens up behind them overtaking the entire left-hand page of the book. As they head off, hand in hand, toward the Washington Monument, the boy says: "But I'd rather have my grandpa here, taking me to the river, telling me to button my jacket because it's cold. I'd rather have him here."

These words are a child's truth. Glory carries no weight. His grandfather is gone forever. No monument, no history, no honor can compensate for that. These simple words make a stronger antiwar statement than can be found in volumes of learned prose. What matters, this picture book says, is that war takes important people away forever; no matter what gets put up afterwards, the hurt is there, and it never goes away.

In contemporary American culture—on TV and in the movies, on magazine covers in supermarkets, in computer games and simulations

—children encounter representations of death, real and imaginary. Often, these are unmourned deaths—brutal, frightening, and incomprehensible. Picture books, however, afford children opportunities to learn gradually about death in formats that respect their needs and that emphasize both the value of life and the importance of memory.

Two books on this subject, both published in 1995, were brought to my attention by colleagues while I was at work on this manuscript, and I mention them here because, in my view, they deserve long life and a wide readership. *Old Pig*, by Margaret Wild and Ron Brooks, tells the story of a grandmother and granddaughter who have lived together "for a long, long time" and share all aspects of their daily lives, right up to the last day of the grandmother's life, a day for which she carefully prepares. Although the word "death" is never spoken, the meaning here, unlike that of *What Miranda Knew*, is clear. There is no confusion about what is about to happen. Old Pig finishes tasks left undone (such as returning her library books) and then, she says, she wants to "feast" on life; she wants to enjoy all her senses for the last time. She wants to look, listen, smell, taste, and touch! She and Granddaughter notice how the warm earth smells and "how the clouds gather like gossips in the sky"; they taste the rain. Granddaughter helps Old Pig into her bed at nightfall and then opens the curtains of the window to let in the moon. The illustration on this page is a direct visual quotation of *Goodnight Moon*, even to the pictures on the wall of the cow jumping over the moon and the scene from *The Runaway Bunny*—except that here the roles are reversed, and it is the grandmother who is in bed and the child who is up and alert. Death and sleep, as we saw at the beginning of the chapter on bedtime, are brought together. Granddaughter climbs into the bed with Old Pig "and for the very last time Old Pig and Granddaughter held each other tight until morning." *Old Pig* is a book about process—about the dignity, grace, and tenderness with which life can be brought to a close.

The New King, by Doreen Rappaport and E. B. Lewis, is set in nineteenth-century Madagascar. A little Malagasy boy, Rakoto, heir to the throne, mourns his young father, who has died during a hunt. As

From *The New King* by Doreen Rappaport, illustrated by E. B. Lewis. Copyright © 1995 by E. B. Lewis, illustrations. Used by permission of Dial Books for Young Readers, a division of Penguin Putnam Inc.

in some of the most sensitive books we have seen, the medium here is watercolor. Lewis, an inspired artist, paints images of beauty and sorrow. After being told of the tragedy by his mother, Rakoto refuses to be held; he breaks away and runs screaming down a corridor to look for his father. He begs each of the supposed wise men of the kingdom to bring his father back to life. The doctor's face, as he softly admits his incapacity, is riven with grief. Finally, Rakoto goes to the "Wise

Woman," who, on a page in which the moon shines out against a darkened sky, tells him an old Malagasy tale: God tells the first human couple that they must die but that they may choose to do so in the manner of the moon or of the banana tree. The moon shrinks until it disappears but then grows large again, whereas the banana tree dies but first sends forth a new generation of life that sprouts up all around it. The man at first prefers to die like the moon because this means living forever, but the woman persuades him otherwise. The moon, she says, is always alone with "no one to care for and no one to care for it," but to die like the banana tree would mean to have children one could love while one lives and who, when one is gone, would carry on one's work in the world. With this message in his ears, the new young king, a tear slipping from his eye, his lower lip pushed out to keep from crying too hard, walks into the future. He holds tightly to his mother's hand, and a crescent orb shines before them, framed by a doorway. The image reminds us of many books we have opened together imaginatively in these pages.

The New King is one of those rare books in which theme, imagery, and text blend seamlessly; it is an exquisitely accessible book for American children of both genders and all races about a nonwhite, non-American child of a previous century, a child who, when he looks straight into our eyes from the cover of his book, we recognize at once and understand. In his long-ago and faraway story, we find ourselves.

☞ Chapter 4 ☜

Behave Yourself

With varying overtones of irritation, pride, and chagrin, we adults sometimes use the terms *mischievous* and *disobedient* to describe children's behavior. These terms have, however, a built-in bias: they portray actions from our own vantage point. As far as the children are concerned, mischief and disobedience do not tell the whole story. They leave out wish and impulse, playfulness, and, above all, curiosity—the pressing need to make sense of the world and to find out what is really going on in it. Alive to these other dimensions and to the inner struggles they often produce in small children—who desire at the same time to remain in the good graces of those they love—the books I discuss in this chapter portray child characters who behave disobediently, are punished in one way or another for their misdeeds, and remain beloved by their child readers from one generation to the next. The awareness that the nuanced approach in each of these books has rung true with so many children may foster a corresponding tolerance in adults for actions that, in real life, can seem downright aggravating. Each book offers insights in the arena of social development—an arena that, unlike that of physical maturation, cannot readily be taken for granted.

I consider first three books in which children's high energy, exuberance, self-assertiveness, or frustration impels them to behave transgressively. *Where the Wild Things Are*, *Pierre*, and *Angry Arthur* each attempt to enter the inner world of their characters and to depict children's feelings after they have been disciplined and/or when a limit has been set that makes them angry. Next, I will compare styles of parenting vis-à-vis disobedient children in three works by Beatrix Potter— *The Tale of Peter Rabbit*, *The Tale of Tom Kitten* (1907), and *The Tale of Squirrel Nutkin*. Finally, I will consider two long-lived picture books in which child characters disregard specific rules and are duly punished, albeit in strikingly different ways. These are *The Story about Ping* (1933) and *The Poky Little Puppy* (1942). Other books will be taken down from the shelf as needed for comparative purposes.

Where the Wild Things Are

This slender volume, written and illustrated by Maurice Sendak in 1963, is undisputably one of the most successful children's books of the last half of the twentieth century. After winning the coveted Caldecott Medal (awarded to the most distinguished picture book of its year), *Where the Wild Things Are* went on to achieve international repute. It has been translated into numerous foreign languages, has proliferated in the form of soft toy replicas of its characters, continues to appear in American stores from coast to coast, and has been recreated as a full-scale opera with stage sets by Sendak and a score by the English composer Oliver Knussen.

The format of *Where the Wild Things Are* is sophisticated and ingenious. Its words and images reinforce each other in complex ways to create crosscurrents that affirm children's needs for fantasy while gently pushing them in the direction of grown-up behavior. Its plot is advanced by means of both words and images. In other words, certain elements of its theme are pictorially represented. Briefly told, a little boy named Max is shown performing "mischief of one kind and another." He is called a "WILD THING" by his mother (to whom he retorts, "I'LL EAT YOU UP!"). He is then sent off to bed without his supper. A forest grows in his bedroom, and Max sails off at length on an ocean in a "private boat" to the place "where the wild things are." There he tames the so-called wild things by magic (he stares into their eyes) and participates with them in a "wild rumpus." After making them "stop!"

From *Where the Wild Things Are* by Maurice Sendak. Copyright © 1963 by Maurice Sendak. Printed in the United States of America. All rights reserved. First Harper Trophy edition 1984. Used by permission of HarperCollins Publishers.

and sending *them* off to bed without *their* supper, Max suddenly feels lonely and wants "to be where someone loved him best of all." He resists the appeal of the wild things (who urge him to stay by protesting that they love him so much they want to eat him up) and says a firm "No!" to them. At last, he sails back "into the night of his very own room," where he finds his supper waiting for him, "and it was still hot."

Three points are worth highlighting before we examine the book in detail. First, its overall graphic design provides a setting that fosters a safe milieu for private fantasies by the child who is listening. Second, Max's mother, an invisible character, parallels the reader of the story by providing a facilitating context for the little boy's imaginative adventure. Max's limit-setting mother exists only through her child's perceptions and distortions and, perhaps, through the recurring symbolism of the moon. Her voice is heard only once. Third, the story unfolds in a very important place—namely, the child's own bedroom, his most familiar and private external space (the symbolic meanings of which I touched on earlier with respect to *Goodnight Moon*). Here, that private space is transformed by Max into an arena for the enactment of an inner drama.

Writing about the formation of dreams, Sigmund Freud (1900) expressed the idea that thoughts, ideas, and words may be transformed into pictures by the mind during sleep. By means of its extraordinary design, *Where the Wild Things Are* almost literally illustrates this idea. The book begins with verbal language—that is, with ordinary everyday communication—as the child listening to the story hears his or her parent's reading voice. The words and pictures at first take up equivalent amounts of space on each page and are equal partners in telling the story. Page by page, however, this balance begins to change. The words (and the reader's voice) diminish: the printed text shrinks in relation to the size of the pictures until finally, when Max (and the child listening) are fully transported inside their own imaginary worlds, the pictures expand to fill up all the available space. On three double-spread pages in the center of the story there are no words at all. Fantasy completely overtakes reality. The reader's voice vanishes. And, just as Max has been transported into the place where the wild things are by means of a "private boat" (named "MAX"), the child listening is likewise transported in these pages to the realm of his or her own private imagination. Because the transitions from word to image are effected so gradually, the experience is not overwhelming. Furthermore, of course, even at the climax of Max's orgy with the wild things, the child hearing the story is not alone: parent and child are still physically together, turning the pages of the book.

Later, as fantasy subsides, the pictures diminish in size, and the world of words reasserts itself. Voice returns, and, along with Max, the child who is listening now returns from the land of wild things to the comfort and safety of verbal reality, to Max's familiar bedroom, and to his supper, which has retained its warmth. Thus, the very design of this fascinating book carries rich psychological overtones.

Sendak's drawing style is characteristically linear and precise. His carefully executed graphics inform the viewer that he is in control—of his medium, surely, and, perhaps by implication, of his message too. Like other artists whose work is intensely linear (for example, Bosch, Blake, Dali, or Magritte), he achieves a kind of exaggerated hyperrealism along with this sense of conscious control. It is remarkable that the wild things themselves, even in their most frenzied orgiastic incarnations, are never entirely frightening but instead seem rather goofy, humorous, even strangely lovable—a bit like parents who can become, evanescently, monsters, or like children who (like Max) can become beasts. Sendak has stated (see Lanes 1980) that his inspiration for the wild things came from his Eastern European Jewish relatives. When they visited his parents' home, they ate everything in sight, pinched his cheeks because he was the youngest in the family, and told him that he was good enough to eat.

The story begins with Max wearing his "wolf suit" and making mischief. We see him acting up in a number of ways, and here the pictures elaborate the text, enriching it and filling it in, while the words themselves serve mainly as instructions to us for the focus of our gaze. Max's wolf suit possesses exaggerated appendages—pointed ears, claws, and an enormous bushy tail—reminding us that the symbol of the wolf is, in our culture, a complex one redolent of many themes, not just of threats of devouring and being devoured (the "I'll eat you up" of "The Three Little Pigs" and "Little Red Riding Hood") but of sexual seduction as well. Additionally, almost as if to undercut such associations, Max's costume looks suspiciously like a baby suit, a sleeper or pajama. This aspect works to mitigate its alleged aggressivity but also, importantly, to reveal the deep wisdom that a child's naughtiness can be, in part, an outgrowth of his very smallness and of his frustration at his own helplessness.

What is the mischief here? Max has strung up a small animal doll, perhaps symbolic of a little brother or sister. He messes up the house.

He ignores the verbal content of two books by stepping on them, thus proclaiming his emancipation from the rule of language, law, and order. With an enormous hammer, he bangs a nail into the wall. From a certain perspective, we can interpret the house as signifying the mother herself and his behavior as a thinly disguised attack on her—she being the powerful provider (and withholder) of good things. Although from many parents' point of view Max's behavior here might well appear destructive, we are given some pictorial clues that his activities are, from his own vantage point, constructive as well. As he messes things up inside his mother's house, he seems simultaneously to be building a tiny house for himself—a sort of tent, a private space, as it were, that will be replicated later on in the story both by his "private boat" and by the royal tent under which he sits when he becomes "king of where the wild things are."

On the next page, Max's mischief continues. Here, in addition to the symbolic attack on his mother, we observe an assault with a fork against a little white dog who might almost be a double for Max himself, dressed as he is in his fuzzy white suit. This dog, incidentally, is a representation of Sendak's beloved Sealyham terrier, Jennie, whom he memorialized in several works and to whom he dedicated *Higglety Pigglety Pop!* (1967). The child is clearly twinned with the animal, and the doubling of the image suggests a further biographical association that is irresistible. Sendak, in choosing "Max" as the name of his naughty protagonist, links this name to his own, Maurice, which is a cognate for the German "Moritz," thus inviting an association to the two devilish young pranksters of the *Max und Moritz* cartoons by Wilhelm Busch. The comic strip is a closely related form to the picture book (especially for Sendak), in which word and image, temporal and spatial models, are brought together. Sendak not only knew *Max und Moritz* but also acknowledged his indebtedness to it and to another famous cartoon strip, *Little Nemo* by Winsor McCay, which, as I mentioned earlier, he quoted in the opening pages of *In the Night Kitchen*.

One 1865 *Max und Moritz* cartoon especially relates to *Where the Wild Things Are* (see Robinson 1974). In it, a peasant woman smiles in anticipation of her dinner. She washes a plate in the basement of her house, while on the hearth above a panful of little game hens is roasting. A small white dog, not unlike Sendak's Jennie, barks, and two naughty boys, Max and Moritz, gleefully dance around the chimney on the roof while, with a fishing rod, they clandestinely reel up the woman's dinner through the chimney, one roast hen at a time. Themes of oral greed, reversal of deprivation, and children's secret wish to triumph over a mother are given full play.

In the second drawing of *Where the Wild Things Are*, we note the predatory expression on Max's face as he grasps at the dog's erect tail and the shadowed stairway, which lends an air of mounting tension to the scene. A drawing by Max hangs on the wall—implicitly a self portrait as a monster with plenty of teeth and bristly hair (including a beard), eyes like breasts, and a horn. Gleefully, his naughtiness fuses with a polymorphous sensuality and exuberance.

On the third page, Max's behavior finally provokes a response from his mother. She, as discussed, never appears visually in the book and exists entirely through the child's experience of her, again, in a double sense—both in terms of the character Max and in terms of the child listening to the story, who can project into the blank an image of his or her own mother. Having made mischief and incited this off-stage mother into calling him a "wild thing," Max now expresses the wish to eat her up, to destroy her by incorporation. Incidentally, the notion of a "wild thing" and the phrase itself may well have been inspired by the common Yiddish expression "wilde chaye," which Sendak undoubtedly heard during his childhood years in Brooklyn, because it was frequently used as an epithet for obstreperous children.

The principal dynamic here goes something like this: Max has been bad (implicitly, to his mother); his mother now has been bad (according to Max) to him. Therefore, Max openly expresses the wish to devour and destroy his mother (that is, to destroy the consequences of his own aggression). What happens next of course is that he *loses* her. He loses food, and food equals mother. In the illustration, the expression on his face conveys more clearly than words his response to this painful consequence of his behavior. His screwed-up countenance proclaims defiantly: "I'll show you!" To avoid unpleasantness, to counteract shame, guilt, and the knowledge that he has upset his mother, he will deny the loss. We can almost see him resorting magically to a plan of triumphing over this "bad" mother who has sent him to his room without his supper. Here the image does not illustrate or expand on the text but *responds* to it in a kind of counterpoint: word versus image equals child against mother.

In the fourth picture, Max magically transgresses the limit set by his mother. As a forest grows in his bedroom, we see his victory over any feelings of anxiety or loss. Again, words and image form a contrapuntal ensemble, and, in the next pair of pages, Max covers his mouth with the paw of his suit to hide his smile and conceal his secret pleasure. Finally, his room completely disappears, and the forest takes over. In this sixth picture, the many-treed forest that supplants his bedroom can be read as emblematic of what is mysterious and feminine (as in, for example, the forests of "The Sleeping Beauty" and "Hansel and Gretel"), but also, if you choose to read psychoanalytically, as the forbidden insides of the mother's body, with all its treasures multiply represented.

What about the moon? Beginning with Max's banishment and loss of his mother, it has remained with him, its shape, size, and position changing from page to page whenever it appears. At this particular point in the story, for example, the moon is ambiguously both crescent and full, and Max prances directly under it. It is hard to resist interpreting these omnipresent orbs as representations of Max's distant but reliable mother—an interpretation borne out, as I have suggested, by the ubiquitous presence of the moon as a similar symbol in so many picture books for young children, two of which are direct antecedents of *Where the Wild Things Are*: *Goodnight Moon* and *Many Moons*, by James Thurber.

As fantasy overtakes reality in this sixth picture, we can see Max only from the back. The rear view facilitates possibilities for reading in. Once again, it permits each child to supply and project his or her own face and feelings into the image. Max has assumed the pose of a necromancer, a shaman casting a spell.

Having created and entered his own alternative world (like Harold with his purple crayon), Max in the seventh picture now faces us fully and smiles with an expression of smug self-satisfaction. He is sailing along in his boat on an ocean of rhythmic waves, soothing and symbolic of new birth as well as of the return to a place that existed before loss and without boundaries. For the first time in *Where the Wild Things Are*, the illustration exceeds its limits and transgresses the space previously reserved for written words. From this point on, the pictures encroach on the domain of words until print is entirely crowded out.

It is significant that Max is provided with a "private" boat, because a focal aspect of his fantasy is his denial of his dependence on his "bad" punishing mother. Here now, with sails rigged, floating independently in his private sailboat, the little boy is completely free. Like Mickey in his fighter plane in *In the Night Kitchen*, he is the captain of his fate. The idea of privacy is also relevant to the relationship between the child listening to the story and the reader, in that it gives that child license to create a private fantasy of his own while following the story.

As picture achieves hegemony over word, space prevails over linear time, and Max travels "in and out of weeks and almost over a year"— an evocation of the timelessness of all imaginary adventures.

Now, however, in the eighth and ninth pictures, Max must meet the creatures of his own disavowed aggression. They appear to him as monsters, "wild things." Just as Max's mother had called *him* a "wild thing," so he now projects wild thingness onto these fanciful creatures. He brings his mother's pejorative epithet to life. Interestingly, there are several wild things, not just one. Their multiplicity reminds me of the psychoanalyst Wilfred Bion's (1967) notion of "bizarre objects." The idea behind this term is that, for defensive purposes, a mental strategy may come into play that operates on a "divide and conquer" principle, one that fragments the enemy in order to vanquish it more effectively. Similarly, the wild things have multiplied in Max's imagination. Yet, like the brooms of the Sorcerer's Apprentice, they now seem not less dangerous but all the more urgently in need of control.

The monsters themselves are marvelous illustrations of a child's typical fantasies of his parents combined into formidable creatures. They possess the secondary sexual characteristics of both males and females and a superabundance of appendages—including horns, claws, teeth, tails, and hair. They also resemble, in these details, Max's self-portrait at the beginning of the story and thus indicate his underlying identification with them.

By the tenth spread, the illustration has literally superseded the text. Max is now in the process of taming his wild things. By performing this act, he ingeniously reverses a young child's helplessness vis-à-vis his punishing parents and his own destructive impulses. Bypassing the slower, more difficult path of true reparation that acknowledges guilt and loss, Max achieves omnipotence by magic—by the act of staring into the monsters' eyes. To understand the force of this magical staring, we might just think of the frequent equations we make routinely between the visual and the oral—such as "he devoured her with his eyes." Staring can suggest a potential violent intimacy; like Max's wolf suit, it condenses various strands of sexuality and aggression. Above all, what matters is that Max *does* triumph over his wild things, that even in his fantasy the little boy never gets destroyed by them.

In the eleventh picture, Max acquires a crown and scepter and becomes king of the wild things. Because he is still intact and in control, he can afford to take pleasure in a frenzied frolic with them. He gives his permission by crying, "And now, let the wild rumpus start!"

The next three pages form the book's centerpiece. Narration is suspended. Words fall away. Pictures reign triumphant. We are transported into a realm of pure play, pure daydream, pure wish fulfillment. At the height of the orgy, however, Max is still king; the pages of the book itself still provide a tangible boundary, and, as suggested above, the child is still alone *within* a holding environment jointly created by imagery, text, the reader's presence, and the contributions of his or her own psyche—alone securely as an achievement.

As I reported earlier, however, one mother told me that during this wordless middle section of *Where the Wild Things Are*, she and her little son do not merely sit still turning the pages. With a gleam in her eye and a mischievous grin, she confessed that they actually get up to "join" the wild things and, whooping, stomping, prancing, hooting, whirling and cavorting about the room, enact their own rumpus. Such moments of shared parent-child playing create the rapport that makes cultural experience a source of ongoing pleasure throughout life.

Another reading of Max's voyage to the land of the wild things could easily locate this picture book on a continuum with a rather sinister centuries-old tradition in Western literature in which civilizing white-skinned male conquerors sail off to cannibal islands to tame and convert the "savages" they find there. Such narratives often portray native dwellers as primitive, crude, and animal-like and show them as being subdued by what their "untutored" minds consider "magic." Thus Max, the quintessential little white male hero, can be read as a colonialist, staring brashly into the eyes of a tribe of hirsute, scaly, bestial natives, dark-skinned and racially "other." This cultural reading blends with the psychological one I have been developing and casts Max problematically as a plucky victor over primitive forces of instinct and aggression—forces, however, portrayed by imagery that is, in terms of today's raised consciousness, far from innocent.

On the fifteenth spread, a major shift occurs. The silence is suddenly broken as Max tells his wild things to "stop!" In sending them off to bed without their supper, he is doing to them precisely what was done to him by his mother. In replicating her speech act, he identifies with her and invokes her in her absence. And now, having vanquished and banished his wild things, Max becomes once again just an ordinary little boy who feels depleted, vulnerable, and alone. His wild, frenzied activity has left him tired, hungry, and yearning for home, longing for his mother—whose loss he only now begins to suffer. Missing her, "he smells good things to eat."

As Max allows himself to experience sadness and separation, he is shown wondering whether—as a consequence of his behavior—he may have actually destroyed his mother or lost her forever. The picture shows him, still crowned, pining at the door of his regal tent (an imaginative recap of his naughtiness on page one). It is hard to resist associating this image to I Samuel 18:10, where the biblical Saul is described as tormented by evil spirits and longing for the sweet sounds of David's lyre. The music, in this analogy, can be likened to the soothing sounds of a parent's reading voice. In silence, evil spirits are terrifying, but, with the return of a gentle voice, a sense of melancholy may ensue.

Accepting his need and his loneliness now, Max gives up being king of where the wild things are. He relinquishes the fantasy of unlimited power and total independence. He starts to go back. Verbal language reasserts itself, and the pictures begin to recede.

The wild things, however, will not let go of him so fast. By repeating to Max exactly what he said to his mother ("we'll eat you up"), they inadvertently betray the double entendre of this expression. The desire to incorporate the loved object in order to possess it is connected to the desire to incorporate the loved object in order to destroy it. Both wishes stem from the paradigm of the baby at the breast, and both deny the independent existence of the mother. She is, in this fantasy, nothing more than a need-fulfilling object for her child.

Max, however, says "No!" This lusty *negative* constitutes a powerful *positive* assertion of himself. Every child must learn to say no to him- or herself as well as to others, and the negative therefore possesses enormous power to define the boundaries of the self. By saying no, Max returns to the realm of boundaries—he moves toward reality and away from fantasy. We now see the reintroduction of his boat. He is going back. But, interestingly, the boat does not present us with the side marked with his name—an indication, possibly, that the boat no longer needs to be quite so "private." As the pictures diminish in size and the domain of verbal language reasserts itself, Max rides along on its waves, traveling developmentally from the land of private image to the realm of public words. Notice his strength and pleasure in this capacity to say no and to stop his own playing—and not only to stop but even to wave good-bye with a smile.

As Max sails back from the timeless land of make-believe, the child listening is also eased back. In the next-to-last picture, the safe boundaries of Max's bedroom are reinstated. His wolf's hat is beginning to slip off his head. The picture is a repeat of page three. Familiarity has been restored. Best of all, his supper is waiting for him. His invisible mother has survived his assaults. She still loves him; she is still feeding him. Max and the child who has heard and seen the story have each lived through it and survived. Visually, the table, bowl, and moon in this image are explicit quotations from the bunny's bedroom in *Goodnight Moon*, which, as we have discussed, deals tenderly with the issue of bedtime separation.

On the last page of *Where the Wild Things Are* there are no more pictures. The child listening to the story just hears the reader utter the final words, "and it was still hot." Love is ongoing and warm; it occurs in the realm of language. The child experiencing this exquisitely crafted book may be helped over time to understand that he and his loved ones can survive the ravages of their own destructive impulses. It takes a parent who is comfortable with her own wild things, however, to be able to enjoy reading this story again and again and to experience it fully with her child.

In conclusion, then, I believe that this picture book has been successful over so many years because of the skill with which Sendak demonstrates two major developmental agendas of early childhood: first, the push toward language and socialization, toward the acceptance of limits, losses, and diachronic time; and second, the pull toward impulse, wish, and desire. What Sendak makes patent is the awesome power of fantasy and imagination to inform as well as to deform, to inspire as well as to derail each child's unique journey toward maturity.

Before saying goodbye to *Where the Wild Things Are*, I would like to compare it briefly with a work in another medium—namely, Maurice Ravel's short 1925 opera, *L'Enfant et les sortilèges* (The child and the magic spells), which has a libretto by Colette. This plot of this work is similar to that of Sendak's story, and I believe a comparison will bring an important issue to light.

In the opening moments of the Ravel-Colette opera, the protagonist, a little boy like Max, is portrayed as irritable and bored. He expresses his wish to hurt the family cat, to destroy the furniture, and to punish his mother. His response to his mother's initial affectionate overtures to him is a grimace. Like Max's mother, she responds to his surliness by depriving him of food. She says she will give him only dry bread and no sugar for his tea.

Flying into an immediate rage at this news, the little boy attacks every object in sight, including a small squirrel. Magically, as the music swells, these attacked objects grow enormous and monster-like. Like wild things, they retaliate against the boy, forcing him to flee outdoors, where the mayhem continues. As in Sendak's tale, when the little boy assaults the objects around him as if they were all bad, the whole world seems to turn bad too. Objects and small animals, imbued now with the child's anger, grow gigantic and threaten to engulf him, puffed up as they are by his own disowned aggression. But when the child stops for a moment and notices that the squirrel has actually been wounded in the fray, he feels a rush of pity for the creature. He binds the squirrel's paw and, with that act of kindness, everything instantly changes. When the small boy responds to a creature in need, the objects return to their normal size. As he whispers softly "Mama," the animals sing that he is a good and well-mannered child, and the opera draws to a harmonious close.

The similarity of this plot to that of Sendak's picture book is evident, but there is one profoundly important difference. In *Where the Wild Things Are*, the defiant child is returned to normalcy purely as a result of his own unfulfilled needs and longings. Exhausted, Max feels hungry and lonely and wants to be "where someone loved him best of all." In the Colette libretto, the motivation is quite different. The naughty child is returned to normalcy not when he feels sorry for himself but rather when he takes compassion on a fellow creature, when he experiences empathy toward a hurt animal and can identify with his mother by performing a spontaneous act of reparative kindness toward it. In the opera, it is not a small boy's hunger for food or lack of love for himself that dispels the "wild things" or "magic spells" but rather his capacity to notice the suffering of another and, beyond that, to acknowledge his own responsibility for that suffering by performing an act of goodness. It is kindness that returns life to normalcy and brings the work of art to its healing finale.

Sendak's story is, ethically speaking, shallow. Max, like Mickey, puts on a solo performance. He is strictly alone. He is capable of strong feelings when it comes to his *own* desires, hurts, and lacks, but at no point does he give back anything to anyone or return the kindness that we must assume has been shown to him. The link between harming and healing that is so beautifully portrayed in *L'Enfant et les sortilèges* is completely missing from Sendak's work. Consequently, *Where the Wild Things Are* is a book that, although enjoyed by many parents and children, is not universally admired. It has proved quite disturbing to some. Its message lacks a reciprocal dimension—a dimension that, in today's world, perhaps more than ever, needs to be emphasized—a dimension, moreover, that no child is ever too young to grasp.

Pierre

Pierre, the "ethics" tale from Sendak's *Nutshell Library* of 1962, was cited briefly in chapter 2. Here, I want to consider it as a felicitous representation of a particular form of disobedience that is well known to all parents of toddlers, namely, passive aggressive behavior.

Beginning with a prologue in limerick form, *Pierre* is highly stylized in its format. This formality is psychologically useful as well as aesthetically pleasurable in that its unfamiliarity may distance and defend children somewhat from its potentially frightening contents. Rather than the common English name "Peter," a name by no means dissociated from Beatrix Potter's earlier disobedient little character, the choice of the more foreign-sounding "Pierre" may likewise serve to defamiliarize the title character slightly and forestall an immediate identification with him.

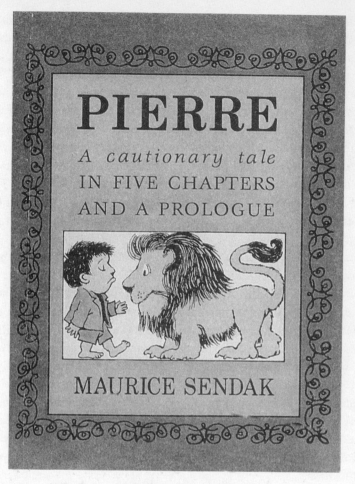

From *Pierre: A Cautionary Tale*. Copyright © 1962 by Maurice Sendak. All rights reserved. Used by permission of HarperCollins Publishers.

Pierre is a child who responds to his mother's affection, her offer of breakfast, and so on by saying the words: "I don't care!" His mother, after her efforts have been to no avail, leaves in defeat, and his father appears. To each of his father's commands, threats, bribes, and entreaties, Pierre reiterates: "I don't care!" His mother and father now depart together, and a hungry lion arrives on the scene. To all of the lion's questions, such as whether Pierre realizes that the lion can eat him up, whether he would like to die, and whether, finally, he has anything else to say, Pierre produces his classic retort. On the page following this interchange, we find a conspicuous gap: Pierre is missing. The lion now fills the entire space occupied previously by both figures. He looks very smug, and the accompanying text is terse: "So the lion ate Pierre."

Arriving home, Pierre's mother and father find a sick lion in their son's bed. Suspecting the worst, they assault him and inquire about their child. Predictably, the lion replies, "I don't care!" On the next page, a doctor shakes the lion upside down and Pierre falls out on the floor. Curiously, the text says that when Pierre falls out, he "laughed because he wasn't dead." In keeping with Judaic motifs previously observed in Sendak's works (*In the Night Kitchen* and *Where the Wild Things Are*), Pierre's surprising laughter at this moment of survival might be interpreted along biblical lines. It evokes Isaac (Yitzchak: "one who laughs"). For, like Isaac-Yitzchak in the story of the Akedah (the "binding") in Genesis 22:1-19, the boy here too survives here what can only be experienced by a child as the extremity of parental abandonment.

Now, after being hugged by his mother and queried by his father (note the gendered behavior of the parents), the little boy reassures them both, and together they all ride home astride the lion. Perched on the lion's head, Pierre finally shouts, "Yes, indeed I care!" The lion remains with them "as a weekend guest," and, as in all true fables, the last line informs us of the moral: "CARE!"

Pierre's lion, a memorable creation, condenses many aspects of a child's inner life. He represents the little boy's previously disowned aggression (his dismissive "I don't care!"), which now turns against him in the form of a hungry beast. The lion, in other words, is in objectified form the very negativism and oppositionalism that originally irritated Pierre's parents. He also represents Pierre's image of his parents as a potentially threatening and punitive entity. Pierre, after all, does not attack his parents directly; he adopts a contrarian stance by which he can aggress against them by not responding positively. He *won't* eat. He *won't* go to town. In fact he turns the milk pitcher, bowl, broom, and himself quite literally upside down.

As I mentioned earlier, this upside-down motif figures prominently in the drama. A small panel of drawings frames the book, ornamenting both the table of contents and the final page. Taken together, this sequence of drawings depicts Pierre performing a headstand. The last drawing, in which Pierre actually stands on his head, shows his right arm rising from the ground and his right leg bending, as if to indicate that he is about to flip over one more time and come right side up. Thus, a process is implied. The drawings suggest that although a child may indeed turn himself upside down, he can right himself as well. The same motif plays an important part in the dramatic action: not only does Pierre infuriate his father by talking to him from a feet-up posture early on, but later the lion, having swallowed Pierre, must be turned upside down in order to release him.

The lion, we note, comes onstage only after Pierre's parents leave. By abandoning him, his parents turn bad and threatening, so it seems to him, for they have played their trump card and lost. To leave him behind is to exercise the parents' ultimate power: to desert him. In this sense, the lion also represents *that* badness (from a child's point of view)—the badness of his abandoning parents. Pierre's mom and dad also leave Pierre without anybody around on whom to vent his feelings. Those feelings therefore turn back against himself and must be confronted. Hence, the lion. And the lion not only threatens Pierre with words but also actually eats him up (Pierre disappears from the page). Before this happens, however, Pierre is informed that, after being eaten, he will be *inside* the lion; in other words, things will be *inside out:* the child's own angry feelings will consume him. The motif of upside down extends then to encompass the theme of inside out.

Significantly, when the parents do return, they do not hesitate to vent their ire directly on the lion (Pierre's mother pulls his hair while Pierre's father lifts a chair to strike the beast). At no point in the story, however, does either parent strike Pierre. It is the child's triumphant naughtiness they attack, his disobedience, his negativistic behavior—symbolized by the lion—not the child himself. This important distinction is made by both pictures and words. It implies that the love of these parents for their child is ongoing and will survive the ravages of developmentally induced negativism.

Both parents verbally and pictorially conform to conventional 1960s gender stereotypes. Pierre's mother calls him "darling," offers him food, and cries and hugs him when he emerges from the lion. His father disciplines him, criticizes him, commands him, reasons with him, bargains, and asks him whether he is all right when he reappears. These typical gender roles are reinforced by the parents' canonical garb of the period: high heels, fur-trimmed coat, and whimsical hat for the mother; moustache, overcoat, and fedora for the father.

In the end, not just Pierre but also his parents are shown riding home on the lion, thus indicating that mastery of aggression is an issue not only for children but for entire families. Riding—a symbol of control and mastery—occurs in *Where the Wild Things Are*, too, where Max rides one of his wild things in the orgy scene. It matters very much, finally, that Pierre's lion does not depart ignominiously but stays on with the family. In this way, negativism and oppositional behavior are seen as themes that will not vanish altogether but need to readdressed from time to time by everyone.

Pierre is a wonderful little book that makes a deep impression on children; once heard, it is not easily forgotten. A demonstration of its lasting power was given to me after I had delivered a lecture on picture books to the psychiatric staff of a New York hospital several years ago. At lunch afterward, one young psychiatrist told me the following anecdote: as a resident, he had seen a female preadolescent who was chronically truant at her junior high school and had already been treated by several other therapists to no avail. When assigned to a therapist, the disheveled girl simply sat mute and refused to cooperate in any way with her treatment. At his first scheduled meeting with her, she failed even to appear. The following week, however, after having been found wandering dangerously on the railroad tracks in the vicinity and picked up by local police, she was ushered into his office. Sitting as far from him as possible with a half-blank, half-sullen expression, she said nothing for a long time. Finally, in response to his gentle prompting, she said very quietly: "Just call me 'Pierre.'"

The young man was startled. Suddenly, he recalled the image of Sendak's upside-down character, the lion, and the words "I don't care!" and realized what his patient was trying to say. Through his memory of the picture book read to him in his own childhood, he was able to grasp the reference, to laugh with warmth at their shared understanding, and to establish the beginnings of rapport with the unhappy girl.

Angry Arthur

Angry Arthur (1982), an artful book by Hiawyn Oram and Satoshi Kitamura, was brought to my attention by a childless colleague in her late thirties. She told me that she had read it countless times to her small nephew, who brought it to her on each of her visits and proclaimed it to be his favorite book in the whole world.

The protagonist is a little boy named Arthur whose mother says "No" when he asks to stay up past his bedtime to watch a television show. As in *Where the Wild Things Are*, the rule-enforcing mother is not given full frontal pictorial representation. We do glimpse her, however, once from the back. In the beginning of the book, we become aware of her presence by noting her legs and apron, plus a massive brown shadow that falls dramatically across the page, delimiting the darkened area where her sullen toddler sits with his arms crossed and his brow furrowed as he stares at the vacant TV screen. Because Arthur's mother is never depicted full-face, the image opens up a fertile field, as we noted in Sendak's work, into which each child encountering the picture book can project his or her own parental imagery.

Arthur's mother's limit is unequivocal: " 'No,' said his mother." This maternal "no," both here and in *Where the Wild Things Are*, triggers a far-reaching response. A mother's "no," in other words, motivates the action of both plots. These feminine "nos" constitute in each case a specifically *social* limit. Mothers in our culture, despite or because of their feminine gender, have been assigned the role of teaching the "civilized" values of self-restraint and self-control to their pleasure-seeking toddlers. From the evidence of picture books, fairy tales, and children's literature more generally (see Bettelheim 1976; Tatar 1992; Warner 1994), it is noteworthy that the mother's "no," rather than the father's, is represented as coming first and proving the more difficult for children to handle. It is the maternal "no" that threatens children with withdrawal of love at a time when vulnerability is at its peak—withdrawal of love from the very parent who, again traditionally in this culture, is supposed to supply that love unconditionally.

As an aside, I want to mention a book that depicts and actually ap-plauds unconditional love on the part of a mother for her (boy) child. This is a book that, like Sendak's *Where the Wild Things Are*, makes no demands on the receiving child for any kind of reciprocity. It is also, not coincidentally, a book from the 1960s, when American culture was undergoing dramatic changes that deracinated youth and glorified their supposed emancipation from tradition.

The Giving Tree (1964), by Shel Silverstein, has been a favorite pic-ture book for over three decades. Despite its widespread appeal, how-ever, this book presents views of both mothers and children that can be regarded as deeply troubling. As in so many of the books I have considered here, its principal characters are a mother and her little boy thinly disguised. Silverstein uses unadorned black line drawings (only the jacket of his book has any color). This visual minimalism—along with the rhetorical devices of repetition and reiteration and the text's glorification of what to some might be considered ennobling self-sacrifice—lend the work the aura of myth.

A tree explicitly gendered feminine ("she loved a little boy") is its title character. A small boy plays under her, gathers her leaves, and makes a crown so that he can be king of the forest (we may think of Max, created just one year earlier, who crowns himself king of the wild things). The boy climbs up on her and swings from her branches. He eats her apples and sleeps in her shade. The boy loved the tree, and "the tree was happy" (this is the book's refrain).

As the boy grows older and physically larger, he stays away from the tree for long periods of time, and she is often alone. It is interesting, as an aside, to notice that the tree is described as being alone when the boy is away; this notion jibes with children's early fantasies of being the sole love object of their mothers. It is a notion that implicitly denies the mother's independent existence. Like the book as a whole, it presupposes eternal, all-encompassing symbiosis between a mother and her child.

When the "boy" does return to the tree, he always asks her for something. His demands and her acquiescence constitute the sole interaction between them. He asks for money with which to buy things (the tree gives him her apples to sell), for a house in which to live (the tree gives him her branches), for a boat in which to sail far away (the tree gives him her trunk so that she is left with a mere stump). And after each demand and corresponding gift, the text states: "The tree was happy." Happy despite being continually depleted, even unto lifelessness. Meanwhile, although the illustrations show the boy change in respect to size and physiognomy—he grows from toddlerhood to young manhood to wizened old age—he is referred to throughout as "boy." The terms of his relationship with his mother, despite the passage of time, remain static.

Eventually, after a prolonged period "away," the "boy" comes back for the last time, a very aged man, and he tells the tree that his teeth are not fit to eat her apples, that he is too old to swing on her branches, but that he now needs a quiet place to rest. The "tree" says kindly to him:

"An old stump is good for sitting and resting." The old man sits down on her then, and the last words of the book are, predictably: "The tree was happy."

Insatiable and entirely self-centered, Shel Silverstein's "boy" encounters no limits for his demands. Although he ages visibly, he remains a child throughout his life. Like the mother in *Love You Forever*, who perversely continues to treat her growing son as if he were a perpetual infant, this character likewise treats his mother as if he himself were frozen in time as a baby. Meanwhile, his self-effacing mother participates in the fantasy by taking pleasure in the extremes of self-sacrifice to which she is driven by his demands. She enjoys depleting herself in order to please him. What is presented here as a paradigm for young children is thus a nonreciprocal view of human relationships, both across genders and across generations. Or a sadomasochistic folie-à-deux.

How can we account for the appeal of this book? Some speak of its kindness, its generosity of spirit, its glorification of self-sacrifice. Yet, it is a *mother*, not a father, who is giving all. It is a mother who is portrayed as lonely but happy; a mother who never protests; a mother who is, by the end of the book, reduced to a dead stump. I would argue that the ongoing popularity of *The Giving Tree* speaks volumes about the persistence of such myths in our culture. Given the gendering and the inequality of its protagonists, I doubt the innocence of this book. A more ethically sound paradigm, I believe, would involve genuine rhythms of give-and-take. As Selma Fraiberg (1959) pointed out, it is just as dangerous to ask too little of children as it is to ask too much. Immediate gratification renders the development of the higher powers unnecessary. Shel Silverstein, in this book, asks far too little. But perhaps, in another way, he asks far too much. For *The Giving Tree* makes sense to me only if we can imbue it with irony and a touch of parodic humor — and irony is a rhetorical device that cannot be understood by a toddler.

To return to *Angry Arthur*, when Arthur's mother sets the limit for him, he threatens her, warning her that he will get angry. This retort is reminiscent of that of Max, who likewise refuses to capitulate to his banishment. "Get angry," is Arthur's mother's reply, which is interesting to consider. Depending on how it is read, these two words can seem a dare—confrontative, indifferent, and abandoning (as in, "So what; I don't care what you do, say, or feel")—or, empathically, they can offer permission for the child to experience his own emotion, secure in the knowledge of her ongoing love (as in, "It's okay for you to get angry; I can deal with it"). In fact, the rest of the book is devoted to an exploration of the visual means for representing anger—specifically the anger of small boys in the face of their mothers' refusal to grant their wishes.

Arthur's anger does not turn inward and smolder silently. It does not work masochistically against his own body, as might happen, for example, in the case of a female character. (I will discuss that solution further when I consider *Madeline*.) Here all the world around little Arthur must be made to suffer. His rage moves outward from his own body and upsets the cosmos that envelops him. It turns his house into a shambles, shatters windows, strews shards everywhere, blows down lampposts, detaches billboards, demolishes buildings, overturns cars, creates disastrous floods. Finally, it swells into a "universe-quake." Representing the repetitive, compulsive nature of a temper tantrum in richly colored inks on dramatic double-spread pages, the artist, Satoshi Kitamura, gives us one splendid image after another. My favorite portrays the splitting, multiplication, and reduplication of the child's scowling self as he plummets across the sky in a propulsive jet stream. This illustration always reminds me of the many wild things that appear so suddenly on Max's island.

Each double-spread image ups the ante as Arthur's anger ravishes the environment until at last, by the end of the book, it has expanded to overwhelm and fragment the entire universe. Importantly, however, just as we saw in *Where the Wild Things Are*, the rage has fueled not only destructiveness but also a spurt of imagination and glorious creativity. On the last page, we find Arthur exhausted; his exertions are over, and he rests peacefully in his own bed, which now floats high in the sky on what the text calls "a piece of Mars." Wonderfully true to life, the little boy, depleted after all his high adventures, can no longer remember what it was that caused his anger. "Can you?" the text asks its reader. But we, too, mesmerized by the graphic intensity and imaginative artistry of the images, cannot remember either. In this way, by recreating Arthur's experience for the reader, the book not only describes or portrays but also powerfully induces the disorganizing function of rage and its power to temporarily dismantle the very function of memory. Reading this picture book becomes a direct and unforgettable experience for each child (and parent) encountering it.

Notwithstanding its unique combination of artistic merit and psychological acuity, *Angry Arthur* does perpetuate a familiar gender stereotype. It is difficult to imagine a female character thus presented—her rebelliousness and rageful feelings against her mother so magnificently valorized and aggrandized. Little girls encountering this picture book must find the message more complex. For although girls are manifestly invited to identify with Arthur in his lusty vengeance, some of them may also sense that they are covertly required to disidentify with him and to sympathize with the role of his limit-setting mother. Whereas the combativeness so exquisitely depicted here is encouraged in little boys, who must, it is commonly believed in our culture, separate and differentiate themselves from their mothers, such combativeness is discouraged in little girls, who are taught early on that they should seek safety in sameness with their mothers rather than stage frontal rebellions against them. To study this book is to ponder such issues anew and to reconsider our discrepant tolerance for the expression of "universe quakes" in boys and in girls.

The Tale of Peter Rabbit

By 1989, Beatrix Potter's classic tale had already sold over seven million copies in English alone and had been translated into over a dozen languages, including Latin (Foote 1989). Briefly, it is the story of four little bunnies, Flopsy, Mopsy, Cotton-tail, and Peter, who live with their mother under a fir tree. Mrs. Rabbit warns them at the start not to go into Mr. McGregor's garden because their "Father had an accident there; he was put in a pie by Mrs. McGregor." After giving them this warning, Mother Rabbit sets off through the woods to the baker's, wearing her red-hooded cape and carrying a basket, thus evoking for us — except for her very English green umbrella — another famous female figure in a red-hooded cape who walks through a forest (although Red Riding Hood bestows rather than fetches good things to eat). After she leaves, Flopsy, Mopsy, and Cotton-tail go off to gather blackberries. Peter, however, "who was very naughty," squeezes under the gate and enters the forbidden garden. He eats a great many vegetables of different varieties until he feels ill. Suddenly, he is spied by Mr. McGregor who comes after him with a rake, crying "Stop thief!" Frightened, Peter loses his shoes and his buttons, begins to cry, is nearly caught, but manages to hide in a near-full watering can. Eventually, seizing a moment when Mr. McGregor's back is turned, he slips out of the garden under the gate and runs all the way home. His mother, wondering what became of his clothes, puts him to bed with a dose of chamomile tea. "But Flopsy, Mopsy, and Cotton-tail had bread and milk and blackberries for supper."

The Tale of Peter Rabbit was originally written as part of a letter that Beatrix Potter had sent to a boy of six. This child, Noel Moore, had been stricken with poliomyelitis, and it is possible that his illness triggered in the author some memories of her own suffering from rheumatic fever, which likewise caused her pain and difficulty in walking (see Grinstein 1995). Surely, illness is closely linked in this tale with the notion of punishment, and twin fantasies seem to underlie it: if you are bad, an external form of chastisement will be visited on you; similarly, when an accident or mishap occurs, you must surely have done wrong in order to have deserved it. This linkage illuminates the fact that Peter's disobedient entry into Mr. McGregor's garden results in making him sick. Because illness and punishment are common childhood events, their connection in the story constitutes a powerful reinforcement of such myths (see Sontag 1978).

Why, indeed, *does* Peter disobey his mother and go into Mr.

McGregor's garden? Beatrix Potter refers simply to "naughtiness," as though that were a sufficient explanation—a fixed character trait. Her notion of "naughtiness" seems reminiscent of the "tragic flaw," which has figured for centuries as a way of interpreting the intentions and actions of certain literary characters. In Sophocles' *Oedipus Rex*, for example, the fateful trait of rashness and impulsivity has been claimed to be what caused Oedipus to act as he did (see Michels 1986). The problem with such explanations, though, is that if a great story *were* to hinge merely on a single character trait, we would be hard-pressed to explain its persistent appeal. On the other hand, by evoking an everyday term like "naughtiness," Beatrix Potter may have meant to indicate a trait not peculiar to *some* children but common to all; for, despite differences in frequency and boldness (differences significantly influenced by gender), the term *is* perhaps generally applicable.

Nevertheless, it is striking that the naughty protagonist is male and the obedient "children" are female. Wait: How can we be sure that "Cotton-tail" is not a good little *boy?* The answer lies in Potter's illustrations: for, whereas Peter sports his now-famous blue jacket, the three other bunnies are identically garbed in red capes, like their mother. The gendering is explicit: good is to girls as bad is to boys. Moreover, even *three* good little girls cannot compete with the antics of one bad boy. Peter's popularity has always outweighed that of his sisters, dear as they are, and Beatrix Potter herself apparently never understood why. With respect to her animal hero, she was baffled by what she saw as the secret of his charm.

But was Peter Rabbit naughty or merely curious? If naughty, how so? Was he naughty because he disobeyed his mother? Because he trespassed, like Goldilocks, in territory that did not belong to him? Because he ate, without permission, vegetables that were not his own? And how do young children negotiate these many meanings? For some, it is not Peter Rabbit at all who is bad but Mr. McGregor: after all, isn't *he* the "thief," the one who wants to steal little Peter and eat him up? This interpretation stems from the need of young children to identify with a thoroughly good character and project the bad onto somebody else. By creating a text fertile enough to nourish these many meanings, Beatrix Potter assured the longevity of her art. Yet another explanation also makes a great deal of sense (see Grinstein 1995). Peter Rabbit, in entering Mr. McGregor's garden, behaves, it has been suggested, counterphobically. In other words, immediately after hearing his mother's injunction and the horrifying story of his father's demise, he rushes off to do precisely what his father had done. He does exactly what he has just been warned *not* to do. This act is motivated not by defiance but by the need to master the anxiety that his mother's story has mobilized in him. He reenacts his father's behavior in the hope of making it come out all right this time. He wants to become the hero that his father failed to be.

Young children, encountering *The Tale of Peter Rabbit* and spellbound by it, often understand its details quite differently from the way adults do, and it is fascinating to ponder their interpretations, for we can no longer recover and reconstruct our own first responses to it. Take, for example, Mother Rabbit's warning. To an adult, her words are dire. It is horrible to contemplate being killed, cooked, and eaten. To a three- or four-year-old, however, the notion of a father (rabbit) being "put in a pie" is very strange, so much so that it needs to be glossed. One three-year-old girl, when asked what it meant, said maybe he was in a *chocolate* pie, her image thus transforming what was potentially frightening into a benign and pleasant scene: the father enjoyed being there, in the midst of all that chocolate. I was reminded by her words of the chocolate bunnies that are often given to children in springtime (we were reading the story in April) and of the fact that American children, unlike the French, do not ordinarily conceive of rabbit as meat. This girl's life experience, in other words, had given her no reference for the intended meaning in the text, so she invented her own. She went on to explain further that Peter was going into the garden to find the father and bring him back. And when a little boy who was also listening to the story asked why in the end Father Rabbit never did come back, she explained to him—with a knowing look on her face—that the father was still in the pie; in other words, that he was simply in some other place and temporarily inaccessible.

What intrigues me particularly about such interpretations by children are the implicit assumptions that underlie them. In the three-year-olds with whom I have worked, I have noted a striking liberation from routine psychological distinctions that adults unproblematically make—say, between active and passive, the doer and the done-to, the eater and the eaten. For these children, the fact that Father Rabbit was "in a pie" seems less threatening partly because of this fluidity. One boy, also three, explained that indeed Father Rabbit *had* been baked in a pie; when questioned as to what happened next, he explained that the McGregors *had* eaten him and he *was* dead but that this was all right because "they" could make another father rabbit by baking him up and making him in a pie. Thus, as long as the transformational possibilities stay fluid, an endlessly reassuring universe can exist, and notions of absolute finality, irrevocable loss, and irreversibility are obviated. With respect to issues of good versus bad, most of the three-year-olds saw Mr. McGregor, rather than Peter, as the bad guy. But, when probed, one child thought that the farmer was trying to trap Peter not in order to kill and eat him but to keep him as a pet. Again the child pulls back from finality and brings present life experience to bear on the fictional narrative. Listening to these three-year-olds' voices, I have pondered the weight of different motivating factors in their observations—whether, in other words, the interpretations they furnish represent principally childish naïveté or are more defensive in nature. In most instances, I suspect that they represent some combination of the above joined with loops and flourishes of imagination.

Common to most three-year-olds was a take on the story that I did not foresee but which seems in retrospect perfectly understandable; namely that, at that age, what creates suspense for them is not the threat of Peter's demise and oral destruction at the McGregors' dining table but rather his prolonged and precarious separation from home, safety, and mother. The plot these children discern seems to run as follows:

a bunny does what is called bad by his mother (who knows bad from good) and is chased by a bad man with a rake; the little fellow finally makes it home but arrives there much too sick to have anything but tea. Subtleties, unless brought to their attention, are rarely perceived as intended. For instance, at one point in the story Peter gets caught by his buttons in the gooseberry net and begins to cry; little sparrows encourage him, imploring him (as Beatrix Potter puts it) to exert himself. None of the children I read to grasped the idea that the birds were trying to enable Peter to help himself. They thought instead that the birds actually freed the little rabbit from the net. Yet, importantly, the notion of *helping* comes through. Likewise for the overall plot: its salient elements get through. In a book of this density, the youngest child can discern a thread that, in subsequent readings, gets overlaid with colorful and ever thicker threads until a dazzling cloth of associations is woven up about it. Avatars of its philosophical conundrums and psychological complexities are experienced, I am convinced, even by the youngest minds, and it is because of this that the book exerts an irresistible magnetism, pulling us back through the years to its pages.

It may seem obvious but is worth mentioning that Beatrix Potter is as fully gifted an artist as she is an author. She illustrates each of her stories with softly colored, delicately lined drawings that reflect her keenly observant eye, deft hand, and clever, often droll imagination. For example, she portrays the bearded McGregor menacing Peter with his rake while calling him a "thief." In so doing, she creates a visual simile: the *tines* of the rake are like *teeth*. Thus, the matched fears of being eaten up (put in a pie) after having just eaten up Mr. McGregor's vegetables gain concrete pictorial representation. Elsewhere the angry farmer's hobnailed boot is shown about to descend on the little rabbit, who has just knocked over the farmer's flower pots. This image draws power from an age-old tradition in Western and Middle Eastern art where, in stone, wood, and metal, victors are conventionally depicted as vanquishing their enemies by standing over them with a raised foot before crushing them.

Shrewdness and tenderness in unique proportions characterize

Beatrix Potter's art. Every gesture in her small pictures is carefully observed. Her acute sensibility joins with insights into animal behavior (note the varying positions of Peter Rabbit's ears when he is contemplating mischief, or surfeited and sick to his stomach, or alert, frightened, or exhausted). Thus she produces pictures that give far more than graphic form to her tales. Long after people have forgotten the precise details of her stories and what befalls her characters, they retain images of long-tailed Johnny Town-mouse, or fat little Timmy Willie with his fateful wicker hamper, or prickly Mrs. Tiggy-winkle with her iron, her apron, and dress tucked up behind, or Jemima Puddle-duck going "pit pat, paddle pat" down the garden path.

The Tale of Tom Kitten

Surely, this Instruction which I enjoin upon you this day is not too baffling for you, nor is it beyond reach. It is not in the heavens, that you should say, "Who among us can go up to the heavens and get it for us and impart it to us, that we may observe it?" Neither is it beyond the sea, that you should say, "Who among us can cross to the other side of the sea and get it for us and impart it to us, that we may observe it?" "No, the thing is very close to you, in your mouth and in your heart, to observe it." Deuteronomy 30:11

This biblical passage has always struck me as upbeat and encouraging—a "come on, you can do it!" text. But the book we are going to consider now is about just the opposite: it is about commands that cannot be carried out. It is about demands that are unreasonable rather than doable. It is about what happens when parents give children instructions that are baffling for them and quite simply, beyond their reach. When this sort of situation occurs, it is a good bet that disobedience and mischief will ensue.

The Tale of Tom Kitten relates the story of Tabitha Twitchit, a mother cat who has invited her friends over for tea. In anticipation of the party, she scrubs and combs her three kittens and dresses them up in what

Beatrix Potter describes as "elegant uncomfortable clothes." When it is clear that Tom, the only boy, has outgrown his jacket and burst his buttons, Mrs. Tabitha refuses to acknowledge the reality of the situation and perversely sews the buttons right back on again. Indeed, an acknowledgement of reality (or, we might say, this mother's failure to acknowledge reality) is perhaps the leitmotiv of the story and an important one for the subject of mischief, disobedience, and punishment. After dressing her kittens up, this very preoccupied mother cat sends them off to the garden to get them out of her way while she prepares buttered toast for her guests. She enjoins them not to get dirty and, to that end, to walk only on their hind legs. Of course, this would be an impossible task for any kitten, even one wearing, as Beatrix Potter puts it, just his or her own "dear little fur coat" — but with the "uncomfortable" civilized finery they have on, the command is preposterous.

The kittens naturally falter. They tread on their party clothes, try to jump and climb on their hind legs, and end up soiling and losing all their clothes, "shedding buttons right and left," until finally the rhythmic sounds of "pit pat paddle pat! pit pat waddle pat!" announce the arrival of the puddle ducks, who try on all the kittens' clothes and then, eventually, plunge into the pond with them. Mrs. Tabitha Twitchit, returning to the garden to find her kittens with no clothes, smacks them vigorously and packs them off upstairs behind closed doors before greeting her guests, to whom she blatantly lies, giving out the false excuse that her kittens are in bed with the measles (as though being sick were preferable to being dirty). On the second-to-last page of the book, we see that, during the tea party, the kittens were making a wild rumpus, for when their mother goes upstairs to retrieve them, she finds that the floor of her bedroom is heaped with clothing and shoes, the side curtain of her bed is partly torn down, and one kitten's ears are just visible from inside its sagging canopy. Mrs. Tabitha's startled expression bodes no good, and on the last page, we see the silly puddle ducks diving down in the lily pond for the clothes, which had all come off because, by the time the ducks got into them, they had already lost their buttons.

Throughout this story, our sympathies are solidly with the kittens and against the mother, whose decorous desires take no account of her children's needs, capabilities, or preferences. On the book's jacket, fat little Tom stares wide-eyed at us, his ample body squeezed uncomfortably into an ill-fitting blue jacket (reminiscent of Peter Rabbit's) and his trousers so small at the waist that they have already sprung open. His ears are perked up, and he seems to be saying: "Oh, dear. This can't last. Whatever shall I do?"

Throughout the book, clothing assumes an overriding symbolic value. In drawings of animals with human characteristics (see Goldstein 1995), clothes conventionally stand for differences between the animal and human kingdoms, between the so-called natural and civilized realms; thus, to dress up an animal is to make him or her seem human. Yet, Beatrix Potter adds a twist to this convention. Clothes assume the added role of marking the difference between adult standards of behavior and the supposedly unfettered, instinctual desires of children. Peter Rabbit, for example, begins fully dressed but, after he disobeys his mother and pursues his own desires by sneaking into Mr. McGregor's garden, he loses all his clothes and ends up quite naked. Thus, in Beatrix Potter's pages, there is occasionally a reversal of the usual paradigm, and Tabitha Twitchit's kittens may seem even more like children without their clothes than they do with them. Or do they? And what about Peter Rabbit? Do we feel more sympathetic toward the animal characters when they are dressed or undressed? Beatrix Potter's works cause our feelings to shift as she explores, both visually and textually, the question of where to locate a child's evolving self.

The Tale of Tom Kitten makes us ponder the thought that, although children need to be given tasks that match their developmental capabilities (something Mrs. Tabitha Twitchit fails to do), they need, at the same time, to be perceived by their parents as growing in these very capabilities, so that the tasks required of them can increase in difficulty, complexity, and level of responsibility. To wear and take care of clothes is surely to assume the burdens and restrictions of civil society, but it is also to participate in the richness, variety, expressiveness, and communicative possibilities of that society. Beatrix Potter, while emphasizing the former in this tale, creates a subtle work in which values are not totally polarized and the fluidity of possibility is maintained. Concretizing that notion, she does not end the story with a scene of bitter retributive strife between mother and children but rather with a calming touch—with illustrations, in fact, not of the cat and her naughty kittens at all, but rather of the lily pond and the puddle ducks. In liquid images, the story is brought to a gentle close, its emphasis placed on the importance of an ongoing search rather than on anger and punishment.

The Tale of Squirrel Nutkin

Little Squirrel Nutkin, in this "tale about a tail," can be seen as the quintessential twit, that exasperating child who ceaselessly annoys, badgers, irritates, and finally manages to push the limits of adult patience past its breaking point. Nutkin can be contrasted with Sendak's Pierre, who merely refuses to comply with what is asked of him. Squirrel Nutkin becomes a positively infuriating, obstreperous nuisance. Throughout the story, a cohort of red squirrels paddle in tiny rafts made of twigs to an island where they go to gather nuts. This island, however, is not entirely safe. It is inhabited by a dangerous owl, Old Brown, who likes to sleep all day and whose doorway stands in the hollow of an oak tree. To placate him, the squirrels bring him a unique peace offering on each nut-gathering excursion. In addition, out of implied fear and respect, the squirrels politely ask for his permission to proceed with their gathering. The owl, apparently dozing, never deigns to respond verbally to them. He accepts, however, each gift that is presented.

Nutkin, "who had no respect" and was "excessively impertinent in his manners," cannot rest content with this state of affairs. A little troublemaker, he attempts to rouse the fearsome owl and to wrest a response from him. With each visit to the island, the little fellow ups the ante, and suspense builds. The fuzzy chestnut-colored squirrel bobs up and down in front of the great owl, poses riddles to him, tickles him impudently with a nettle, peeps brazenly into his keyhole, skips in front of him, laughs, sings, and shouts. But Old Brown continues to say "nothing at all." Tension mounts and reaches its height when, in an outrageously transgressive act, Nutkin at length takes a running jump and lands right smack on the head of the resting bird. At this point, a loud squeak is heard, and the other squirrels scamper away in terror. When they creep back, they discover that Nutkin is now in the great owl's pocket. Intending to skin him, Old Brown takes the little fellow inside his hollow and holds him up by the tail, but Nutkin pulls so hard that his tail breaks in two. Forever after, Beatrix Potter informs her readers, he stutters and throws sticks if you ask him a riddle.

What interests me especially about this story is the brilliant way in which it illuminates the underlying motivational factors that determine the sort of behavior in children that often seems gratuitously difficult. Beatrix Potter reveals that such behavior may stem from at least two readily understandable sources. The first is curiosity (as manifested by the fact that Nutkin does not merely disturb the owl with nonsensical antics but in fact actually asks him questions, poses riddles to him, seems to want to learn something from him). A second, more emotionally resonant motive is the poignant desire of every creature to be responded to. Old Brown never deigns to address the squirrels. He never looks at them, indeed declines to dignify them with any reciprocity whatsoever. This passivity leaves little Nutkin unsatisfied. He wants to be noticed. He wants to be paid attention to. Furthermore, as his antics grow ever more infuriating, Old Brown gives him no warning of impending retaliation. No limits are set for his behavior.

In a way, the parental behavior here (on the part of Old Brown) is the obverse of but also, paradoxically, the equivalent of, that portrayed in *The Tale of Tom Kitten*, where the demands on the children are manifestly unrealistic but fully expressed by Tabitha Twitchit. In *Squirrel Nutkin*, on the other hand, it seems that the children must already know how to behave and must have so fully internalized the parental prohibitions that they require no outside help whatsoever. Only Peter Rabbit's mother, we might say, provides a middle ground—between Old Brown, who abdicates any parenting role until the story reaches its harsh and punitive end, and Tabitha Twitchit, whose rules are self-serving and unfair and lead also to chastisement. Alone among these figures, Mrs. Rabbit demands of her children what is eminently doable. She gives them *alternatives* to the forbidden act: "You may go into the fields or down the lane, but don't go into Mr. McGregor's garden." Furthermore, she takes the trouble to *explain* to them the purpose behind her rule and the reason for her concern. Her reason, moreover, has to do not solely with her own interests, as in the case of Tabitha Twitchit, but also with the safety and best interests of the children themselves.

The Story about Ping

Originally published in 1933, still widely distributed and dearly loved by children, *The Story about Ping* by Marjorie Flack and Kurt Wiese came racing back into my mind quite suddenly one day when I was an undergraduate in college. I had signed up for an advanced European history seminar with a very austere professor who began the semester by warning us that we could expect to be called on at any time during class to answer questions on the assigned reading, and that no student who had failed to complete the assigned reading was welcome in class that day. This was an intimidating way to begin the semester. Nevertheless, he was an erudite scholar, a superb lecturer, and, as I found out later, a charming gentleman. I stayed. Once during the course of the semester, however, I was in anguish. I had failed to complete the assigned reading for the day, but nevertheless went, almost by force of habit, to the hall where the class was being held. Standing before the closed door in turmoil, I wavered as to whether I should go in. On one hand, not to enter would be to miss a fascinating class; on the other hand, to go in meant risking the embarrassment of being asked a question for which I was unprepared. As I stood there with books and notebooks, wondering what to do, the story of Ping suddenly rushed back into memory. I took a deep breath, pushed the heavy door open, walked shyly in, and sat down at the seminar table.

Ping is the story of a little duck who runs away to avoid humiliation. Every day of his short life, all the ducks who live with him on a house boat "with two wise eyes on the Yangtze River" go ashore to hunt for good things to eat. When the shadows grow long, the Master of the boat gives a call, and the ducks all return, lining up to march in single file over the bridge, back to the boat for the night with their families. Ping is careful never to be last in line, for the last duck back receives a spank with a stick by the Master of the boat. Yet one day, inevitably, Ping's head happens to be underwater when the call is given and he fails to hear it. Looking up, he sees that all the other ducks have already begun their march over the bridge and that, if he returns, he will be the very last one. Not wanting to be spanked, Ping hides in the reeds on the shore and watches as the wise-eyed boat sails away with all his relatives aboard.

In warm, grainy, hand-colored images, master illustrator Kurt Wiese, who spent six years in China as a young man, details Ping's adventures on the great river as he tries to find his way back to his familiar surroundings. Finally, after several dangerous escapades, he hears the boatman's signal, "La-la-la-la-lei!" and spies the wise-eyed boat. Paddling toward it as fast as he can, Ping realizes that the last of his forty-two cousins will have already marched over the bridge by the time he gets there and that, once again, he will be the last duck aboard. This time, however, he marches up to the bridge and, as the rod descends, unflinchingly accepts his punishment. The final picture shows him in a bed of yellow hay, happily surrounded by a flock of quacking relations—home again at last.

The appeal of this charming book is that it engages with a choice faced by all children at one time or another—namely, whether to submit to or avoid the rules of society, and beyond that, whether to face or try to evade punishment after breaking the rules. Ping is unintentionally late, but he intentionally avoids his punishment. The beauty of his story lies in its very simplicity. It can be made to fit a great variety of real-life situations with similar underlying dynamics. Ping's story, after all, is about individual freedom, which may lead to isolation and danger, versus participation in a community, which means acquiescing to strictures on that freedom or paying the price for transgressions against them. The little yellow duck is lovable because his impulses make such perfect sense: he does not want to be punished (who does?), and he tries to avoid the unpleasant consequences of his behavior while at the same time wishing to remain united with, and in the good graces of, his family. Perfectly reasonable goals. But Ping is naïve, for, as we know, combining them is not quite so easy in life.

The Story about Ping thus gives children a chance to vicariously experience an ethical dilemma that is bound to recur throughout their lives. The fact that its protagonist is a small yellow duck and that the setting is faraway, long-ago China serves both to distance and to foreground its profoundly philosophical theme because, as I indicated earlier, metaphor is central to the power of rhetoric. *Ping* creates a scene to which—as happened to me when I was in college—other scenes can be felicitously referred. Several images remain ensconced in my memory: the little duck, having been captured by a strange family and kept on their houseboat, overhears the news that he is to be cooked for dinner that very night. He is placed under a basket, and standing on the criss-cross shadows made by light filtering in through its interstices, he watches sadly as the spaces between the shadows grow pink with the setting sun. I can still remember my own mingled feelings of sting and relief, my "ouch" and my "whew," when he runs over the bridge to safety and is struck by the Master's stick.

The Poky Little Puppy

One of my friends, a psychiatric social worker whose practice involves mothers and young children, described the following scene. A mother and her little son are arriving at playschool on the first day of the season. They are a few minutes late, and the mother's face wears a resolute look. She is determined to march steadily along through the corridor toward the classroom. But the little boy is moving very slowly. With his unheld hand, he touches the concrete wall, allowing his palm and fingers to trail along its surface, feeling its bumpy texture. He lingers; he dawdles. His mother impatiently jerks him along, but it is clear that he wants to make this journey at a very different pace. Perhaps he wants, quite literally, to *feel* his way into the new situation.

Similarly, have you ever seen a toddler stop in the middle of a walk to bend down and peer intently at something on the ground? Or squat down unexpectedly to pick up a fascinating treasure? The *Poky Little Puppy* (1942), by Janette Sebring Lowrey and Gustaf Tenggren, evokes such moments as well as the slow time that is also a feature of *Goodnight Moon*. The poky little puppy *is* that curious child for whom the environment, as for Shakespeare's Miranda, seems a "brave new world," a world of endlessly entertaining caterpillars, lizards, frogs, toads, spiders, grasshoppers. Or, for city children, pieces of trash, scraps, pebbles, even dust. When I took my sixteen-month-old daughter, years ago, to Stonehenge, the contrast in our perceptions was dramatic: while the adults in the group were staring up in wonder at those awe-inspiring prehistoric monuments, little Rivi was equally absorbed: filling her tiny hands with pebbles, she sat on the ground, her eyes cast down, thoroughly engrossed in her own compelling discoveries.

The story of *The Poky Little Puppy*, to all young children's immense delight, rewards the slowest, most curious puppy. He is the one who, each time he and his siblings disobediently dig a hole under the fence and wriggle through it to explore "the wide, wide world," receives a treat—one delicious dessert after another until, at the end of the story, proper adult values reassert themselves, and this poky little puppy is duly sent off to bed "without a single bite of shortcake." In the meantime, however, the book brings together two of the most salient motifs of early childhood—curiosity about the world and the pleasures of tasting sweet food. Its gentle images and rhythms portray a benign universe in which, despite maternal prohibitions, these agendas can be pursued in tandem. Not surprisingly, the mischievous puppy is gendered masculine, and the "someone" who puts up the sign that says: "DON'T EVER DIG HOLES UNDER THIS FENCE!" turns out to be the mother. She is, however, a mother who knows how to prepare rice pudding, chocolate custard, and strawberry shortcake, and she is, moreover, a forgiving mother who, when the puppies make amends by filling up the hole they dig, is ready to treat them accordingly.

Poetic phrases such as "roly-poly, pell-mell, tumble-bumble" and "through the meadow, down the road, over the bridge, across the green grass, and up the hill" require notice, as does this book's graphic design, for the perspective of the pictures alternates between up and down, high and low, near and far—between an adult's and a child's eye view. The caterpillar, lizard, toad, grass snake, and grasshopper, for instance, are drawn large in scale, as seen close up—whereas as the puppies themselves, on top of the hill or under their colored blankets, are beheld from a slightly greater distance. The varying perspective of the images thus mirrors what is being communicated in the text: namely, a tender friction between wandering young explorers and their concerned, protective parents.

The Poky Little Puppy, like the other picture books described in this chapter, represents a struggle between points of view. Children's disobedience seems invariably to involve crossing a boundary that has been set by adults, whether by messing up the house (as in *Where the Wild Things Are*), turning things upside-down (as in *Pierre*), refusing to go to bed (the way Arthur does), trespassing (like Peter Rabbit), getting one's clothes soiled (in the manner of Tom Kitten), making a nuisance of oneself (like Squirrel Nutkin), refusing to take one's punishment (remember Ping), or stealing out to explore the world (like the poky little puppy). But, we must ask, what do such boundaries feel like to young children? Not as fixed and permanent. Rather more like fences (used metaphorically, as we have just seen, in several books) that— whether physical, emotional, intellectual, or social—*can* perhaps be bypassed. This is in part because, growing and changing, each child keeps testing his or her developing strength against the resistance. (Maybe this time it will break.) And, as children's minds and bodies grow, some barriers do break from a child's push. Others crash for external reasons, and some never yield. Because only experimentation can reveal which barriers are likely to be retained, mischief and disobedience are probably necessary. To explore classic picture books is thus to discover how children expand their worlds through misbehavior—and how mischief can be a surprisingly constructive, and even creative, means by which children adapt to, and seek to revise, societal and familial boundaries.

~ Chapter 5 ~

I Like You Just the Way You Are

A dynamic, energetic woman I know went directly from college to medical school and without skipping a beat, segued into a distinguished career in pediatrics in a large city hospital. Her husband, during those years, became a surgeon. Notwithstanding the pressures of training, research, and the beginnings of their clinical practice, the couple managed during this hectic period to become proud parents of three daughters. One afternoon, their youngest daughter, Debby, then about four years old, was playing in her room with a little boy when, passing by the doorway, her mother overheard the following exchange: "Let's play doctor," suggested the boy; "*I'll* be the doctor." Debby, without a moment's hesitation, concurred. "Okay," she agreed, "You can be the doctor; I'll be the nurse."

My friend stood transfixed. Here she was, a medical doctor for over a decade, and the holder of an academic rank and a hospital position fully equivalent to those of her husband. Equality, not gender bias, had been the watchword in their home; yet, like a dandelion in a well-tended lawn, the atavistic stereotype was cropping up before her very eyes. Had she failed as a role model for her daughter? Who or what had nurtured this seed? Baffled, my friend pondered this instance of bias. Her daughter's unhesitating acquiescence troubled her; she was concerned not only that Debby had not chosen to be the doctor, but also that she had not even acknowledged that role as a viable option for herself.

No matter how powerful a figure a mother cuts with her daughter, the mother soon discovers that other competing influences are at work. Although children's primary identifications are within the family, stereotypes, values, and tastes are communicated independently to children by the surrounding culture, and these influences take root deeply in fertile young minds. To focus interpretive attention exclusively on the nuclear family—as mental health professionals are wont to do—shortchanges the effect of these cultural influences and fosters the sort of limited thinking about causality that results in, for example, my friend's assumption that *she* was somehow directly responsible for her daughter's momentary self-identification as a nurse rather than a doctor.

On the contrary, cultural influences matter increasingly and dramatically. "Latchkey" children, an extreme example, are now a widespread phenomenon in contemporary American life. In homes where television substitutes for the presence of live human beings, these children see and hear, in the intimate settings of their living and sleeping quarters, much that falls outside the purview of parental awareness and judgment. Such children exist at the far end of a continuum that includes us all. Debby's alacrity in choosing the role of nurse on one particular occasion was hardly a cause for alarm. Considering the rich background of images available to a typical American four-year-old, this role may well have seemed an attractive option to her rather than a negative or diminished one, as it did to her mother. We can imagine a variety of sources for whatever propelled her toward her choice, including, perhaps, her wish not to quarrel with her friend, who had already unequivocally announced his own preference (a preference no less culturally inflected).

As children and adults, our ways of seeing are shaped by that which necessarily lies outside our awareness at any given time. But this fact does not mean that we should abdicate our right to learn as much as possible about the sources of our views or forfeit our right to question, and possibly revise them. As guides for young children in a democratic society, such ongoing cultural interpretation seems a civic obligation as well as a privilege. Change comes slowly—first, through an awakening to attitudes and circumstances hitherto taken for granted, such as the persistent (but absurd) notion that girls must be nurses and boys be doctors. Despite present-day medical school statistics, which show a rise in the number of women in training to be physicians, this notion hangs on stubbornly as cultural myths do, long past the time when they reflect an accurate picture of reality or have social utility in restricting reality. In other words, when little girls actually believed that only boys could be doctors, they rarely aspired to this position. Thus, myth can function as a constraint upon reality. When, however, a deep sense of injustice arises, calls for change can be heard, and conscientious reformers arise to create new images that seem more equitable. I believe that this is just in fact what many authors and illustrators of picture books have been doing for years—putting forth images and ideas that deeply alter our world.

In this chapter I will consider several books that address the theme underlying Debby's self-identification as a nurse rather than a doctor: the theme of the young child's relationship with her- or himself. In addition to exploring the world at large, each young person is simultaneously engaged in a fascinating project of self-discovery. This self-discovery begins with the physical—with tasting, touching, seeing, hearing, smelling, and moving in space. In one of his most influential papers, Freud (1923) addressed this topic and expressed his view that the ego, or self, derives first and foremost from the body. Freud implied that it is through our experiences with and in and from the perspective of our own bodies that we gradually come to know who we are. Our comfort with and acceptance of our individual bodies is therefore fundamental to our well-being. Each child's own idiosyncratic body is a locus of primary knowledge. At every moment, his or her sex, race, temperament, current state of growth and development, range of abilities, sociocultural background, and milieu operate together. Each child must gradually come to terms with these variables and learn to function optimally within their horizon. Using the senses and moving about, a child quickly takes advantage of the amazing potential of the human body—for pleasure, for learning, and for relating to others— and, in the process, also becomes aware of its limitations. These limitations of the body are in some instances permanent and in other cases merely temporary. Moreover, the sociocultural myths and prejudices that shape this process of self-discovery are, as we have seen, inseparable from it. Thus, self-acceptance on a physical level—that is to say, feeling genuinely at ease with one's own body—is, in our culture, not a given but an achievement, for girls especially, perhaps, but for boys as well. Once attained, however, this rootedness in the body can become a source of incalculable strength; it can enable a person to go forth on any course in life with a stable core, a secure base.

Because this theme is both so crucial and so difficult for children to negotiate, it has long been a popular subject for picture books. Each book in this chapter deals directly with the theme of body image and the formation of identity in early childhood. There are two groups of books. The first cluster consists of classics from the decade of the 1930s that have appealed to several generations of parents and children. Even before naming them, I want to anticipate that, in grappling with this recalcitrant theme, we must expect to be drawn into some fierce tugs-of-war, to feel the pull of opposites. By now we should be alert to this, for we have already observed it at work elsewhere in these pages. I noted, for example, the tension between a child's wish to gratify her impulses versus the equally powerful wish to please others and retain their love by doing the right thing, obeying the rules. In this chapter, the terms of inner conflict are somewhat different, but the structure remains intact.

Now Open the Box (1934), by Dorothy Kunhardt, depicts with whimsy, charm, and pathos a small child's struggle between the wish to remain lovably small and the necessity of growing up. *Noodle* (1937), by Munro Leaf and Ludwig Bemelmans, portrays the competition within a young person between the longing to transcend the body given at birth and the need to accept and actually cherish that very body with its own unique characteristics. *The Story of Ferdinand* (1936), by Munro Leaf and Robert Lawson, needs no introduction: it records a child's effort to sustain his sense of self despite continuous outside pressures to conform to norms that do not match his special temperament and world view. *Horton Hatches the Egg* (1940), by Dr. Seuss, a classic avant-garde text, radically reverses gender stereotypes. *Wee Gillis* (1938), by Munro Leaf and Robert Lawson, tells the story of a young boy's valiant attempts to incorporate elements of both parents' worlds while at the same time creating an identity that is uniquely his own. Each of these works, over a span of more than sixty years, has demonstrated its capacity to expand the inner life of children.

A second group consists of books that inscribe the process of self-discovery and bodily acceptance in more highly inflected cultural settings. *Madeline*, by Ludwig Bemelmans, dates from the same period as the previous books and speaks paradigmatically to issues of gender. Madeline is, of course, a prototypically exuberant little girl who is compelled to learn, through the medium of an appendectomy, some of the cultural meanings of her femininity. *Willy the Wimp* (1984), by Anthony Browne, addresses, in highly ambivalent terms, issues of race as well as gender. *Dandelion* (1964) and *Corduroy*, both by Don Freeman, speak to the importance of childhood friendship as a way of validating body image with respect both to race and gender. Each of these books has attracted a large following, and each raises questions worth serious reflection.

Now Open the Box

Dorothy Kunhardt is best known as the gifted author of *Pat the Bunny* (1942), an incredibly long-lived and often imitated book for the very youngest child that combines visual, verbal, tactile, and olfactory experiences. Even earlier, however, she wrote and illustrated a book entitled *Now Open the Box* (1934), also addressed to toddlers. The shape of this book is interesting. Nearly twice as wide as it is tall when closed, it opens out to form an elongated shape with its text hand-printed on the left-hand page. The text is composed of rhythmic run-on sentences and word repetitions that mirror not only the shape of the object itself but also the tendency of young children to join one idea to the next and to use the same words over and over when telling a tale. The right-hand pages are reserved solely for pictures. Only twice does the image completely take over both sides of the book, and these are at climactic moments in the story.

In striking yellow, red, and black images drawn with a bold freedom, spontaneity, and clarity, this book narrates the story of a tiny circus dog who is beloved because of his miniscule size. Parenthetically, the double-entendre of the dog's name, Peewee, suggests not only his smallness but also, associatively, a young child's way of referring to a bodily function over which he or she is attempting to gain control. Thus the name possesses its own inherent fascination and creates a further subliminal bond of identification between the toddler and the animal character. Because more than a half-dozen of the books discussed in this chapter employ animal characters, it is important to recall that, psychologically speaking, no small part of the attraction of such books for young children has to do with the fact that animals can perform openly a range of bodily functions that human adults prefer to keep private or hidden. This insight was articulated by the Hungarian psychoanalyst Sándor Ferenczi in 1913, when he wrote up his observations of little Arpád, a five-year-old boy obsessed with roosters, in his classic essay "The Little Chanticleer." It is a point reiterated recently by Henry Louis Gates, Jr. (1997), who argues that the privacy practiced by humans in such matters results in valuable social gains (Freud doubtless would have agreed).

Now Open the Box begins with a rotund, tall-hatted, big-footed circus man who gathers an expectant crowd each day by promising them that, if they step inside his red tent, he will reveal what is inside a tiny yellow box. Each time he does so the miniscule red dog Peewee appears. Everybody loves Peewee at once. He has only to *be*. Unlike the other circus entertainers depicted in the book—the clown riding a two-headed donkey, the lady standing on her head on an umbrella holding a pair of scissors with one foot while balancing a cup of warm milk with the other foot, the lady who hangs in the air by her nose, the rolling snake—Peewee does not have to perform in order to justify his existence. He merely emerges from his box and, like a newborn infant (especially as viewed, not without an admixture of wonder and envy, by its older siblings), he is unconditionally and universally admired.

"But one day," Kunhardt writes, "a terrible frightful awful thing happened. One day little teeny weeny weeny weeny Peewee started to grow." Double-spread pages reveal this process, which continues until finally, with tears streaming from his eyes (a vertical line of black dashes), the circus man explains that, because he is no longer tiny, Peewee is no longer unique. He has become just like any ordinary dog. Therefore, because he cannot do any tricks, he will not be permitted to remain in the circus; he will have to be sent away. At this point, a complex double-spread image studded with vertical dashes portrays all the circus performers—the little dog himself and all the characters previously encountered—in tears. The scene, despite (and actually because of) the humor of its characters, is one of pathos. Manifestly straightforward, it taps directly into one of young people's deepest anxieties—the envy and fear of being replaced by a new love in the form of a newborn sibling. It invokes children's normal feelings of inadequacy vis-à-vis adults (who are more accomplished) and babies (who need no accomplishments). It elicits fears of abandonment and of loss of love.

At this point, however, just as "poor little Peewee started to go away and never come back to the circus any more . . . a wonderful splendid beautiful thing happened." As he walks sadly away, the simple red shape of the animal suddenly begins to enlarge. Page by page, this new growth spurt is dramatized by repeated slightly larger images. Finally, Peewee towers over the circus man himself, who proclaims that, because he is so lovely and *big*, Peewee may remain in the circus. At this point, an enormous yellow box replaces the tiny one, and, in a recap of the first scene, the circus man once more invites the crowd to come inside his tent: "People," he shouts, "this is my dear little circus dog Peewee and he is the hugest most enormous dog in the whole world and I love him dearly."

This apparently simple picture book, by using the pictorial device of amplifying its principal image page by page, conveys subtleties of psychological wisdom. Children who encounter it may come to understand, by means of projection and identification, that being lovable does not necessarily mean staying small (that is, refusing to progress or regressing in imitation of an envied infant or one's former self). Being lovable, furthermore, does not necessarily mean being able to perform tricks for an audience (that is, being able to behave in ways that will please others). Rather, the child is shown here to be worthy of love simply by virtue of his growing and continuing to develop.

The final words of the book read: "Every time the circus man said he is the hugest most enormous dog in the whole world and I love him dearly then little Peewee felt VERY HAPPY INDEED!" And because the form of the circus man's invitation and the images of the yellow box at the beginning and end of the story remain similar, *Now Open the Box* stresses another important psychological point, namely, that there is always *continuity* between each child's former self and his changing self. In addition, casting the principal adult character as *male* rather than female serves first to perpetuate but then importantly to critique the representation of fathers as providers only of provisional love—of love, in other words, that is conditional upon its being deserved rather than freely bestowed. Here, the "father," in the guise of the circus man, after threatening at first to reject Peewee, restores Peewee to his affections when it is clear that he is actually going to continue growing. Another reading, on the other hand, might see the father here as exemplifying a typical provider of conditional love. After all, he reaccepts Peewee only when the dog again becomes unusual and distinctive, albeit in a different way—extra big instead of extra small—the point being that, to be loved by your father, you need to be special in some way, out of the ordinary. Both readings fit, and we can therefore deduce that the father's role, as symbolically represented here, is ambiguous—as it ever was and continues to be, both in life and in children's literature. Think, parenthetically, of the fathers you can recall from well-known European fairy tales—absent (in "Snow White"), ineffectual (in both "Hansel and Gretel" and "Sleeping Beauty"), demanding of the impossible (in "Rumpelstiltskin"), overly protective (in "Rapunzel"). The good father is, in this canon, a rare commodity.

Now Open the Box implies, nevertheless, that, if children are to form stable, resilient selves, they must gradually and never without some pain relinquish the idolization of infancy and accept their growing bodies with whatever unique potentialities and limitations these afford. There is no stasis; there is no return.

The next four books, because they too date from the decade of the 1930s, remind me to note here that, although my focus throughout this book has been on what I take to be enduring *psychological* themes, my purpose is not to ignore or diminish the importance of the relevant historical questions that might also be posed. It is startling to notice that, during the same decade in which these American picture books extolling diversity, individuality, and self-actualization were being written and distributed, in Europe, the theme of identity was, in picture books being published for young children, linked to an ideology of hatred that produced persecutions and atrocities. Widely circulated Nazi picture books published in the mid-1930s depicted the Jew as a sly fox or, in one book, as a poisonous mushroom—blond German youngsters are shown learning to distinguish Jews from so-called Aryans just as noxious fungi must be differentiated from safe, edible species. To reflect on this discrepancy is to recognize both the contingent nature and the awesome power of a child's early acculturation and to be reminded that the right to self-discovery requires vigilance. In times of relative peace and economic stability this lesson may be all too easily forgotten.

Noodle

In 1936 and in 1938, Munro Leaf and Robert Lawson produced *The Story of Ferdinand* and *Wee Gillis*. And in 1937, Leaf and Ludwig Bemelmans created *Noodle*—the story of a dachshund whose short front legs make it difficult for him to dig because the dirt he displaces always flies up and hits him in the stomach. The dimensions of his body, in other words, do not permit him to do comfortably what he yearns to do.

Noodle's name, like Peewee's, conveys innuendoes that require notation: it refers to his shape and also to a favorite food of many children.

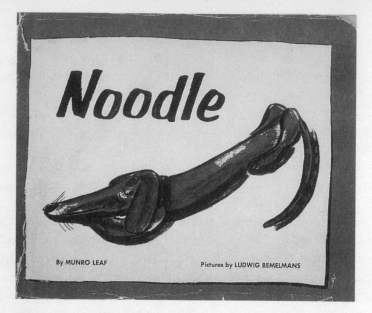

From *Noodle* by Munro Leaf, illustrated by Ludwig Bemelmans.
Illustrations copyright © 1937 Ludwig Bemelmans; copyright renewed.
Reprinted with the permission of Simon & Schuster Books for Young
Readers, an imprint of Simon & Schuster Children's Publishing Division.

Small, like Peewee—short specifically—this character ideally serves a
child's projective needs: he loves to dig, and he wants to transcend
his size.

One day, after much labor, Noodle unearths a wishbone and expresses a desire to be some other size and shape than he currently is.
Later, with the bone in his mouth, he emerges from a deep hole that
he has dug. He is surprised by a white, airborne, dog-shaped creature,
who arrives onomatopoeically in a "whirr and a buzz and a flip-flap
of wings." She is the "dog fairy," and her presence may remind us
of another character, the "Blue Fairy" who swoops down similarly in
Disney's *Pinocchio* (1943) to grant the little woodenhead his wish to

be, not precisely some other size and shape, but some other substance (flesh rather than wood).

Thus, Noodle, by burrowing in the ground, symbolically unearths the bedrock issue of body image and identity formation with its concomitant disappointments, longings, and conflicts. Digging down into the earth at the cost of considerable discomfort, the dachshund comes up with a *wishbone*. The form of this familiar object, with its protuberances, is repeated in various guises throughout the book and assumes in context a vaguely suggestive androgyny. Adumbrated are covert wishes to be the sex one is not (to have both male and female genitalia) as well as to alter the details of one's body image. Visual innuendoes abound, as in the picture where Noodle pokes his nose into the hollow earth to smell the bone. Furthermore, by strategically matching the shape of the printed text on the left-hand page with that of the picture on the right (this occurs just three times, when the question of body image comes to the fore), Bemelmans creates graphic schemata that reinforce the textual message and its psychological import.

Noodle learns from the dog fairy that he will be granted his wish but that he must choose his new size and shape within just a few hours. This "time limit" comments wryly on the gap (previously discussed) between children's and adults' experience of the passage of time. After visiting a nearby zoo and interviewing several of the animals there as to their feelings about *their* various sizes and shapes, Noodle returns home, where, like an ordinary toddler, he eats his lunch and then settles down to take his afternoon nap. By having him query a male zebra first, then a married female hippopotamus, then an unmarried female ostrich, and finally a male giraffe, Munro Leaf makes explicit the relevance of gender to each child's gradual sorting out of bodily identity. Finally, when the dog fairy returns with her whirr and her buzz and her flip-flap of wings to grant him his wish, Noodle tells her he has decided to remain "Just exactly the size and shape I am *right now.*"

Thus, an elastic message of reassurance (Noodle stretches, metaphorically, but returns to his original state) occurs here in a context of whimsy and warmth. Bemelmans's art, despite its sophistication, reminds us uncannily of children's own linear drawings. Older children, who continue to enjoy this book, often come to associate it with other tales involving wishes and fairies and to appreciate its poetic devices, such as alliteration and onomatopoeia, which strengthen the effect of its urgent, ongoing theme and variations.

The Story of Ferdinand

The intense black-and-white line drawings of *The Story of Ferdinand* are designed with an elegance that works magic, taking small boys and girls both out of and deeply into the recesses of their inner selves. I have never met anyone who, having once encountered this book, was able to forget it. Everyone, moreover, recalls it with affection.

The first page presents an exotic image of a faraway castle in Spain—the time-honored metaphor for what is greatly desired but seemingly unattainable. Page two, by contrast, zooms in on the protagonist, an endearing young calf absorbed in regarding a wild flower on which a butterfly has momentarily alighted. Unlike the other lusty young male animals of his species, who snort, cavort, jump, and butt, Ferdinand prefers sitting quietly under a cork tree just smelling the flowers.

Like many children, however, Ferdinand has a concerned mother. Seeing him across the pasture alone in his favorite spot, she worries about him and asks him why he does not play with the other young bulls. Ferdinand shakes his head and pushes her away gently with his hoof. This tender image, by marking the outline of Ferdinand's beloved cork tree, makes patent, in the form of a black line that bisects the page, the invisible psychic barrier that exists between a child and his or her solicitous mother. Ferdinand's good and sensitive mother simply withdraws at this point; graciously and wisely, she leaves her son alone. As she does so, departing to the tinkle of her bell inscribed "MOTHER," the shadow she makes on the grass mirrors that cast by the tree under which Ferdinand sits. Thus, pictorially but not verbally, an important message is conveyed: namely, that by allowing her child the

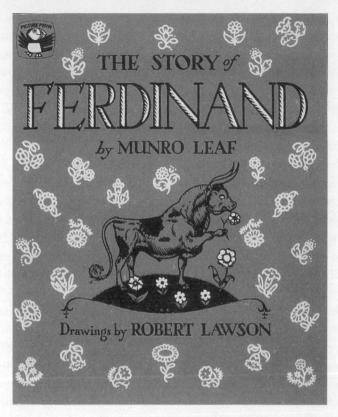

From *The Story of Ferdinand* by Munro Leaf. Copyright © 1936 by
Munro Leaf and Robert Lawson, renewed 1964 by Munro Leaf
and John W. Boyd. Used by permission of Viking Penguin,
a division of Penguin Putnam Inc.

freedom to be what he wishes and needs to be, this mother does not
rupture her bond with him but, rather, preserves it. Respecting his privacy, not violating it, she strengthens and protects him. Her recogni-
tion of his individuality and her ongoing love for him, despite his push
away, make the story's eventual denouement psychologically possible.

Ferdinand grows bigger, and, as is true for many human children,
his changes in height are recorded each year—in his case, by grooves

carved into the trunk of a tree. After some time, five men come to the meadow to pick the biggest, roughest bull for the bullfights in Madrid. On a tautly designed page, we are shown close-ups of these strange judges. Each one wears a bizarre and distinctive hat, and their inscrutable, vaguely menacing faces capture en masse the eerie sensation that the sight of unfamiliar adults can arouse in children. Even close up, they remain mysterious. They are quintessential aliens with the power to strike terror.

Whereas the other young bulls vie to attract the attention of these men, Ferdinand retires to his beloved cork tree to sit quietly and smell the flowers. But wait! Suddenly, in a zoom-lens image, he lowers himself upon a startled bee who stings him instantly. We see his hind legs kick into the air in an electric image. We can almost hear his bellow, his snort of surprise and pain. When the strangely hatted men see his leap, they mistake him as being fierce, and we watch sadly as they cart him away, dejected, for the bullfights in Madrid.

Ferdinand of course refuses to fight. Despite the provocations of the banderilleros, picadors, and even the matador, whose costumes are prefigured by the men in strange hats, the young bull maintains his own boundaries as he once did vis-à-vis his mother. Like her love, those boundaries of body and self remain intact. He simply sits in the center of the ring and smells the ladies' flowers. Gentle by nature, not tempted by violence into violence, he survives. In the end he is returned to his cork tree in the meadow, where, in peaceful contemplation, he remains.

Crossing gender lines by means of a character to whom both boys and girls can relate, this book condenses wisdom made theoretically explicit nearly a half-century later by psychoanalysts Margaret S. Mahler, Fred Pine, and Anni Bergman (1975) in their research on the separation-individuation process as it occurs between mothers and children. Yet a disquieting undercurrent persists here in the black silhouette of Ferdinand, who faces away from us under his tree. This image may unintentionally betray a measure of sadness, belying the book's final words, "He is very happy." I wonder whether, in trying to valorize a position that is not the norm, to purvey the message that it is all right to be yourself—in this case, to be a gentle, nonbellicose male—this wise old book leaves some sensitive children knowing uncomfortably that the road for those who defy social (and gender) stereotypes is never easy, despite a loving mother and an early victory.

Horton Hatches the Egg

Another book that defies gender stereotypes appeared just four years after *Ferdinand*. Published, therefore, after the outbreak of World War II but before most Americans had any inkling of their forthcoming involvement in it, this book by Dr. Seuss deserves to be seen as an avant-garde work in the literature for small children. Memorable for its oft-quoted refrain:

> I meant what I said
> And I said what I meant
> An elephant's faithful
> One hundred percent,

Horton pulls no punches; it zestfully and unabashedly makes use of every device imaginable—rhythms and rhymes, zany illustrations, humor, pathos, suspense, and empathy—to treat a question of perennial fascination to children: where do babies come from, and what are mommy's and daddy's respective roles in the reproductive process? It not only gives no biologically intelligible answers to these questions but also treats them as open to construction, possibility, and imagination. As revolutionary as this book was in 1940, it is no less so today, when the issues it implicates are in the forefront of public debate and even legal action.

A silly, lazy bird whose name, Mayzie, rhymes with her most salient personal quality, has laid an egg in her nest but feels bored, uninvolved, and restless as she sits on it day after day. When an elephant named Horton passes by her tree, she pleads with him to take her place for a while and sit on her egg while she goes off to Palm Beach to have a vacation in the sun. Unsure of his ability to comply with her request,

From *Horton Hatches the Egg* by Dr. Seuss. Trademark and copyright
© 1940 and renewed 1968 by Dr. Seuss Enterprises, L.P.
Reprinted by permission of Random House, Inc.

Horton hesitates, but Mayzie, reminding him of his qualities of gentleness and kindness, persuades him to stay. When he agrees ("since you insist"), she flies off with a grin and a "Toodle-oo!"

Thus Mayzie, in one fell swoop, reverses the stereotype of the all-giving, self-sacrificing mother with an almost staggering redundancy.

She is flippant and self-indulgent. Mayzie is not, however, entirely devoid of responsibility, for she conscripts a proxy before abandoning her egg, and Horton, as she shrewdly senses in advance, turns out to be an excellent bet. I wonder, even so, just how much our negative feelings toward Mayzie are conditioned not only by her manifest behavior but also by the parade of images we have internalized of her opposite—the totally absorbed, devoted mother. Does Mayzie shock us in part because we see her through scrims of grandiose, unrealistic expectation?

Several pages after she is gone, we find Horton sitting on her nest, his brow furrowed, his face puckered as rain pours down on his head and he is pelted by the high winds of a terrible storm. Mayzie, on the other hand, has arrived in Florida. Her eyes are closed in blissful tranquillity; she luxuriates on the fronds of a palm; warm sun soothes her; children play with a beach ball beneath her; striped umbrellas adorn the sand. Having such a wonderful time, she decides never to return to her nest. She is hardly the conscientious, self-sacrificing parent—or, to be precise, parent-to-be, for this book is really about pregnancy, not parenthood. Viewed in the light of current controversies over the status of a fetus; the relative rights and responsibilities of women, men, unborn children, and prenatal care, *Horton* presents a challenging picture. Radical and unsettling, it is at the same time filled with hope.

Horton, with the complications of gender, possesses the same plot structure as the Solomonic story in Kings 3:16-28 in which two prostitutes come before the King, each claiming a living child to be her own. When Solomon calls for a sword and offers to cut the baby in half so that each woman can have part of him, the woman who cries out that she would rather see the baby in the arms of her rival than dead is declared the true mother and awarded the child. *Horton* has, moreover, the same theme as a Chinese classical play, *The Circle of Chalk* (ca. 1300 A.D.), in which a concubine is similarly awarded her disputed child by the emperor because she refuses to allow harm to be done to him. Finally, *Horton* prefigures Bertolt Brecht's reconfiguring of this drama in *The Caucasian Chalk Circle* of 1944-45, in which Grusha, a serving girl, saves the life of a baby boy abandoned by the governor's wife during a palace upheaval. After caring for him at great risk to herself, Grusha is asked to return the baby to his birth mother. The judge Azdak places the child in a circle on the ground, and when Grusha refuses to pull him out for fear of hurting him, declares her the rightful parent. The final lines of Brecht's play could well be a motto for *Horton* as well:

> Take note what men of old concluded:
> That what there is shall go to those who are good for it,
> Thus: the children to the motherly, that they prosper
> The carts to good drivers, that they are driven well
> And the valley to the waterers, that it bring forth fruit.
>
> (Brecht 1947, p. 189)

Here, in a startling equation, the male elephant Horton takes the place of the prostitute or the concubine in the ancient versions. Shortly, in this chapter, I will look at another book in which masculinity and femininity are remapped in reverse (*Willy the Wimp*), and the place of a male coward is filled by a girl. In *Horton*, the loving, loyal role normally given to a woman is filled by a male. Common to both equations, despite their manifest difference, is that in each, the female character is portrayed in a derogatory way.

Horton, unlike Mayzie, makes a commitment. Promising to sit on her egg and to keep it warm until her return, the kindly, awkward, massive elephant props up her tree with forked branches so that it will withstand his bulk and then settles himself down on the nest to wait as long as necessary:

> And he sat
> and he sat
> and he sat
> and he sat

—a uniquely female experience during gestation. Icy snow and sleet assail him, and we see poor Horton whitened, icicles pendant from his ears and trunk. Friends mock and tease him. Hunters come with rifles to attack him and end up capturing him and selling him to a circus. Thus, he suffers adversity on the part of natural forces, through "human" derision, and by being the victim of overt aggression. A Promethean or Christlike figure, he is scorned and sold. While listening to *Horton*, young children who know Babar will recall him as another beloved elephant who likewise was sold to a circus and humiliated. But unlike Horton, who is displayed to the jeering hordes as a curiosity, King Babar is forced to perform in costume for circus crowds and to sleep in a narrow stable of straw "like a donkey" (see *The Travels of Babar*).

When the circus lands in Palm Beach, Mayzie and Horton confront each other again. Just as they are disputing whose egg it is, the shell cracks, bursts, and a little creature hatches out. The newborn has not only wings but also an elephant's ears, tail, and trunk; because of Horton's faithfulness to it, it resembles him. The people cheer and send Horton home with his little elephant-bird, who perches cozily on his waving trunk. Like Ferdinand, Horton is happy. "Happy,/One hundred per cent!"

But the last picture of Mayzie remains disturbing. Shunted off to one side, the neglectful mother looks ugly, mean, and angry. Her punishment fits her crime. Having abandoned her nest, she is now excluded. And her banishment mars the happiness of the final scene. Ultimately, this is an either/or story in which one parent (here, surprisingly, the "father") is good and the other distinctly bad. The tale ends with no integration of parental roles. And yet that would be desirable, especially for little girl readers, whose feelings about this story may be highly complex.

Wee Gillis

After a lecture I gave a year or two ago, a distinguished elder physician came over to show me a threadbare 1938 copy of *Wee Gillis* inscribed in uppercase letters on a dizzy slant with his name, "*STANLEY*." This tattered object, he reported with pride, was his all-time favorite chil-

From *Wee Gillis* by Munro Leaf, illustrated by Robert Lawson.
Copyright © 1938 by Munro Leaf and Robert Lawson, renewed
1966 by Munro Leaf and John W. Boyd, Executor of the Estate
of Robert Lawson. Used by permission of Viking Penguin,
a division of Penguin Putnam Inc.

dren's book. As in *Ferdinand*, we are gifted with the artistry of Robert
Lawson. We have the play of near and far, the careful placing of image
on page, the sense of being taken deep inside the psyche while vast out-
door spaces are being negotiated. In this book, a young Scottish boy
must choose between being like his mother's Lowland relatives (who

drive longhaired cows through the mists) or his father's Highland relations (who stalk stags among craggy hills of heather and thistle).

The story of *Wee Gillis* encapsulates every child's struggle to find a way to be like both parents, who are themselves different from each other, and yet to be different from each of them as well. To be original. To be oneself. As his mother's relations berate his father's and vice versa, Wee Gillis watches and listens to all the voices. He decides to spend successive years in the Lowlands and in the Highlands, just to try things out. During the period he lives with his mother's clan, he eats a heaping bowlful of oatmeal each morning—a ritual he repeats in a nearly identical scene later on in the Highlands, where the only change is that the cattle horns on the wall have been replaced by antlers. Thus, the repeated breakfast scene establishes a pictorial continuity between his two parents, who are never themselves actually depicted. And, as we have seen so many times, the fact that the boy's parents do not appear graphically within the pages of the book works psychologically to open a fertile field of projection for the child encountering it.

Wee Gillis's lungs grow strong from shouting for the cows through the heavy mists in the Lowlands. We observe him in a delicate drawing composed of thousands of tiny dashes and hatches, no line longer than an eighth of an inch. The following year, he travels up to the Highlands and must hold his breath for hours as he learns to keep perfectly still so as not to frighten the stags. His body develops year in and year out as he alternates between parental domains, and his lungs grow incredibly strong.

At last, his Uncle Andrew from his mother's clan and his Uncle Angus from his father's side go with him to a medium-sized hill halfway between the Highlands and the Lowlands, where he must choose his destiny forever. In a brilliant pictorial accelerando, Wee Gillis's opposing uncles plead, demand, grow angry, and finally turn abusive. Suddenly, they notice that a large stranger has appeared and is sitting silently on a rock nearby with something beside him. As they watch, he picks it up—an enormous sack with sticks protruding. The stranger closes his eyes, takes a big breath, and blows into it. Nothing happens, and the man almost weeps because, as it turns out, he is a bagpiper who has made himself a new instrument that is simply too large to play. Although the uncles try one by one, eager to outdo each other and to prove their relative strength to Wee Gillis, each fails.

Now, at this sensitive moment, the text and pictures marvelously conspire to capture every child's shy unspoken wish: "because Wee Gillis looked so *wanting-to*, the large man asked him if he would like to try. / Wee Gillis said: 'Aye,' so he did."

Using his body as he has developed it through both the paternal and maternal identifications, the boy holds his breath as he had learned to do when stalking the stags in his father's territory in the Highlands. Then, in repeat images, he blows with all his might as he had learned to do when calling the longhaired cows with his mother's relations in the Lowlands. His uncles fall off their rocks with surprise as the bagpipes fill with air and an enormous screech breaks forth. The large man teaches the boy how to make music, "and now Wee Gillis is welcome down in the Lowlands and up in the Highlands, but most of the time he just stays in his house halfway up the side of a medium-sized hill and plays THE BIGGEST BAGPIPES IN ALL SCOTLAND."

In this marvelously inventive picture book, art—music—is thus proposed as a solution, a means of resolving inner conflict. The child, having internalized strengths gained from both parents, creates something utterly new, something that is fully his own and that sets an example for the future. On the final page, a new generation of children watches admiringly while Wee Gillis, like Orpheus with his lyre, plays his bagpipes. Originally made sixty years ago, this small masterpiece seems even more poignant today, when so many children must find a way to make music out of the discord they encounter daily in the lives of their families.

Madeline

Two years before Pearl Harbor, a picture book about a little girl who lived in Paris was published. Madeline is arguably still the most beloved female character in picture books. Her creator, Ludwig Bemelmans, was a painter living in France before the war and had a daughter named Barbara about the same age as his heroine. He himself had, after a road accident, experienced a brief stay in a French hospital. A half-century later, adults who grew up with Madeline still have her indelibly fixed in some ivied *hôtel-de-ville* of their imaginations. More in vogue than ever, she reappeared a few years ago in stores all over the country as a little rag doll, scar and all.

Beyond chantable rhymed couplets and whimsical drawings, *Madeline*'s longevity must be traced to its uncanny grasp of the inner life of children. It parlays subliminal messages that both reflect and perpetuate longstanding cultural myths about the feminine gender.

The book begins in an old vine-covered house in Paris in which twelve little girls live together with Nurse Clavel. A *dozen* little girls — surely, a highly significant number, especially in the setting of a convent school. They break their bread, brush their teeth, sleep, and do everything else in two straight lines. They all conform to the expected pattern: submission, passivity, cleanliness, and order. Notably, if one were to choose three activities in which to depict little boys, I doubt they would be eating, tooth-brushing, and sleeping. Bemelmans, of course, should not be held accountable for the broader cultural meanings of his choices for conscious artistic decisions carry a valence that, in the wide swath of cultural context, remains open to ongoing interpretation.

The girls smile at the good and frown at the bad. In Paris, in front of the rounded arches of L'Opéra, they are taught that giving, nurturing, feeding, and extending kindness to animals are desiderata. The person in this picture whom the girls are supposed to emulate is gendered feminine. In the Place Vendôme, by contrast, beneath the looming phallic obelisk, evil is gendered masculine. And the sort of evil it is — stealing — is the very sort of acting out that has long been associated in the clinical literature with female perversions. By contrast, on the manifest level (also not without import), it is a dangerous *man* who is depicted as having stolen what might be (mis)taken for a wealthy woman's handbag.

On the page that tells us that the girls were sometimes very sad, a soldier limps by on crutches, thereby eliciting their sympathy. The image of the man with a wounded, bandaged foot is reminiscent of a syndrome that has been described in clinical literature whereby certain women who are plagued by the unconscious envy of men and by accompanying wishes to harm and mutilate them can permit themselves to love only damaged men, men who are in some way maimed or inferior (one thinks, in this context, of Jane Eyre and Rochester).

On the next pages, we see the girls walking in two straight lines with umbrellas and balloons in rain and shine, respectively. And we are reminded that weather, as so often in literature, transparently externalizes the inner moods of characters.

Madeline is the smallest. Clearly, this is a desirable characteristic for girls: "small" being a code word for insignificant, dependent, and nonthreatening. She is not, however, we are told, afraid of mice, and at this point the heroine's reversal of gender stereotype begins: females are *supposed* to be afraid of mice. In fact, another little girl in the accompanying illustration has climbed up on a chair in terror, thus instantiating the paradigm that Madeline rejects.

She loves the wintertime, with its snow and ice. By skating merrily along among the snowflakes, Madeline rebels yet again, for women in our culture are traditionally supposed to prefer cozy warm indoor spaces that surround the hearth over the rugged elements. (This idea can be traced back to ancient Greece; think, for example, of Euripides' *Bacchae*.) On a visit to the zoo, Madeline coolly pooh-poohs the toothy tiger, while the other girls cling fearfully to the skirts of their nun. Miss Clavel's tent-like image as she shelters them in this picture has always seemed like that of a madonna. But at some moments Miss Clavel illustrates the childhood fantasy of the perfectly asexual mother. Under duress, later in the story, she acquires an unmistakably phallic shape.

While fishermen placidly await their catch on the banks of the Seine in the next picture, daredevil Madeline teeters on the edge of the Pont Neuf. Frightening the nun with her derring-do, our small heroine now seems ripe, after this display, for some kind of comeuppance. Little girls cannot be allowed this much deviation from the norm. So, in the middle of the night, Miss Clavel is suddenly awakened and, fearing that something is amiss, turns on her light.

Sitting up in bed, Madeline cries and cries. A doctor is called in, a cue that whatever punishment fate decides to mete out to this feisty little girl will be played out on the stage of her own body. This is of more than passing psychological interest, because for girls and women in our culture it is often the body of the self rather than that of another or the external world (as in *Angry Arthur*) that becomes the locus for enactments of fantasy and aggression.

At the phone, the doctor dials "DANton-ten-six" and tells the nurse that it is an appendix. This phone number has always seemed to me a reference to the French Revolution, to the insurrectionist Danton who, like Madeline, rebelled and was put down for it. Danton is famous for his rousing lines: "Il nous faut de l'audace, encore de l'audace, et toujours de l'audace, et la France est sauvée." (We must have boldness, more boldness, and always boldness, and then France will be saved.)

All the little girls cry as Madeline departs in the arms of the doctor. In this dramatic illustration, the defiant little girl has become a true victim. Limp and passive, she finally incarnates a feminine gender ideal, one who is carried helpless *down* the stairs in the arms of a strong male figure. She may remind some readers of the paradigm image of Scarlett O'Hara as she is carried *up* the stairs by Rhett Butler in the movie version of *Gone with the Wind*, which coincidentally appeared in precisely the same year that *Madeline* was first published.

The juxtaposition of the next two drawings wonderfully conveys the way the passage of time, or its eclipse, is experienced by a traumatized child. On the left, we see a white ambulance, with its red light, screeching past the Eiffel Tower as it speeds through the darkness to the hospital. On the right, we see what Madeline saw when she awoke two hours later. Martyred now and thus totally feminized, she is here, in her absence, represented by gender-coded props: a vase of flowers and a lacy curtain.

A smiling nurse brings in her food on a tray, and we are explicitly shown the crank on her hospital bed—an apparatus of unfailing fascination to every child who encounters one. Furthermore, the cracks on her ceiling look precisely like a rabbit. In portraying this, Bemelmans sums up with graphic genius the many tedious hours of lying on one's back staring at the ceiling, hours that are implicit in nearly everyone's hospital experience.

Ten days pass quickly by, and one bright morning Miss Clavel decides that it would be a fine day for the girls to visit Madeline. They buy flowers from a vendor's cart near a typical Parisian kiosk, and each child carries one large daisy, her round face solemn under its beribboned straw hat. Tiptoeing in, they all say "Ahhh" when they see Madeline surrounded by toys, candy, and a dollhouse from her Papa.

The image of Madeline in her bed surrounded by her trophies can be read as a rather graphic depiction of the rewards a girl may receive (from her father and, by association, later in life from other male admirers) for assuming her designated gender role. Associations abound to the candy, flowers, gifts, and "toys" that will come to her in the future from other men. Recall Manet's *Olympia*, in which we see an erotically posed woman on a bed about to receive a gift of flowers sent, we can imagine, by some grateful or would-be suitor.

And now the pièce de résistance: Madeline stands up on her bed and, in a theatrical gesture, raises her polka-dotted pajama top to reveal her scar to her astonished schoolmates. The aptness of this image is that it not only provides the mise-en-scène that has so often been pointed out by authors writing about perverse scenarios (see Kaplan 1992; McDougall 1982); it also plays on the confusions of little girls about their own bodies, about the actual location and description of their genitals.

The little girls say goodbye to Madeline and leave in the rain. Once more, feelings are externalized as weather. Again they return home and break their bread, brush their teeth, and go to bed. But this time all their faces bear frowns: nothing can ever be quite the same.

In the middle of the night, Miss Clavel is again awakened and turns on her light. Again, something is not right. At this point, the child attending to the story may become mesmerized by the sight of the mother nun metamorphosing into a terrifying, elongated, black diagonal shape. Miss Clavel, fearing disaster, runs fast and faster. She asks the children to say what is troubling them. And all the little girls cry out that each one wants to have her appendix out too.

On the final page, print that gets smaller and smaller as we read toward the bottom tells us that Miss Clavel bids the little girls goodnight and thanks the Lord that they are well. She tells them to go to sleep, turns out the light, closes the door, and then, the text says: "and that's all there is—there isn't any more."

Or is there? In this enchanting book subliminal messages abound about ways of perceiving the world and of being in the world. A work of art of this stature remains ever open to ongoing interpretation. Each interpretive lens applied to it will add a layer of richness to our experience of it, and no reading should be taken as a warrant for abandoning others. I hope that a deeply psychological reading such as the one I have provided will awaken the reader to unexamined assumptions of his or her own as well as to those embedded in its pages. My goal, however, is to encourage all readers to continue to read and cherish *Madeline*—which remains, as ever, charming, wise, and brilliant, but like all important and influential works of art deserves to be questioned as well as adored.

To study *Madeline* in this way is to confront the enduring rigidity of our gender ideals, their pugnacious tenacity, and their viselike grip on us—a grip that has scarcely relaxed throughout the course of this turbulent century, as we have moved from catastrophic war to restless peace and back again to war, and from generosity and tolerance back again now to nostalgic moralisms and myopias.

Willy the Wimp

As I have shown, many famous and popular picture books available throughout the United States characterize little boys as naughty, oppositional, and adventurous. One thinks of the flagrantly disobedient

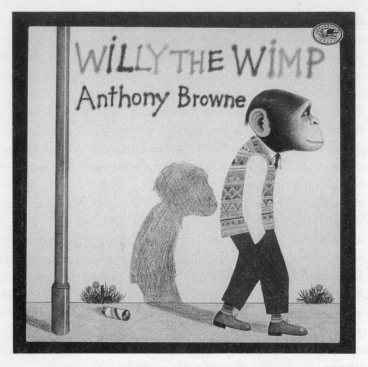

From *Willy the Wimp* by Anthony Browne. Copyright © 1984 by
Anthony Browne. Reprinted by permission of Pantheon Books,
a division of Random House.

Peter Rabbit, of the devilish little Squirrel Nutkin, of the venturesome
yellow duck Ping, of notorious Max with his wild things, of Pierre and
the hungry lion, Harold and his purple crayon, angry Arthur. It is no
news that boys in our culture learn early on the unacceptability of their
so-called feminine wishes; they are taught to feel ambivalent, for example, about gentleness.

Willy the Wimp, written and illustrated by Anthony Browne in 1984,
explores this motif in complex ways. I write about it not to recommend
it but to interpret it, because, to my amazement, I have discovered that
it has achieved a high level of popularity.

The title page is broken through by a fist, indicating that aggression will figure as a prominent theme. And to emphasize the link between aggression and gender, I note that "willy" is slang for penis. The protagonist, a pale, stoop-shouldered young chimpanzee, is dressed in an argyle sweater, polka-dot tie, striped pants, and shiny brown-laced shoes. We are introduced to him by the words, "Willy wouldn't hurt a fly." Gentle and polite to a fault, Willy does not shoo away the insect that buzzes in his face, and he avoids stepping on other insects when he walks. He even says "I'm sorry" when others inconsiderately knock into him. Thus, right from the start, the qualities of gentleness, reticence, and the abhorrence of cruelty are caricatured by exaggeration, made to seem ridiculous. Young children are encouraged to laugh at Willy while also, of course, identifying with him as an (anti)hero whose reactions mirror the genuine feelings of many little boys. Children are, in other words, compelled, while laughing at him, to repudiate a part of their own genuine feelings.

When a large gorilla rudely jostles him on the street, Willy apologizes, although what has happened is clearly not his fault. What sort of message is conveyed here? The ability of a child to say the words "I'm sorry"—that is, to express regret—indicates an acceptance of responsibility and an acknowledgement of possible complicity in the face of wrongdoing. It represents a major developmental achievement, for it signifies that the same child who, at a previous stage, needed to project all badness outward and preserve himself as entirely good can now acknowledge his own capacity for harm and accept both the badness and the goodness that coexist within him. Saying and meaning "I'm sorry" are, as we saw in *The Accident*, extremely important in the moral life of a child. By caricaturing Willy's apologetic stance and making fun of his tendency to say "I'm sorry," the text here works against the tide of early moral development. In the interest of humor, it burlesques and covertly undermines the agendas of other children's books that elicit empathy and push their young readers toward higher levels of moral awareness. One outstanding such book, also featuring male characters, is Dr. Seuss's *Bartholomew and the Oobleck*. There, humor contributes to a humane message: the protagonist teaches a silly, selfish monarch that even kings must learn to say the magic words "I'm sorry." On the other hand, Willy's apology to a telephone pole at the end of *Willy the Wimp* renders the phrase nonsensical.

At night under stars and a full moon, a black cityscape serves as backdrop, and Willy is harassed by a "suburban gorilla gang" whose members call him a wimp. The biggest attacking gorilla has Willy's neck in a viselike grip while another restrains his hands behind his back. Through the imagery alone, not the words, we see how insidiously messages about gender can slide into messages about race. What we observe is a gang of big, tough, black kids who are beating up on a sissy white boy. Or perhaps, as one African-American colleague pointed out to me, this image can be read as dark-skinned black kids attacking a lighter-skinned black boy. In any case, there can be no escaping the racial slur. The gorillas have much darker skins than Willy, and they are dressed differently. In contrast to his preppy look, they sport cool jeans, denim jackets, sneakers, and distinctive red hats.

Back home after this attack, the little chimpanzee sinks into a pink armchair. More than the physical assault, what rankles is the humiliation of having been called a "wimp." This sheds light on the deep level of denial that smolders in the words of the old playground rhyme: "Sticks and stones can break my bones, but names will never hurt me." Willy's wounded feelings remind us that words can and do hurt. Even nicknames conferred by others, rarely chosen by the named, possess a strange potency and cannot easily be evaded. "Willy the Wimp," of course, combines sexual insult with its general offensiveness.

Ensconced in his pink armchair, Willy holds a comic book with an end-cover picture of a character who is not precisely Superman but a kind of "Super Gorilla," a pictorial detail that is never mentioned in the text but that can be read as emblematic of the book as a whole. This animal Superman flexes his biceps in a menacing gesture and looks as though he is about to zoom off the cover. His canonical blue, red, and gold suit bring to mind Superman's alter ego, the mild-mannered, bespectacled Clark Kent. Unremarked in words—and therefore needing to be pointed out explicitly to children by a reading adult—this tiny image symbolically encapsulates a central theme of this entire book, namely, the uncertain relations between masculine strength and tenderness, between bravery and faintheartedness, between what is on the outside and what is within.

Willy spies an ad in the comic book. Adjacent to a drawing of a brawny, grinning gorilla, bold black letters read: "DON'T BE A WIMP! MAIL THIS NOW!" Immediately, he sends away for the promised instruction manual, and over the next twelve pages, this self-deprecatory little chimpanzee makes heroic efforts to refashion himself to conform to the masculine gender ideal. He jogs daily and adheres to a phallic diet of all bananas. He learns how to fight, works out at a body-building club, takes up weight lifting. We watch him grow larger, darker, and hairier. Finally, when "Willy looked in the mirror," Browne writes, "He liked what he saw." What, however, does Willy see?

Pale yellow daffodils adorn the wallpaper that surrounds this great new macho Willy. Do they perhaps betoken a symbolic feminine presence that cannot be entirely exorcised? Meanwhile, his former self, shy and stoop-shouldered, persists imagistically in the form of a black-and-white photograph that rests unobtrusively on the bureau next to the mirror. Through these details, the picture belies or expands the meaning of the accompanying text. Within the range of Willy's gaze was not merely his tough new gorilla-self but also the old chimpanzee self and the flowers. Or should we take him at that moment to be blind to these reminders, so that the details work only on the readers, like a species of visual irony? At the centerpoint of the page our gaze meets Willy's genital area clothed in fire-red jockey briefs—a visual reference to the hats of his bullies earlier on and a sign that his nickname no longer holds.

Suddenly, in an uncanny repeat scene of the gorillas' attack on Willy, the place of the helpless, victimized little *boy* is taken by a *girl*. Instead of Willy, little Milly is held now in a viselike grip by the gorilla gang leader, who also grabs her purse. The visual equation is patent: the passive, helpless, vulnerable position is gendered feminine: wimp equals girl. On the following page, Milly has been left on the ground by the gorillas, who are running away. We notice Willy's looming shadow in the foreground and presume that it is he who has sent them fleeing. *By being able to scare, Willy has changed from a wimp into a hero.* Big, strong, and alarming now, he attracts the girl, and, on the next page, we see Milly covering his face with lipstick kisses in gratitude for her rescue.

Willy now marches cockily down the street smiling to himself that he is truly a hero, no longer a wimp. On the final page of the book, however, he bumps absentmindedly into a telephone pole, whereupon he shrinks back instantly to his original size. His last words are addressed to the pole: "I'm sorry!"

What actually happens here? However one reads this book, its brazen promulgation of a prevalent macho ideology, not to mention its insidious visual promotion of racial urban stereotypes, cannot be evaded. Irony, as I have suggested, is a mode appropriate to adults whose attitudes are securely formed, but it can be easily misunderstood by young children, whose values and beliefs are still being formed. Our culture continues to perpetuate the notion that to be worthwhile, lovable, and effective as a human being, a man requires prodigious physical strength and a frightening demeanor. At the same time, we fear and disdain this image. Little Willy, despite his concerted efforts, fails in the end to achieve his goal. His outside has changed, but his inside, apparently, has not. He is therefore portrayed as ridiculous.

To summon the Superman image, however, may possibly be to suggest a solution—one in which outside and inside do indeed differ from one another but coexist as legitimate aspects of masculinity. The mild Clark Kent, flinging open his jacket to reveal the bulging muscles and iconic *S* of his alter ego, suggests a reading of this picture book that valorizes *both* aspects of a little boy's persona, tough and gentle, but without mockery of either. This message, however, is one that any parent prepared to read this book to a child must supply in conversation. It is a message that appears only covertly in these pages and one that, if it is conveyed at all, comes garbled with other confusing messages that require considerable unraveling.

As this picture book reveals, a small boy, when striving to live up to narrowly conceived ideals of masculine appearance and behavior, often retains a host of feelings that may not find outlets in socially valorized norms. Within the book's pages such feelings are permissible. But at the same time, a complex cultural object such as this is clearly riddled with ambivalence and needs in various creative ways to be resisted. For however one may decide to interpret its bewildering takes on masculinity, its racial prejudice and gender bias are frighteningly clear.

Dandelion

Dandelion (1964), by Don Freeman, is the story of a thick-maned lion who, when invited to a party by a giraffe, gets himself so bedecked for the event that his hostess fails to recognize him and slams the door in his face. The invitation she has sent out reads: "Come as you are," an instruction that, as one little girl who heard the story pointed out matter-of-factly but not unsympathetically, the lion does not obey: "He didn't come like he was, like the invitation said to." He was punished, in other words, for not following directions.

Jennifer Giraffe's invitation resonates strongly with small children because, as we saw in *The Tale of Tom Kitten*, dressing up for special occasions can be fun for them but at the same time a source of potential discomfort and distress. Partly, this discomfort occurs because the fancy clothes require an altered standard of behavior. By telling her guests to "come as they are," the giraffe hostess means to convey an initial message of self-acceptance: "just be yourself." You need not, in other words, disguise yourself and adopt a different persona in order to engage in social activities. You do not have to walk on your hind legs only, as in the *The Tale of Tom Kitten*.

Dandelion, whose name of course is a pun that will need to be pointed out initially to the youngest child, does just that. He goes to his barber and gets himself all dandied up for the party. What is fascinating here is that, as we watch Dandelion being transformed—his hair shampooed by a male kangaroo; his nails manicured by a female rabbit; his mane frizzed, curled on rollers, stylishly coiffed by the kangaroo—

the illustrations evoke less a barber shop than a beauty salon. When this book was read to four-year-olds in Cambridge, Massachusetts, several of the children became confused about Dandelion's gender after his hair was styled. Although most of the little girls were willing to continue to recognize him as male, one little boy declared with certainty: "He's (*sic*) a girl!" The unreflective use of the masculine pronoun in this pronouncement of altered gender designation reveals the confusion that attends it. I also find it significant that a boy rather than the girls could not accept Dandelion's continued masculinity in spite of his newly "feminized" appearance. Without overinterpreting such a minor event, it seems to me that this difference in part reflects the effort made in our culture to teach boys very early on to dissociate themselves from anything remotely "feminine," whereas we tolerate a far wider range of cross-gender identifications in girls. A girl need not be ashamed of wearing her brother's jeans, but a boy cannot walk outdoors wearing his sister's skirt. This idiosyncratic cultural discrepancy is absorbed at a tender age, and I think it accounts for boys' discomfort at such moments relative to girls'. Parenthetically, four-year-old children who listened to *Willy the Wimp* also expressed, on occasion, a similar uncertainty about his gender. In relation to the dark-skinned larger-bodied gorillas, for example, on several pages they saw Willy as feminine. "Now he's a girl," said one boy about a picture in which Willy, shown wearing striped tights, kicks his leg in an aerobics class. This subject of gender is, arguably, the central aspect of every child's identity.

An argument could be made in favor of books that in fact complicate gender imagery and do not buy immediately into the stereotypical representations. By making children encountering a picture book unsure of how to categorize the representation, unsure whether a given character is a girl or boy, the book forces them to question and ponder the matter. Gender becomes an issue that can no longer be taken for granted. At the same time, however, there is something to be said for secure perception, for feeling that you can accurately apply the information you have acquired, especially at the beginning of knowledge.

The musical *The King and I* (1951) by Richard Rodgers and Oscar Hammerstein II has an especially delightful passage in which the King of Siam betrays his uncertainty about what he "absolutely knows" and his confusion about conclusions that he concluded long ago. But this royal state of epistemological doubt, which may be healthy albeit stressful for too-complacent middle-aged adults, is probably not the optimal one for very young children, who are continually being propelled into it by their own naïveté. A fine, but perhaps wiggly, line needs to be drawn here. Whereas I have little patience for books that offer pat, simplistic answers (books that can be read once but do not summon us back), I would tend likewise to turn away from books that actively confuse children. After all, the overriding agenda for a picture book is to please and to comfort, as well as to instruct. These books, most often read at bedtime or to calm children when they need it, should generally not introduce messages so unsettling as to belie this ulterior purpose.

What happens to Dandelion is that, after Jennifer Giraffe closes the door on him, a storm blows up. In the wind and rain, his curls and elegant finery are soaked and spoiled. He sits down on a step and waits to dry off after the downpour. When he makes a second attempt and rings the doorbell again, he looks much more like his usual self. The giraffe answers the bell, and this time she greets him with warmth. She tells him that they have all been waiting for him. Later, over tea and taffy, she describes the silly-looking lion who had come to the door earlier on, and Dandelion, laughing, admits that it was he. Jennifer Giraffe, upon hearing this, becomes so flustered that she entangles herself in her long pearl necklace and apologizes in embarrassment for not having recognized her friend. The book ends a bit like *Noodle*, with Dandelion promising that "From now on I'll always be just plain me!"

One detail here unobtrusively conveys a message about gender difference in our culture. Dandelion is enjoined to come as he is. When he ignores that injunction and tries to pretty himself up, he is, as we have seen, rejected, humiliated, and abandoned. He is accepted only when he looks ordinary and down-to-earth. But what about Jennifer

Giraffe? Surely she does not wear a long strand of pearls every day. No, *she* is clearly "dressed up" for the party, and her ornamentation is not only illustrated but also specifically mentioned in the text—mentioned, however, in passing, with no comment on its implicit gender discrepancy. It is precisely this sort of unremarked discrepancy that supplies the context in which four-year-old girls can accept Dandelion as himself even when he is dressed up whereas little boys cannot as readily do so, for they have been made wary and anxious lest a dramatic change in appearance betray the possibility of deeper, more threatening changes.

Before leaving *Dandelion*, there is another point that deserves comment. The lion, after all, goes to enormous lengths to please his hostess, to make himself handsome for her, to obtain a bouquet for her, but then, when he arrives at her door, she rudely rejects him. This scene, which occurs at midpoint in the story, is painful and disturbing. To be rejected by one's friend on the basis of one's appearance, to be turned away, to feel that one's efforts to please have met with disapproval, is a blow to one's self esteem. And in this case, it is the lion's physical self that is at stake—it is his body that has been spurned. Several four-year-olds, when this moment in the story arrived, were asked what *they* would do if their friend would not let them in. Each child became quite emotionally involved and agitated. One little girl began to shout: "If I were him, I would say, 'Hey! Come on! Come on! It's *me!*'" Two other children saw the situation as a problem that needed to be solved by just getting themselves past the closed door and inside the friend's house. One, probably with Santa Claus and the big bad wolf in mind, announced that he would sneak down the chimney. Another dismissed that plan as unrealistic and said: "I wouldn't do that; I'd hide in the basement and come up!" When confronted with the ongoing unsolved problem—namely, that their hostess still would not be able to recognize them—they seemed baffled and could not come up with a solution that would assure their acceptance. It was as if they believed that, if they could just somehow get inside the friend's door, acceptance would be automatic. And this is, after all, a wonderful way to feel. Unfortunately, however, it is clearly *not* the way all American children have been allowed to feel, especially children of color and children disadvantaged in other ways.

Corduroy

Corduroy, also by Don Freeman, is a quintessential tale of unconditional love and loyalty. Like the other books I have examined that draw upon that particular format, albeit in a variety of ways—including *The Story of Babar*, *The Runaway Bunny*, *Where the Wild Things Are*, *The Giving Tree*, and *Love You Forever*—the giver of this bountiful love is female and the recipient, male. Here, a teddy bear is cherished despite his imperfection: a button has been lost from his overalls. He sits on the shelf in a department store with other dolls and toys waiting to be chosen and taken home by a child. Yet when Lisa, an African-American girl, walks by the shelf with her mother and decides instantly, in a clear case of love at first sight, that this is the very bear she has always wanted, her mother points out his imperfection and refuses to allow her to buy him.

A group of four-year-olds, listening to *Corduroy*, were asked, upon seeing the first page—where the little bear is flanked by a clown, a white rabbit, a blonde beribboned doll, and a stuffed giraffe—which toy they would each choose if they were Lisa. At this initial point in the story, having established no loyalty yet to Corduroy, the children gave a variety of answers. Rachel wanted the doll. Another child announced unashamedly that she wanted *all* of the toys on the shelf. Only a little girl who had previously heard the story replied staunchly that she wanted Corduroy. When Lisa's mother rejects the bear on the following pages, the children were again asked this question. It was put to them in a particular way: "Would *you* buy a bear with a button missing?" Sensing now, perhaps, the unfairness, the discrimination against the title character, nearly all of the children loyally responded that, yes, they would buy the bear and that, yes, they wanted Corduroy. Only one child, a girl, held out, claiming that she wanted a new bear. I wonder whether this child's latent feelings of empathy for Corduroy's unmet need for acceptance might have been mobilized if the question had been put to her after the following page, where Lisa's mother is shown pulling her reluctant young daughter away from Corduroy, and the sad little bear is left all alone on the shelf with his one button, watching forlornly as they depart.

Notably, at this juncture in the story, Corduroy behaves differently from nearly all of the little "boys" I have discussed so far. He wants very much to be loved. This in itself is remarkable. Most of the boys in the picture books that I have considered do not need to wish for love; they are loved simply because they exist. Moreover, Corduroy does not sit around waiting for love to happen. He makes an effort to do something to make himself lovable. He does not (as in the standard "Sendak solution") attempt to triumph in fantasy over the "bad" mother who will not love him as he is (Max), or go it alone (Mickey), or pretend he doesn't care (Pierre). He does not get angry. He does not wait passively, whine, or make demands on others to help him. He does not misbehave out of disappointment. Instead, wanting love and figuring that he needs another button to achieve it, Corduroy goes off adaptively to search for one.

Apparently, children derive enormous gratification and inspiration from this active approach. When interviewed about her favorite picture books, one Harvard undergraduate, a Chinese-American student, mentioned *Corduroy* right away and praised the book for taking just this stance. She emphasized that Corduroy had tried and failed, and that he had not been content to await his fate helplessly. This, she said, was why she loved the book so much.

In search of his missing button, Corduroy wanders through the department store, mounting the escalator in two dramatically designed scenes that capture young children's endless fascination with moving stairways and evoke Babar's earlier enthrallment with a department store elevator (he rides up and down so often that the red-capped elevator boy finally has to admonish him: "This is not a toy, Mr. Elephant"). Finally, on the furniture floor, Corduroy spies a button fastened to a mattress. With all his might, he begins to pull on it. Sewn tautly, of course, into the fabric, the button springs back, sending the small bear careening head over heels into a standing lamp. When it crashes, the massive, yet kindly night watchman on patrol comes running to the spot. This watchman turns out to be a dead ringer for the ducks' beloved savior, Michael, in Robert McCloskey's classic *Make Way for Ducklings* (1941), Michael being arguably the most famous police officer in American children's literature.

The button scene in Corduroy is central. It is actually right on the button, because it captures precisely the sort of quirky and, from an adult's point of view, utterly unpredictable misapprehensions about the world that children have all the time. Young children at first do not understand what is happening on these pages, and some think that in fact Corduroy *has* found his button. When a child hearing the story actually gets to the point of being able to laugh at Corduroy's mistake, we know that a cognitive milestone has been reached. For me, the scene rings true. It brings back those hilarious "surreal" moments in James Thurber (1945) when he describes adult metaphors that he had understood concretely as a child and that therefore had seemed unintelligible to him: the man who could not put his foot down, for instance. Here, of course, the ultimate point of the scene is that Corduroy cannot have his lost button back. He cannot find it himself. The missing button needs to be supplied to him, in the end, by someone who loves him — but by someone, importantly, who loves him *without* it.

Lisa returns to the store and, with money she has saved up in her piggy bank, she purchases the stuffed bear. Thus, we learn that she too does not wait to be loved or expect the bear to be given to her; she, like Corduroy, actively pursues the object of her desire. Upon returning home, her first act of affection is to sew a new button on his overalls. As she does this, however, she speaks important words of reassurance: "I like you the way you are," she says, "but you'll be more comfortable with your shoulder strap fastened." She says, in other words, "I am not doing this because there is something wrong with you the way you are or because I myself need you to be different." Her act is unselfish. It is a gift. It is thus completely unlike, say, that of Aylmer, Nathaniel Hawthorne's despicable protagonist in his story *The Birthmark* (1846), who tries to perfect his apparently defective beloved (and who destroys her in the process). Here, little Lisa assures her bear that he is equally acceptable to *her* with or without his button but that she wants *him* to be happy. In the Hawthorne tale, with genders reversed, the beloved, Georgiana, states initially that she is perfectly content to go on indefinitely with her tiny birthmark; it is her lover who regards it as a blemish and who feels he cannot love her until it is removed. He acts in his own interest. Lisa acts in the interest of Corduroy. Lisa, moreover, adds something (love) that is missing; Aylmer, on the other hand, takes something away (life) that is already there.

I was fascinated to learn that, years after they had first read it, some of the college students whom we had interviewed misremembered this crucial scene. Their memories not only missed its point entirely but also undermined it. As they recalled *Corduroy*, these young adults thought that the little girl had returned to buy the bear precisely because he had succeeded in finding his button and was therefore now whole and acceptable. The message of the book in that case would have been something quite different: love as conditional, as earned, as the result of meeting the standards of others. This would be a very contrary message to those conveyed in *Now Open the Box*, *Noodle*, *Ferdinand*, or *Dandelion*. In trying to understand why these undergraduates had subverted the theme of *Corduroy*, my research assistant, Sandra Y. Lee, made a powerful suggestion. She spoke of a certain cynicism that creeps in as children grow, a doubt about the possibility of unconditional love that, she implied, might stem from what young people perceive as the changing reality of their parents' love as it is offered to them. This love, which after all must alter as children grow, can, if its demands increase too precipitously, leave comfort, warmth, and acceptance—the essence of *Corduroy*—far behind, relegating these qualities to a distant memory.

Lisa and her mother are African Americans, and I want now to turn to this fact. *Corduroy* was published in 1968, the year of the passage of the Civil Rights Act and the Poor People's March on Washington, the year in which Shirley Chisholm was elected to Congress, and the year in which Martin Luther King, Jr. was assassinated. During the earlier part of the decade, civil rights boycotts, demonstrations, and marches had occurred. The "I Have a Dream" speech had been made just five years earlier, and the Selma to Montgomery march had happened only three years earlier. In this context, race had become a national issue in America, and Don Freeman, by giving his principal characters dark skin, was clearly making an open statement about it—a statement about love and acceptance of those who may seem superficially different, who may look different in some way, but who are in fact not different. All of the human figures depicted in this book except Lisa and her mother are white, including the doll. And there are over a dozen such figures. Lisa and her mother are clearly "other" from this viewpoint, like Corduroy. From this perspective, when Lisa's mother initially rejects Corduroy, her behavior seems almost counterphobic, as though somehow she must hold her child to standards that are unrealistically, compensatorily, high. When one feels derogated, one often feels compelled to bend over backward to become the opposite of the stereotype. From this racial perspective, when Lisa sews the button on Corduroy and says she wants him to be "comfortable," the meaning of her word extends beyond the physical. It is not only that his strap will hang down and bother him no longer but also that he will no longer feel different; he will no longer perceive himself as an outsider. The issue of race thus blends with the psychological theme of acceptance, but in a positive way—not negatively, as in *Willy the Wimp*. Race is, however, treated in *Corduroy* in terms of 1960s liberalism and not in terms that would necessarily be acceptable today. In today's political climate, at least in some quarters, otherness is seen not as something that must be transcended but as something that should be emphasized and even celebrated.

A final note on *Corduroy*. When the story starts, Lisa appears to be a little girl of six or seven. After she returns to the department store all by herself to buy the bear, she seems a bit older. By the final three pages of the book, where she introduces Corduroy to his new home, sews his button on, and then, on the last page, holds him over her shoulder in the manner of a young mother with an infant, her bodily

proportions have altered, elongated, to those of a pre- or young adolescent. What I find so remarkable about this transformation is that
these barely noticeable but definite changes in her body make visible
the inner changes that are likewise occurring and that we can infer—
her power to achieve her goals on her own, her protectiveness toward
the little bear, and the expression of her maternal feelings.

We have seen in this chapter that, Freud and Piaget notwithstanding,
parents only partially construct—and children themselves only partially construct—the psychic worlds in which they live. Much is given
to them ready-made. Images circulate in the culture that convey gender
and other stereotypes even before we quite realize what is happening.
Before we can catch our breath, children are hooked on fixed ideas, not
only about gender and color but also about size, shape, strength, peck-
ing order, personal attributes, and the meanings of behavior. Many of
these notions are taken in from the surrounding culture without much
awareness, but they remain in the psyche and provide it with deeply
held notions that, once planted, may prove extremely difficult to up-
root.

The artist, however, in attempting to create images for children that
undo rigid stereotypes and to place more fluid pictures of identity
into circulation, encounters a highly complex problem. Such representations must take several crucial factors into account: that children's
physical maturation is still in progress, that their life experience is limited, and that their cognitive and emotional development is similarly
nascent. Children can interpret what is represented to them only in
terms of their own past and present experience. It is impossible for a
child, for instance, to imagine him- or herself in possession of a sexu-
ally mature adult body. Trying hard to remember my own experience
in this realm, I recall a conversation that I once had, as a little girl, with
a fully developed adolescent cousin. I asked her whether she hurt when
she lay down on her stomach. "Why?" she replied. "Because," I said,
"of your breasts. Don't they get crushed?" Young children, moreover,
in their need to make sense of the world and to feel safe in it, crave clo-

sure and certainty. Young children are intolerant of ambiguity. How, therefore, do we achieve balance between their need for surety and security and our desire to challenge stereotypes that restrict children's sense of themselves and of who they can be? Little Debby, for example, should feel equally comfortable choosing the role of doctor or nurse. An artist's challenge for the future may be to create images that free up that choice while keeping the world safe from confusion.

A Glance Forward and Back

With children's increased access to images in the media, there is a debate in our country over the effect on the minds of young people of pictures, art, and visual representation in general. Some believe that the purpose of art is to stimulate the imagination and allow children to go over to the other side, as it were, without leaving home—that is, they believe that art is safe. According to this view, in pictures and in stories a child can confront danger and passion and take extreme risks without forsaking the comforts of everyday reality. He or she can travel to exotic places or backward in time to a glamorous past with minimal effort. Those who hold this view claim that art for children should be given wide latitude with respect to content. Because whatever it offers is experienced in the imagination alone, it will simply enhance the creative life of its beholders. Art and representation serve, at best, to inspire children and, at worst, to siphon off desires that are unrealizable in ordinary life. Proponents of this view tend likewise to see freedom of representation as an absolute good and a basic right in a democratic society.

On the other side of the debate are those who see images as causative with respect to behavior and formative with respect to attitudes. They claim that children reflect what they see. Accordingly, the imagery shown to young children must, they aver, be carefully monitored. In their view, art is not safe. If you show a young child the famous picture of Peter Pan teaching Wendy and her brothers John and Michael to fly, you should not be surprised if that child tries to imitate them by walking out of a window.

Although I believe the first position has merit and is extremely important to claim and to maintain, I also know that when a young child wakes up terrified in the middle of the night, telling her or him that "it was only a dream" does not work instant magic. That reasonable phrase, "it was only a dream" or, by analogy, it was only a picture, a story, movie, TV show, does not have the force of the words "I love you," "I'm here with you now," or "I'll protect you." The child who was frightened by images of a menacing dinosaur, a devouring whale, or a wicked witch still needs to be calmed down. Merely giving a frightened child the information that the scary image belongs to one category of experience rather than another will not suffice. This strategy is inadequate because, although art surely *does* offer an alternative realm of imaginary experience, it also produces a direct emotional experience. The emotions with which we respond to art are as real and powerful as those with which we respond to life. And this is especially so in early childhood.

Young children need plenty of time to sort out the differences between make-believe and reality, dreaming and living, fantasy and fact. To recognize this is to pay attention to the form and content of the imagery we make available to them. It is to understand that, from their point of view, each image has an effect that we as adults do not fully grasp, unless, perhaps, we pay attention. And, by reading to children, by turning pages together with them, we can learn bit by bit about what they are thinking and help them to negotiate the complex cultural messages that are continuously being given to them.

In writing this book, my aim has never been to be comprehensive nor to furnish a definitive interpretation of any single work. I have merely sought to reflect, with you, my readers, on why certain images and words have survived, and on some of the perhaps not-obvious meanings that inhere in them—meanings that, because they are met with at a tender age and are sanctioned by significant adults, gain ascendency over children's imaginative lives and exert influence well into the future.

I would like to end now by inviting you to consider a still highly controversial hundred-year-old book, a survivor from the same period as *Peter Rabbit*. This book was written and illustrated in India at the turn of the century by a Scottish-born mother, Helen Bannerman, for her two small daughters. Shortly thereafter, it was taken to England by a friend of the family and then brought to the United States, where, because it was not protected by copyright, it appeared during subsequent decades in numerous vulgarized editions. In the 1960s and 1970s, with the advent of the civil rights movement, it came to be regarded as blatantly offensive and overtly racist. But *The Story of Little Black Sambo*, despite these strong negative reactions to it, has managed to survive. Why? I do not believe that its survival is due only to racism or that its appeal to children is principally vicious. Children have responded to this story, I believe, because of its intrinsic brilliance and because of its moral and psychological authenticity regarding childhood experience.

The Story of Little Black Sambo was resuscitated last year in two retellings by two American artists and a writer, all of whom felt that its good qualities should not to be made to suffer the fate of its deplorable ones. In 1996 reviews of these recycled versions, such as "Meltdown" by Brian Anderson in the *New York Times* Book Review, "Same Story, New Attitude" by Belinda Luscombe in *Time*, and "Taking a Tiger by the Tale" by Linton Weeks in the *Washington Post*, journalists offered factual information about the original and updated stories and quoted from interviews with relevant parties, including editors, artists, and professors. But none made any attempt to explain *why* the story has been and continues to be so beloved by children. The pleasure it affords them is simply taken as an unquestioned fact.

Indeed, Julius Lester, who retells the story in a designedly African-American voice, adopting the style of the Uncle Remus tales, asks rhetorically on the final page of his 1996 version, entitled *Sam and the Tigers:* "What other story had I read at age seven and remembered for fifty years? There was obviously an abiding truth in the story, despite itself." Lester goes on to write that he thinks "it is the truth of the imagination, that incredible realm where animals and people live

From *The Story of Little Black Sambo* by Helen Bannerman.
Originally published in 1899.

together like they don't know any better, and children eat pancakes cooked in the butter of melted tigers, and parents never say, 'Don't eat so many.' " I agree with him. But I think there is more to it than that.

This is a story about a little boy who is smart as a whip and a true survivor. Children of both sexes can identify readily with him. He is a genuine hero. He has a mother and father who clearly love him and who, not because he does anything special to deserve it (it isn't even his birthday), bestow gifts on him. He is given a Red Coat, a pair of beautiful Blue Trousers, a beautiful Green Umbrella, and a lovely Pair of Purple Shoes with Crimson Soles and Crimson Linings. The colors matter; they specify each item of clothing and lock it in place for children who, in many cases, are just learning to name those colors correctly.

When the little boy goes out for his canonical adventure (as we have seen in so many other books), he walks proudly in the jungle with his new clothes on and meets the first Tiger, who threatens to eat him up. At this point, our young hero, scared to death, bargains with pluck for his life. Good move. To survive, he gives up his new jacket. When the second Tiger appears, he repeats this successful strategy and gives up his pants. When the third Tiger arrives on the scene, however, there is a problem. All he has left are the shoes and the umbrella. Gamely, he offers his shoes, but the Tiger protests that he has no use for them because he has four feet, not just two. At this point, the child, desperate to live, comes up with an ingenious solution. How about having the Tiger wear them as decorations for his ears? And the Tiger accepts, striding off, repeating the refrain "Now *I*'m the grandest Tiger in the Jungle." With the fourth and final Tiger, our hero devises another ingenious scheme to persuade the predator to take his Umbrella rather than his life. He suggests that the Tiger tie a knot in his tail around the umbrella so that his four paws are still free for walking. And this Tiger goes off pleased, convinced that *he* is the grandest Tiger in the Jungle.

But, like anyone who has been forced to give up all his treasures, our now nearly naked little hero is terribly sad and begins to cry. The clothes were important to Little Black Sambo not only because he cared for them, but also because they had been given to him by his parents. Hearing a loud "grrrrr," he fears that the Tigers are returning to eat him up. But of course, what they are actually doing is growling at one another and disputing over which one is the grandest Tiger in the Jungle. This, to my way of thinking, is one of the most psychologically telling moments in the book, for it captures precisely the way children often see adults—that is, talking angrily to one another and arguing over things that make absolutely no sense. By and by, the child realizes that these Tigers are far more interested in their own argument with one another (again like typical adults) than in his lovely clothes, which they have discarded. Bravely and politely, he asks whether they still want the clothes. The tigers cannot respond because they have their tails in one anothers' mouths—another wonderful image—so Little Black Sambo deftly reclaims his possessions and walks triumphantly offstage, while the ridiculous Tigers (adults) chase each other around a tree until they all melt into a ring of butter.

At the end of the story, we see an absolutely perfect scene of retribution. Our hero's mother has made a huge platter of tigerish-looking pancakes out of the melted butter that the Tigers became, and now, instead of the Tigers eating *him* up, Little Black Sambo, plucky and brave and clever, finishes the story by eating *them* up. Every child listening to this story knows that those 169 pancakes must have tasted mighty good.

This is, then, a story that grabs the threads of a child's deepest fears and loves and weaves them into a plot that brings them to the surface and patterns them. And, as we saw in the chapter on bedtime, its repetitions and rhythms are central to this effect. As to the overarching theme itself, consider the importance of food, hunger, and oral aggression in early childhood. Think of the vast number of tales that feature child-eating monsters, witches, wolves, and devouring ogres. Think of the role that oral themes have played in so many of the picture books we have studied here—Mickey baked in the oven in Sendak's *Night Kitchen*, Peter Rabbit consuming vegetables in Mr. McGregor's garden and narrowly avoiding being put in a pie himself, Ping's narrow escape from becoming someone's dinner on a houseboat in the middle of the Yangtze River, the poky little puppy's joyful anticipation of his delicious desserts, Frances's yearning for her parents' layer cake at bedtime, Max's wild things threatening to eat him up and his bowl of cereal that is still hot. *The Story of Little Black Sambo* clearly taps into a theme of enduring significance for young children.

On May 29, 1997, Hortense Spillers, a distinguished professor of

English literature, with expertise in the areas of race and gender and a fellow scholar at the Center for Advanced Study in the Behavioral Sciences at Stanford, held a fascinating discussion with me about *The Story of Little Black Sambo*. Our conversation involved not only the original tale but also the 1996 versions—the previously mentioned *Sam and the Tigers* by Julius Lester and Jerry Pinckney, and *The Story of Little Babaji*, which pairs the original Helen Bannerman text with new illustrations by Fred Marcellino.

Spillers had not seen the story as a child, and she speculated that, *had* she encountered it during the 1960s, she, along with everyone else, probably would have damned it on ideological grounds. But now she found it fascinating. We tried to imagine why a white woman like Helen Bannerman would have chosen to write a story about a little African boy when her goal was to please her two Scottish daughters in India.

It is in the drawings and the names of the characters in *The Story of Little Black Sambo*, rather than its story, that racial slurs are found, and they are unmistakable. The drawings of the characters are, in fact, caricatures of racial stereotypes; they have protruding red lips and white eyes, and, as Spillers pointed out, the mother's face actually resembles that of a pig. This insight brought to mind another famous "mother" figure in children's literature whose face resembles a pig—the Duchess in *Alice's Adventures in Wonderland*, that nasty sneezing character who also addresses her *child* as a pig! The names in the *The Story of Little Black Sambo* are obviously disrespectful toward African cultures and languages: Black Mumbo, the mother, and Black Jumbo, the father— the pair adding up to "mumbo-jumbo," or "nonsense."

Spillers and I, however, came up with the idea of reading *The Story of Little Black Sambo* against the grain, as an anticolonialist narrative. What about seeing the black child as a carrier of civilization, a champion, in opposition to the tigers as representatives of the forces of destructive nature? After all, as we have seen, clothes normally are taken to be the sign of civilization. Here, it is the little African boy who is equipped with a wardrobe and an umbrella—the emblems of culture— which the tigers lack, misunderstand, and have no use for. We wondered, however, why a white woman like Helen Bannerman would want to expose, or would be capable of exposing, colonialism at the height of the Empire, yet the reading fits.

We considered the fact that very few other children in the tales we know are showered with gifts. Hansel and Gretel are, after all, poor, and in fairy tales generally, children must find or earn or deserve their fortune. Madeline, as we saw, receives her bounty only after she has suffered and been rushed to the hospital in an ambulance. Little Black Sambo, on the contrary, is favored with good things gratuitously. He comes very near to losing them forever, however. The plot is therefore unique—a twist on the ordinary. But what about the near loss of his gifts? Does race play a role here? Is Little Black Sambo especially vulnerable to having his things stolen because of his race and social status? Is it going to be especially hard for *this* child to keep the good stuff—that is, what he receives from his parents? Will it be hard for him not merely because he is a child, small and inexperienced, but also specifically because he is a *black* child? Will that factor force him to be unusually clever so as to outwit his enemies?

Trying another interpretation, Spillers and I thought about seeing the tigers themselves as the British colonialist powers—as powers that by force, deception, and terror try to despoil the cultures that existed before they did. After all, the tigers do seem like grand viziers. They strut about. And, like the colonialists, they make bargains with loopholes, as in: "I won't eat you *this time*." We elaborated these cultural readings, and as we looked at the pictures together and talked, the slender story, with its several hundred words, became increasingly complex.

The rewrite by Lester and Pinckney, both African Americans, makes a deliberate attempt to counteract the "mumbo-jumbo" of the original names in Bannerman's text by adopting "Sam" as the sole designation for all members of the family. Spillers admired this strategy because, as she put it, it makes them differentiable on the basis of function rather than proper name. You can tell who is talking even though they all have the same name. I, however, am not quite so impressed by this strategy; I fear that children may find it confusing. In general, we agreed that

Sam and the Tigers may be a bit too self-conscious in its efforts to purify the original text and consequently, more decorative and ornate than necessary. For me, it lacks the elegant simplicity and mythic power of the original. The result, in my view, is a pretty and interesting book but one with less magic.

Spillers and I both, however, fell in love with the tigers in Fred Marcellino's "Indian" version, in which the words of the story have been maintained intact except for the offensive names, which were changed to Babaji, Mamaji, and Papaji. The tale has been reset in India, and each tiger has been endowed with a sardonically menacing pose and a distinctive facial expression to match. Each one of these inimitably drawn beasts embodies a subtle melange of tigerish characteristics and human ones—such as pomposity. And each is both hilarious and scary, just as the plot demands.

Spillers and I, sitting together with the three picture books spread out before us, pondered the changing meanings of a story like this as it circulates in a culture. Books may survive, after all, and mean very different things in different generations, or they may skip a whole era and then resurface. *The Story of Little Black Sambo*, revivified for children on the eve of its centennial, reminds us of the richness and complexity of all our cultural objects. A deceptively simple little book like this can sharpen our awareness of the crucial role that adults have to play as mediators between our children and the images they encounter.

Thus, art is both safe and unsafe, like life itself. Just as we might hold hands with a little boy or girl while walking down a busy city street; just as we might check the nutritional value of food we give them to eat; just so, might we sit down with them and, turning pages together, engage in the task of cultural transmission. A task that blends past, present, and future. A task that never ends. A task that we must not put off. A task that brings the generations together.

Picture Books Cited

(Author listed first, illustrator listed second)

Adshead, Gladys, and Elizabeth Orton Jones. 1944. *What Miranda Knew.* London: Oxford University Press.

Bannerman, Helen. 1899. *The Story of Little Black Sambo.* Philadelphia: J. B. Lippincott.

———. 1996. *The Story of Little Babaji.* Illus. Fred Marcellino. New York: Harper Collins.

Bemelmans, Ludwig. 1939. *Madeline.* New York: Simon and Schuster.

Brown, Margaret Wise, and Clement Hurd. 1942. *The Runaway Bunny.* New York: Harper and Row.

———. 1947. *Goodnight Moon.* New York: Harper and Row.

Brown, Margaret Wise, and Leonard Weisgard. 1947. *The Golden Egg Book.* New York: Golden.

Brown, Margaret Wise, and Garth Williams. 1948. *Wait till the Moon Is Full.* New York: Harper and Row.

Browne, Anthony. 1984. *Willy the Wimp.* New York: Knopf.

Brunhoff, Jean de. (1933.) *The Story of Babar.* Trans. Merle S. Haas. New York: Random House, 1960.

———. (1934.) *The Travels of Babar.* Trans. Merle S. Haas. New York: Random House, 1961.

Bunting, Eve, and Ronald Himler. 1990. *The Wall.* Boston: Houghton Mifflin.

Carle. Eric. 1969. *The Very Hungry Caterpillar.* New York: World Publishing.

Carrick, Carol, and Donald Carrick. 1976. *The Accident.* Boston: Houghton Mifflin.

Carroll, Lewis. (1865.) *Alice's Adventures in Wonderland.* New York: Grosset and Dunlap, 1946.

de Paola, Tomie. 1973. *Nana Upstairs and Nana Downstairs.* New York: G. P. Putnam's Sons.

———. 1975. *Strega Nona.* New York: Simon and Schuster.

———. 1978. *Pancakes for Breakfast.* New York: Harcourt Brace Jovanovich.

———. 1980. *Now One Foot, Now the Other.* New York: G. P. Putnam's Sons.

Dickens, Charles. (1871.) "A Child's Dream of a Star." in *Charles Dickens' Best Stories.* Ed. Morton Dauwen Zabel. Garden City, N.Y.: Hanover House, 1959.

Eldridge, Ethel J., and Kurt Wiese. 1946. *Yen-Foh: A Chinese Boy.* Chicago: Albert Whitman.

Flack, Marjorie, and Kurt Wiese. 1933. *The Story about Ping.* New York: Macmillan.

Fox, Mem, and Jane Dyer. 1993. *Time for Bed.* New York: Harcourt Brace.

Freeman, Don. 1964. *Dandelion.* New York: Viking.

———. 1968. *Corduroy.* New York: Viking.

Hoban, Russell, and Lillian Hoban. 1964. *A Baby Sister for Frances.* New York: Harper and Row.

———. 1964. *Bread and Jam for Frances.* New York: Harper and Row.

———. 1968. *A Birthday for Frances.* New York: Harper and Row.

———. 1969. *Best Friends for Frances.* New York: Harper and Row.

Hoban, Russell, and Garth Williams. 1960. *Bedtime for Frances.* New York: Harper and Row.

Johnson, Crockett. 1955. *Harold and the Purple Crayon.* New York: Harper and Row.

Kipling, Rudyard. 1902. *Favorite Just So Stories.* New York: Grosset and Dunlap, 1957.

Kunhardt, Dorothy. 1934. *Now Open the Box.* New York: Harcourt, Brace, and Company.

——— 1942. *Pat the Bunny.* Racine, Wis.: Golden.

Lamorisse, Albert. 1956. *The Red Balloon.* Garden City, N.Y.: Doubleday.

Leaf, Munro. 1936. *Manners Can Be Fun.* Philadelphia: J. B. Lippincott.

Leaf, Munro, and Ludwig Bemelmans. 1937. *Noodle.* New York: Four Winds Press.

Leaf, Munro, and Robert Lawson. 1936. *The Story of Ferdinand.* New York: Viking Penguin.

Lester, Julius, and Jerry Pinckney. 1996. *Sam and the Tigers.* New York: Dial.

Lowrey, Janette Sebring, and Gustaf Tenggren. 1942. *The Poky Little Puppy.* Racine, Wis.: Western.

Mayer, Mercer. 1968. *There's a Nightmare in My Closet.* New York: Dial.

McCloskey, Robert. 1941. *Make Way for Ducklings*. New York: Viking.

Milne, A. A. (1927.) *Now We Are Six*. New York: Dell, 1955.

Munsch, Robert, and Sheila McGraw. 1986. *Love You Forever.* Willowdale, Ont.: Firefly.

Nelson, Vaunda Micheau, and Kimianne Uhler. 1988. *Always Gramma*. New York: G. P. Putnam's Sons.

Oram, Hiawam, and Satoshi Kitamura. 1982. *Angry Arthur.* London: Andersen.

Ormerod, Jan. 1982. *Moonlight*. New York: Viking Penguin.

Piper, Watty. 1930. *The Little Engine That Could*. New York: Platt and Munk, 1961.

Potter, Beatrix. 1902. *The Tale of Peter Rabbit*. London: Frederick Warne.

———. 1903. *The Tale of Squirrel Nutkin*. London: Frederick Warne.

———. 1905. *The Tale of Mrs. Tiggy-winkle*. London: Frederick Warne.

———. 1907. *The Tale of Tom Kitten*. London: Frederick Warne.

———. 1918. *The Tale of Johnny Town Mouse*. London: Frederick Warne.

Rappaport, Doreen, and E. B. Lewis. 1995. *The New King*. New York: Dial.

Rey, Margaret, and H. A. Rey. 1966. *Curious George Goes to the Hospital*. Boston: Houghton Mifflin.

Rojankowsky, Feodor. (Illus.) 1967. *The Three Bears*. Racine, Wis.: Golden.

Ruthstrom, Dorotha, and Alice Schesinger. 1966. *I'm Suzy*. Racine, Wis.: Whitman.

Scarry, Richard. 1964. *Is This the House of Mistress Mouse?* New York: Golden.

———. 1968. *What Do People Do All Day?* New York: Random House.

Sendak, Maurice. 1962. *The Nutshell Library*. New York: Harper and Row.

——— 1963. *Where the Wild Things Are*. New York: Harper and Row.

———. 1970. *In the Night Kitchen*. New York: Harper and Row.

———. 1981. *Outside Over There*. New York: Harper and Row.

Seuss, Dr. [Theodor S. Geisel]. 1940. *Horton Hatches the Egg*. New York: Random House.

———. 1949. *Bartholomew and the Oobleck*. New York: Random House.

Silverstein, Shel. 1964. *The Giving Tree*. New York: Harper Collins.

Singer, Isaac Bashevis, and Maurice Sendak. 1966. *Zlateh the Goat and Other Stories*. New York: Harper and Row.

Thurber, James. 1939. *The Last Flower.* New York: Harper and Row.

Thurber, James, and Louis Slobodkin. 1943. *Many Moons*. New York: Harcourt, Brace.

Ungerer, Tomi. 1967. *Moon Man*. New York: Harper and Row.

Van Allsberg, Chris. 1981. *Jumanji*. Boston: Houghton Mifflin.

Viorst, Judith, and Erik Blegvad. 1971. *The Tenth Good Thing about Barney.* New York: Simon and Schuster.

Viorst, Judith, and Ray Cruz. 1972. *Alexander and the Terrible, Horrible, No Good, Very Bad Day.* New York: Simon and Schuster.

Walt Disney's Surprise Package. 1944. Stories adapted by H. Marion Palmer. New York: Simon and Schuster, 1948.

Walt Disney's Version of Pinocchio. 1939. New York: Random House.

Weilerstein, Sadie Rose. 1942. *What the Moon Brought.* Philadelphia: The Jewish Publication Society of America.

White, E. B. 1952. *Charlotte's Web.* New York: Harper and Row.

Wild, Margaret, and Ron Brooks. 1995. *Old Pig.* New York: Dial.

Williams, Margery. 1922. *The Velveteen Rabbit.* New York: Avon Camelot, 1975.

Yolen, Jane, and John Schoenherr. 1987. *Owl Moon.* New York: Putnam.

Secondary Sources

Alderson, Brian. 1996. Meltdown: Two New, Rehabilitated Renderings of "Little Black Sambo." *New York Times Book Review*, Nov. 10, p. 34.

All-Time Bestselling Hardcover Children's Books. (Directory). 1996. *Publisher's Weekly*. Feb. 5.

All-Time Bestselling Paperback Children's Books. (Directory). 1996. *Publisher's Weekly*. Feb. 5.

Ariès, Philippe. 1962. *Centuries of Childhood: A Social History of Family Life*. Trans. Robert Baldick. New York: Vintage.

Axline, Virginia M. 1969. *Play Therapy*. New York: Ballantine.

Baudelaire, Charles. 1956. *The Mirror of Art*. Trans. and ed. Jonathan Mayne. Garden City, N.Y.: Doubleday Anchor.

Bettelheim, Bruno. 1976. *The Uses of Enchantment: The Meaning and Importance of Fairy Tales*. New York: Knopf.

Bion, Wilfred R. 1967. *Second Thoughts*. London: Heinemann.

Blum, Virginia L. 1995. *Hide and Seek: The Child between Psychoanalysis and Fiction*. Urbana: University of Illinois Press.

Bower, T. G. R. 1977. *The Perceptual World of the Child*. Cambridge, Mass.: Harvard University Press.

Brecht, Bertolt. (1945.) *The Caucasian Chalk Circle* in *Parables for the Theater: Two Plays by Bertolt Brecht*. Trans. and ed. Eric Bentley and Maja Apelman. New York: Grove, 1947.

Chukovksky, Kornei. 1963. *From Two to Five*. Berkeley: University of California Press.

Coles, Robert. 1989. *The Call of Stories: Teaching and the Moral Imagination*. Boston: Houghton Mifflin.

Donaldson, Margaret. 1978. *Children's Minds*. New York: W. W. Norton.

Edelman, Marian Wright. 1992. *The Measure of Our Success: A Letter to My Children and Yours*. Boston: Beacon.

Eisen, George. 1988. *Children and Play in the Holocaust: Games among the Shadows.* Amherst: University of Massachusetts Press.

Felstiner, John. 1995. *Paul Celan: Poet, Survivor, Jew.* New Haven: Yale University Press.

Ferenczi, Sándor. (1913.) The Little Chanticleer. In *First Contributions to Psycho-Analysis.* Trans. Ernest Jones. New York: Brunner-Mazel, 1980, pp. 240–52.

Foote, Timothy. 1989. A Tale of Some Tails, and the Story of Their Shy Creator. *Smithsonian Magazine,* Jan., pp. 80–90.

Fraiberg, Selma H. 1959. *The Magic Years.* New York: Charles Scribner's Sons.

Freud, Sigmund. (1900–1901.) *The Interpretation of Dreams.* Trans. and ed. James Strachey. *The Standard Edition.* London: Hogarth Press, 1953. Vol. 5.

———. 1923. *The Ego and the Id.* Trans. and ed. James Strachey. *The Standard Edition.* London: Hogarth Press, 1953. Vol. 19, pp. 3–16.

———. 1963. *The Sexual Enlightenment of Children.* New York: Collier.

Gates, Henry Louis, Jr. 1997. The Naked Republic. *New Yorker,* Aug. 25–Sept.1, pp. 114–23.

Gates of Prayer: The New Union Prayerbook. 1975. New York: Central Conference of American Rabbis.

Gates of Repentance: The New Union Prayerbook for the Days of Awe. 1984. New York: Central Conference of American Rabbis.

Gesell, Arnold. 1940. *The First Five Years of Life.* New York: Harper.

Gilot, Françoise, and Carlton Lake. 1989. *My Life with Picasso.* New York: Doubleday.

Goldstein, Judith L. 1995. Realism without a Human Face. In *The Spectacles of Realism—Body, Gender, Medium.* Ed. Margaret Cohen and Christopher Prendergast. Minneapolis: University of Minnesota Press, pp. 66–89.

Golomb, Claire. 1992. *The Child's Creation of a Pictorial World.* Berkeley: University of California Press.

Gombrich, E. H. 1960. *Art and Illusion: A Study in the Psychology of Pictorial Representation.* Princeton, N.J.: Princeton University Press.

———- 1993. What Art Tells Us. *New York Review of Books.* Oct. 21, pp. 60–62.

Grinstein, Alexander. 1995. *The Remarkable Beatrix Potter.* Madison, Conn.: International Universities Press.

Grubb, W. Norton, and Marvin Lazerson. 1988. *Broken Promises: How Americans Fail Their Children.* Chicago: University of Chicago Press.

Haskell, Francis. 1993. *History and Its Images: Art and the Interpretation of the Past.* New Haven: Yale University Press.

Jagusch, Sybille A., ed. 1988. *Stepping Away from Tradition: Children's Books of the Twenties and Thirties.* Washington: Library of Congress.

Kamenetsky, Christa. 1984. *Children's Literature in Hitler's Germany: The Cultural Policy of National Socialism.* Athens: Ohio University Press.

Kaplan, Louise. 1992. *Female Perversions: The Temptations of Emma Bovary.* New York: Doubleday.

Kater, Michael H. 1997. *The Twisted Muse: Musicians and Their Music in the Third Reich.* New York: Oxford University Press.

Kernberg, Paulina. 1987. Mother-Child Interaction and Mirror Behavior. *Infant Mental Health Journal* 8 (winter), p. 4.

Kofman, Sarah. 1988. *The Childhood of Art: An Interpretation of Freud's Aesthetics.* Trans. Winifred Woodhull. New York: Columbia University Press.

———. 1994. *Rue Ordener, rue Labat.* Paris: Editions Galilee.

Lanes, Selma G. 1980. *The Art of Maurice Sendak.* New York: Harry N. Abrams.

Luscombe, Belinda. 1996. Same Story, New Attitude: Two Publishers Resuscitate a Children's "Classic." *Time*, Sept. 9.

Mahler, Margaret S., Fred Pine, and Anni Bergman. 1975. *The Psychological Birth of the Human Infant.* New York: Basic Books.

Marcus, Leonard. 1987. A Moon That Never Sets. *New York Times Book Review*, Jan. 25, p. 22.

Matthews, Gareth B. 1980. *Philosophy and the Young Child.* Cambridge, Mass.: Harvard University Press.

McCrum, Robert. 1996. Personal History: My Old and New Lives. *New Yorker*, May 27, pp. 112–19.

McDougall, Joyce. 1982. *Théâtres du je.* Paris: Gallimard.

Mead, Margaret, and Martha Wolfenstein, eds. 1955. *Childhood in Contemporary Cultures.* Chicago: University of Chicago Press.

Meyer, Susan E. 1983. *A Treasury of the Great Children's Book Illustrators.* New York: Harry N. Abrams.

Michels, Robert. 1986. Oedipus and Insight. *Psychoanalytic Quarterly* 55, pp. 599–617.

Miller, Alice. 1981. *The Drama of the Gifted Child.* Trans. Ruth Ward. New York: Basic Books.

Morrison, Toni. 1970. *The Bluest Eye: A Novel.* New York: Knopf.

Piaget, Jean. 1960. *The Child's Conception of the World*. Trans. Joan Tomlinson and Andrew Tomlinson. Totowa, N.J.: Rowman and Littlefield.

Piaget, Jean, and Bärbel Inhelder. 1969. *The Psychology of the Child*. New York: Basic Books.

Robinson, Jerry. 1974. *The Comics: An Illustrated History of the Comic Strip*. New York: Berkeley Windhover.

Rose, Jacqueline. 1984. *The Case of Peter Pan, or The Impossibility of Children's Fiction*. London: Macmillan.

Rustin, Margaret, and Michael Rustin. 1987. *Narratives of Love and Loss: Studies in Modern Children's Fiction*. London: Verso.

Scott, Carole. 1994. Clothed in Nature or Nature Clothed: Dress as Metaphor in the Illustrations of Beatrix Potter and C. M. Barker. *Children's Literature* 22, pp. 70–89.

Showalter, Dennis E. 1982. *Little Man, WHAT NOW?: Der Stuermer in the Weimar Republic*. Hamden, Conn.: Archon.

Smith, Joseph H., and William Kerrigan, eds. 1985. *Opening Texts: Psychoanalysis and the Culture of the Child*. Baltimore, Md.: Johns Hopkins University Press.

Sontag, Susan. 1978. *Illness as a Metaphor*. New York: Doubleday.

Spiegelman, Art. 1973. *Maus: A Survivor's Tale*. New York: Pantheon.

Spitz, Ellen Handler. 1988. "Picturing the Child's Inner World of Fantasy." *The Psychoanalytic Study of the Child* 43, pp. 433–47.

———. 1989. "Primary Art Objects." *The Psychoanalytic Study of the Child* 44, pp. 351–68.

———. 1994a. "Good and Naughty/Boys and Girls: Reflections on the Impact of Culture on Young Minds." *American Imago* 51, pp. 307–28.

———. 1994b. *Museums of the Mind*. New Haven: Yale University Press.

———. 1996. "Between Image and Child: Further Reflections on Picture Books." *American Imago* 53, pp. 177–90.

Spock, Benjamin. 1946. *Baby and Child Care*. New York: Pocket Books.

Steinberg, Leo. 1984. *The Sexuality of Christ in Renaissance Art and in Modern Oblivion*. New York: Pantheon Books.

Stern, Dan. 1995. *The Family Guide to Collecting Children's Books*. Santa Monica, Calif.: DMS Publishers.

Stern, Daniel N. 1985. *The Interpersonal World of the Infant*. New York: Basic Books.

Suransky, Valerie Polakow. 1982. *The Erosion of Childhood*. Chicago: University of Chicago Press.

Tatar, Maria. 1992. *Off with Their Heads! Fairy Tales and the Culture of Childhood.* Princeton, N.J.: Princeton University Press.

Thurber, James. 1945. The Secret Life of James Thurber. In *The Thurber Carnival.* Harmondsworth, Eng.: Penguin, 1953.

Trelease, Jim. 1989. *The New Read-Aloud Handbook.* New York: Viking Penguin.

Tucker, Nicholas. 1981. *The Child and the Book: A Psychological and Literary Exploration.* Cambridge: Cambridge University Press.

Warner, Marina. 1994. *From the Beast to the Blonde: On Fairy Tales and Their Tellers.* London: Chatto and Windus.

Weeks, Linton. 1996. Taking a Tiger by the Tale: "Little Black Sambo" Loses Racist Elements in Two Retellings. *Washington Post,* Sept. 17, 1996, p. B1.

Whalley, Joyce Irene, and Tessa Rose Chester. 1988. *A History of Children's Book Illustration.* London: John Murray.

Winnicott, D. W. (1956.) The Antisocial Tendency. In *Through Pediatrics to Psycho-Analysis.* London: Hogarth, 1987, pp. 306–15.

———. 1971. *Playing and Reality.* London: Routledge.

Wolfenstein, Martha. 1978. *Children's Humor: A Psychological Analysis.* Bloomington: Indiana University Press.

Wolfenstein, Martha, and Gilbert Kliman. 1965. *Children and the Death of a President: Multi-Disciplinary Studies.* New York: Doubleday.

Index